Messages From "Nowhere"

By Samuel Avital

A collection of observations, visions, dreams, words, poems, situations, reflections, events, memories, and practical exercises from new dimensions of reality

Addressed to almost anyone who is concerned with the human consciousness and beyond, and the purpose of humans on this earth. May it serve as a source of inspiration and application.

Kol-Emeth Publishers
Boulder, Colorado

Other Books by Samuel Avital

Mime Workbook. 1975
Mimenspiel. German edition of Mime Workbook, 1985
Mime and Beyond: The Silent Outcry. 1985
The Conception Mandala: Creative Techniques for Inviting a Child into Your Life. 1992, co-authored with Mark Olsen.
The Silent Outcry: The Life and Times of Samuel Avital (DVD) 1992
The BodySpeak™ Manual. 2001
The Invisible Stairway: Kabbalistic Meditations on the Hebrew Letters. 2003
Haggadah Shel Pessah, 1982, revised 2010
From Ecstasy to Lunch, 2020
Messages from "Nowhere", 2024

Copyright © 2024 by Samuel Avital,
Le Centre du Silence Mime School,
Boulder, Colorado
All rights reserved. No part of this publication may be reproduced, distributed, or transmitted in any form or by any means, including photocopying, recording, or other electronic or mechanical methods, without author's express written consent

ISBN: 978-0-9861196-3-7

Published By
Kol-Emeth Publishers
Le Centre du Silence Mime School
Lafayette, Colorado
www.bodyspeak.com
www.gokabbalahnow.com

Table of Contents

Acknowledgments v
Dedication vii
Eulogy for Raphael Avital ix

INTRODUCTION FROM "NOWHERE" 1
1. Introduction 3
2. Who Am I Who Says I Am Nothing? 7
3. "Their Way is Like That of Animals" 12

KABBALAH ARTICLES AND STORIES 13
1. The Great Shift 15
2. Adam 19
3. The Street Violinist 26
4. Generating Positive and Creative Thoughts 27
5. Balance: The Middle Way of the Tree of Life 29
6. In the Beginning was the Dot 37
7. The Golden Letters 38
8. The Shield of the Beloved 46
9. The Rabbi and the Alchemist 52
10. When a Human is Born to this World 54
11. To Thee My God 56
12. The "Presence of the Living Teacher" 60
13. "Maybe" and "Whatever" 66
14. What Kabbalah Is and Is Not 69
15. The Debate of the Two Twins 76
16. Personal Commentary on "Nothing" 83
17. The Gate Long Shut 87
18. The Awesome and Terrible Story of Rabbi Joseph De La Rheina 88

MIME ARTICLES 103
1. Practical Happiness 105
2. Advice to a Young Mime Artist 107
3. Artistic Zero 109
4. Beyond Opposites 113
5. Mime – The Silent Outcry 116
6. On Being Alert 121
7. On Being an Artist 125
8. Spiritualizing the Art of Mime 131
9. The Harmonious Cell 138
10. The Poetry of Activity 141

52 WEEKS: FROM THOUGHT TO ACTION 143
1. 52 Weeks of Practice: The Journey from Thought to Action 145
2. First Thought, Last Thought 159
3. The Day Map 160
4. The Eye Compass 163

ARTICLES 165
1. What is a Sane and Balanced Life? 167
2. A Look at Myself 171
3. Memes: Dangerous Minefields 175
4. Fear Does Not Exist 178
5. What If? 183
6. 11 Commandments for Students 185
7. Meditation Anesthesia 187

STORIES AND POEMS 197
8. Sefrou, the City of Roses 199
9. Time and Space – TI-PACE 203

- 10. Waiting for the Messiah 204
- 11. The Mother Who Loved Her Son 206

VISIONS FROM NOWHERE 213
1. One Night I Could Not Sleep 215
2. A Dream: The Missing Piece of the Puzzle 219
3. The Vision of the Serpent and the Unicorn ... 221
4. Admission to the Sacred Chamber 224
5. The Listening Ears 226
6. The Vagabond I 227
7. The Vagabond II 232

QUOTES 235
1. Sparks from a Dancing Dot 237
2. Teaching Nuggets 243
3. Words from Samuel 247

ONE MORE THING 253
1. Who You Are, and Who They Think You Are 255
2. Excuses and Becauses 263
3. Excuses 264
4. Becauses 267
5. The Hall of Mirrors 271
6. Opposites 273

DEFINTUITIONS 277

LAST WORD 295
1. Has Intelligence Left the Planet? 299
2. Madness and Sanity on Broadway 304

BIOGRAPHY 309
1. Biography of Samuel Avital 311
2. Heritage of my Families Abitbol, Ezekri, and Elbaz 315

WHAT ARE "THEY" SAYING ABOUT SAMUEL AVITAL? 317
1. Rabbi Zalman Schachter-Shalomi 319
2. Zohara Hieronimus 319
3. Marcel Marceau 320
4. Kenneth Cohen 322
5. Maximilien Decroux 323
6. Masheikh Wali Ali Meyer 323
7. Dr. David Passig 323
8. Mark Olson 323
9. Melissa Michaels 324
10. Moni Yakim 324
11. E.J. Gold 324
12. Shalom Kalfon 325

Memorial to Suzanne Fountain 327
Books by Samuel Avital 329

Acknowledgments

Over the years, I accumulated stories, poems and articles I had written, as I traveled to different places in the world and encountered many life experiences.

What triggered this book to see the light was when Neshamah Ruth Bat-Li-Or Avital (Alessandra Lior) gave me two volumes she printed with a collection of my poems, as a gift for my birthday in 2002. For some time, I wanted to publish that collection, and to call it **"MESSAGES FROM "NOWHERE."** Over this last twenty years, more stories and other poems were added to make the collection complete. I thank you Neshamah, for that precious gift, and your dedication of studying and being with me all these years.

For my friends and family that assisted and helped bring to light this book **"MESSAGES FROM "NOWHERE"** with their generous contributions, both spiritual and material, thank you for your contribution in bringing this book about.

May all these beautiful beings be blessed, and may all their families and friends be at peace with each other, may they cooperate toward that great state of **"being good and acting good,"** and may they find calm and serenity in the midst of activities in our perplexed times.

May the triple blessing from the Torah be with them always in prosperity and development of their spiritual lives both in **"This world"** and **"That World,"** which is also called **"The World to Come"**.

I would also like to thank Devorah Shirah Elkayyam for her invested dedication and personal urgency for editing and revising these writings to be ready to publish at this time.

Dedication

I dedicate this book to my three beloved brothers, my older brother and the firstborn, Raphael Avital, and my two younger brothers, Elisha Avital and Amos Avital. They left the planet during the years of 2021 (Raphael) and 2023 (Amos and Elisha). This book is dedicated to their memory.

The Mayor of Lod Israel wrote a dedication for my brother Raphi, at his funeral. His writing has been translated into English and is included in Hebrew, for those who can read it, following this dedication. A whole plaza was dedicated to Raphael (Raphi) in Lod, called Kikar Raphi, where a plaque has been dedicated to him in the roundabout. May Raphi's soul and that of Elisha and Amos be blessed in Gan Eden.

This book is also dedicated to my past student, Suzanne Fountain, who was among the ten murdered in the mass killing at the King Soopers in Boulder in March 2021.

יאיר רביבו ראש העיר לוד הספד בהלוויה של אחי רפאל אביטל זצוק"ל. 2021 – 1927
נולד בעיר צפרו כ"ה באייר ה. תרפ"ז 2021 – 1927
ביום ראשון כ"ב בניסן התשפ"א Sunday, April 4, 2021

ברוך דיין האמת. היום אנו מלווים למנוחת עולמים את אחד מוותיקי העיר ומדור המייסדים שלה, יקיר העיר לוד, רפאל אביטל ז"ל, שהיה ממובילי רוח העשייה וההתנדבות והקרין מאישיותו הלבבית על העיר, כאיש חסד, נעים הליכות, איש משפחה למופת, אוהב התורה וארץ ישראל, סמל ודוגמא לאהבת האדם.

סיפורו של רפי אביטל הוא סיפורה של יהדות מרוקו, של עלייתה לישראל ושל קליטתה בה. זהו גם סיפור של מדינה בהתהוותה, של העיר לוד בהתחדשותה, ושל אדם, שכל חייו תרם למדינה ולחברה הישראלית – ציוני אמיתי.

בפעילותו ההתנדבותית היה רפי חבר במשך שנים ארוכות במועדון רוטרי לוד ואף שימש כנשיאה, פעל רבות בסיוע למען מעוטי יכולת. בין היתר היה חבר בוועדה העירונית להנצחת זכרם של נפגעי הטרור.

עד לאחרונה היה ידוע רפי אביטל בעיר לוד כמי שתמיד אפשר לפנות אליו בעת צרה, והוא איננו מאכזב.

רפי ז"ל היה אבא וסבא טוב ואוהב למשפחתו, דמות מוערכת ובולטת ואיש אהוד על כל תושבי העיר.

מסכת חייו העשירה מנציחה מורשת ערכית ציונית, שבוודאי עוד תעבור לדורות הבא תנחומיי ותנחומי עיריית לוד למשפחה היקרה, לרעיה פורטונה מזל, ולילדים עמי, אלי, לאה, הדס ומשה.

Eulogy by Yair Revivo, Mayor of Lod, Israel

For the Funeral of my Brother Raphael Avital Z"L. Sun, April 4th, 2021.

Blessed be the Judge of Truth. Today we accompany to rest one of the city's veterans, a member of the founding generation of the beloved city of Lod, the late Rafael Avital. He was one of the city's leaders in the spirit of action and volunteerism, who radiated his heartfelt personality on the city. He was a man of loving-kindness, and pleasant manners, an exemplary family man, who loved the Torah and the land of Israel, a symbol and example of love for mankind.

Rafi Avital's story is the story of Moroccan Jewry, its immigration to Israel and its absorption in it. It is also a story of a state in its formation, of the city of Lod in its renewal, and of a man who all his life contributed to the state and Israeli society – a true Zionist.

In his volunteer activities, Rafi was a member of the Rotary Club of Lod for many years, and even served as president, working extensively to help the less fortunate. Among other things, he was a member of the municipal committee, commemorating the victims of terrorism. Until recently, Rafi Avital was known in the city of Lod as someone who could always be contacted in times of need, and he did not disappoint.

The late Rafi was a good and loving father and grandfather to his family, a valued and prominent figure and a well-liked man among all the residents of the city. The rich order of his life perpetuates a Zionist heritage of values, which will surely be passed on to future generations.

My condolences and condolences to the Municipality of Lod, to his dear family, to Raya Fortuna Mazal, and to the children, Ami, Eli, Leah, Hadas and Moshe.

Translated from Hebrew to English by Samuel Avital.

רֹאשׁ־דְּבָרְךָ אֱמֶת וּלְעוֹלָם כָּל־מִשְׁפַּט צִדְקֶךָ.
תהלים קיט. קס.

**The beginning of Your word is true,
and each of Your righteous judgments is eternal.
Psalms 119. 1**

פְּלָאוֹת עֵדְוֹתֶיךָ עַל־כֵּן נְצָרָתַם נַפְשִׁי.
תהלים קיט. קכט.

**Your testimonies are hidden; therefore, my soul kept them.
Psalms 119. 129**

אַשְׁרֵי תְמִימֵי־דָרֶךְ הַהֹלְכִים בְּתוֹרַת יְהוָה.
תהלים קיט. א.

**Praiseworthy are those whose way is perfect,
who walk with the law of the Lord.
Psalms 119. 1**

לְעוֹלָם יְהוָה דְּבָרְךָ נִצָּב בַּשָּׁמָיִם.
תהלים קיט. פט.

**Forever, O Lord, Your word stands in the heavens.
Psalms 119. 89**

Raphael Gematria

I wrote this gematria of my brother Raphael to detect the inner-hidden meaning of his name. He wears the verb of Healing, as the angel Raphael, and as written below, the abbreviation of the letters of his name contains the contemplation of the great wonders and miracles of the Creator. Next is the numerology of 311 of his name which comes to the word which means summit, then a few sentences that come to the number 311. And so, his soul left this world of lies to the world of truth, the summit infinity, Ein Sof.

רְפָאֵל

רְאוּ פְּלָאוֹת אֲדוֹנִי לְעוֹלָם־וָעֶד
רְפָאֵל = 311 = ש י א
יֵשׁ אַלוּפוֹ שֶׁל עוֹלָם
גַּם מַלְאָכָיו יְצַוֶּה לָךְ = 311
וְאֵין כָּמוֹהוּ בְּכָל הָעוֹלָם = 311
יוֹמָם יְצַוֶּה ה חַסְדּוֹ = 311
עַד לְאֵין סוֹף = 311

Introduction from "Nowhere"

Introduction 3

Who Am I Who Says I Am Nothing? 7

"Their Way is Like That of Animals" 12

Introduction To Messages From "Nowhere"

A Portal to the "Not Yet Known"

מְסָרִים מִשׁוּם מָקוֹם

מְסָרִים מִ " אֵי -שָׁם "

"**NO-WHERE**" in Hebrew is שׁוּם מָקוֹם – ר״ת ש״ם

מְסָרִים מִשׁוּם מָקוֹם is the Hebrew name of the book *Messages from "Nowhere"*

WE KNOW THE classical question: Where does thought come from? Some know how to use their thoughts. But unfortunately, most thinking is according to all the memes (programmed ways of thinking) that were created throughout the history of the world – And so, most of these thoughts and ideas are abused.

Where do thoughts come from? Using careful words, from my humble perception, they come from a source. We don't know the location of that source. We can't see it. We can't even look at it. I call that source "**nowhere**."

I'm embarrassed to dare to explain the unexplainable. But I am going to attempt the unattemptable and dare, for the understanding of my readers. So please bear with me. The intention is for the benefit of all.

Definitions of "Nowhere"

"**Nowhere**" is a term newly used in Le Centre Du Silence, for that which is beyond space and time, beyond silence, and beyond spiritual transmission teachings. It is also a state of mind to aspire to, to protect oneself from this perplexed and confused world. In other words, a source of creativity.

Nowhere is NO THING, the essential present moment beingness.
It is a state of conscious knowing that "I do not know."

"Nowhere" – a Portal to the "Not Yet Known"

"Nowhere" is a portal to the "Not Yet Known." People call it "The Unknown" but I call it the "**Not Yet Known**." When it is known, in essence it is not known at all with words or sound. This "Nowhere" is that which is empty of thoughts, personal history, duality, categories, numbers etc. It is that which is not yet born, and is beyond all human definitions.

"Nowhere" is NO WHERE

"Nowhere" refers to a space that is no space, a no form source from which we all manifest into the density of "this world", a time that is no time, a spaceless space, a source that brings words. It is also known as "spiritual home."

"Nowhere" is NO WHERE

Nowhere is the space between the piano keys, the space between yes and no, the gap between inhaling and exhaling, the space of no thinking – what is called in Kabbalah חָלָל פָּנוּי = empty space. It is the state of "**Between**" and "**No because**."

Nowhere is the NOT KNOWING, the space of being of yes and no, it is "No Where."

Nowhere is the same as NOTHING, NO THING.
In Hebrew, Nothing is **AYIN** אַיִן. If you rearrange the letters, you get **ANI** אֲנִי, which is "I" or "myself". This "**I am**" (**ANI** אֲנִי) is **nothing** (**AYIN** אַיִן).

In Hebrew, nowhere is **the ANI** אֲנִי of the **AYIN** אַיִן and the **AYIN** אַיִן of **the ANI** אֲנִי – **the nothing of myself and the myself of nothing** – אֲנִי אַיִן. (See the article "Who Am I to Say I am Nothing" following this introduction). The kabbalistic term for this is Ein Sof אֵין סוֹף.

The word **ANI** אֲנִי in Hebrew, which is translated as "I am," is the Neshama, the divine spark, which is the activator and the animator of the human body. Through the power of the Creator, the Neshama activates the body, the physical. This Neshama is the spark of the Creator from above חלק אלוה ממעל. (See the article Adam.)

The Neshama is the power of the Creator activating the human body and all created beings. So the body is just a cover, a set of clothes. In other words, my clothes are not what I am. I am not my shirt.

The REAL and True self is the ANI of AYIN (the "I am" of "nothing") and the FALSE/FAKE myself is the ego, which all the time tries to disguise itself as the Real self. "I am" in Hebrew is the essential self, rooted in or connected with the Creator's power. When you say "I am" in English, you are referring to the body. When you say "I am" in Hebrew, you refer to the essential self, the Neshama soul, the divine spark within, which wears the clothes of the body.

"Nowhere" guides you to somewhere.
"Nowhere" is within, inside, it is called "that world," the formless, the unnameable, the invisible, the non-tangible.

Somewhere is without, outside, it is called "this world," the form, the visible, the nameable, the tangible. The physical is a temporary form, the place of opposites.

And so, my little conclusion is that I am a spiritual agent that comes here with a mission. First, my mission is to know the meaning of my being here – and to understand once and for all that the matter perishes and the Neshama is forever. Another simple way to say this is "death does not exist." So the only thing that dies is the physical use of the body, but the Neshama is eternal and continues its own dimension journeys, which are called in Kabbalistic terms, the spiritual worlds.

So, we are "spiritual agents" from "Nowhere," with a mission in "this life" that we have to discover. We discover that mission through individual specific practices of Tikkun, restoration of oneself.

This is through what we call in Hebrew, the Middot – Traits. We must consciously go through our traits and restore them to be balanced physically, mentally, and spiritually. That is one of the ways to discover one's nowhere – that is, to shift consciousness from the limited matrix of duality, and advance the whole humanity to that which is beyond thought, time and space. And we have 40 days and 40 nights of the month of Elul to work out the Middot, so that for the next Hebrew year, we will hopefully be "**inscribed in the book of life**."

That process is called in Kabbalah קְפִיצַת הַדֶּרֶךְ = "**The Jumping of the Way**," which we can refer to as transporting oneself from this limited timeline to another timeline, the next **GREAT SHIFT** from the darkness to Light, from what is "**known**" to that which is "**Not Yet Known**." This is also a process of personal restoration, Tikkun Prati תיקון פרטי.

Actually, this is the shift humanity is making now, and the suffering happening in the world now is part of the process to exit the state of personal slavery humanity has built until now. (See the article, "The Great Shift"). And that is what I call, humanity "**being cooked**", not just to medium but "well-done".

Profound contemplation on the following verse from the book of Job is suggested. It can guide the contemplator to discover messages of how to begin to work on themselves. Deep reflection is needed, in order to find out what this verse truly means, from personal experience:

וּמִבְּשָׂרִי אֶחֱזֶה אֱלוֹהַּ
"...and from my flesh I shall envision Elowah"
Job 19:26

This is a profound suggestion – If by some miraculous event you are reading these words, and you came to here, please consider this. If you read these words and profoundly meditate on not just the meaning, but beyond the word meanings, of this supposedly simple verse, you will discover your own gate or portal to the nowhere. In this way, you will create your own exercise how to enter the nowhere – your own portal to nowhere. This verse has been explored in a kabbalistic way in the Jewish tradition, untold times.

Samuel Avital
Your Friend from "Nowhere"

Important note: I would like to suggest that here, as in some of my other books, I have inserted many kabbalistic ideas, but without using kabbalistic terms. Instead, these ideas are translated into a language that can be understood by all. You may or may not recognize it, but if some of you are familiar with kabbalistic information, you can be a spiritual detective to discover this. In other words, I made a sincere attempt to simplify the complexity and translate the information and knowledge of those ideas, so they can be understood and applied.

Who Am I Who Says I Am Nothing?

"I am not a Human Being, I am a Human Becoming."
—Samuel Avital, Boulder Colorado, 1982

WHO AM I? I am nothing.

How can nothing say it is nothing? Who is this, I, who says I am nothing?

Only constant self-examination can clarify this question. Only self-questioning, particularly in moments of silence and stillness, can lead us back to our source. Only in this process can we cleanse our psychic and physical systems of impurities and restore ourselves.

Who am I? What am I doing here? Almost all spiritual streams deal with these questions, asking us to dare that self-confrontation, that constant search for self-honesty.

For me, as an individual and an artist, that search is structured and guided by my study of the Kabbalah, not just on a philosophical level, but as a program and attitude, a way of life and being.

Who am I? For many years, I resisted the realization of the answer to that classical spiritual question. Like everyone else, when I was young, I experienced a strong sense of personal identity: I am something definite, I am so and so, I am a particular someone. Society's conditioning teaches you that you are only your environment, home, school, friends and a compulsive consumer, etc. And this state of affairs is a very limited view of who you and I really are.

But even then, the Kabbalah taught me that "nothing" is built into "I am." The Hebrew word for "I am" is ANI אני – composed of the three letters: aleph, א noon נ, and י yod. But just slightly change the order of the letters to aleph, yod, noon אין and you have the word AYIN – אין – that means "nothing." "I am" becomes "nothing" so easily, just put the yod in the middle instead of at the end.

So, I grew up being taught that when I said, "I am hurt" I was saying, "nothing is hurt." I am sick, means nothing is sick. I love you, means nothing loves you. That was the programming I grew up with, and throughout much of my life I have dwelled on that, and proclaimed it in many situations and experiences, even facing death. And through this, every moment has been intensified with life. Through this realization, I am focused. I am present. Words cannot explain or express this nothingness. I try to express it by being it, by daring to be myself, by performing it, by teaching it.

What seems to be something is actually nothing. I see you. Who do I see? Nothing. Who is this that lives? Nothing. Everything is nothing. But to be nothing, you have to be something. That is the holy paradox, as is the marriage of all the opposites, male-female, spirit-matter, and visible-invisible.

The Kabbalistic view of the universe is that everything is light. I am a being of light, a spark, encapsulated in this organism, a community of billions of cells working in perfect harmony. This organism is a microcosm, a small world עולם קטן in itself, a miniature universe that functions in a miraculous way. This organism, this animal system, with all its intricacies and complexities of intelligence and language, communicating between its brain cells and the vastness of the rest of its being...the very knowledge of all of this is itself the joy of being nothing.

This knowledge is itself the art of living the ecstasy, of knowing that you know that matter is actually spirit, but of a certain frequency, and that the marriage between matter and spirit is the goal, the destination, and the path itself, of the spiritual quest.

Self-examining the self is like looking in a mirror. What it sees in that reflection is the theatricality of itself; that which is and that which is not bemuses it. All life is theatre. My realization is that I play the role of nothing by being something.

Nothing sees itself wherever it looks. Kabbalah offers the concept of the image of the broken vessels שבירת כלים and shattered mirrors. You look in one piece of a broken mirror and you see yourself, you look in another piece and you see yourself. Put the pieces of the puzzle back together into one whole mirror, and still you see yourself. Every human being is like that. Each piece of mirror, or the whole mirror, reflects the same: I.

When you look at your friend, your mate, your child, who do you see? Always "I," and you see yourself reflected in that I. You look in their eyes, and you see yourself reflected in those little round crystals. That is the idea of the broken vessels, the shattered mirrors.

So who is looking at whom? Who is it that examines the self, and who is examined? The process itself is very purifying, and it re-strengthens spirituality.

All humanity is like a colony of cells, separate but connected. Separate in order to unite. That is the work. So, when we encounter one another, when we meet and talk, there is work to do. There is recognition: I am Thou, Thou art I. I am not you, you are not I. There is no you, there is no me.

But we get lost in the cosmic theatricality of all this. These focal points of energy, these units of consciousness, which we call human beings, pretend to be important, separate, and unique. We worship matter and deny that which activates matter, which is spirit. There's nothing religious about this. It's simply a fact.

But, when you know that you are something that is nothing, that you are nothing that is something – You know that every day is a page in the book of life, and that you are the author, the scriptwriter, the interpreter, the central star role, and the actor player of your life. You have the ability to incorporate the ecstatic vision of Omar Kayyam or Rumi, and the earthy practicality of Lao Tzu, in one breath.

The utterly intoxicated lover of "God," uplifted in ecstasy, becomes grounded and anchored by going "from ecstasy to lunch." The cosmic ping-pong. Otherwise, you can't do your work. That's why the Kabbalah says, that the crown is in the foundation (Keter DeMalkhut – **כתר דמלכות**) and the foundation is in the crown (Malkhut DeKeter – **מלכות דכתר**), in the Tree of Life. That's why the heart center, being between, can reconcile what is above and what is below, the knowledge manifested and practiced. The space between thought and action is condensed.

If you are at the top of your ecstasy, overjoyed, how can you elasticize that moment and make it last, outside of time and space, unless you live fully every moment, whether joyful or sad? You know it's passing, so every moment becomes a privilege, and becomes everlasting, "eternal". Gam Zeh Ya'Avor – **גם זה יעבור** = This too shall pass.

And finally, the wild pendulum of opposites reconciles and comes to a center of silence (Merkaz Hademama – **מרכז הדממה**) and stillness, neither this nor that. There you experience emptiness and nothingness. That is quite a learning situation. That's where you "learn how to learn".

After the play/performance, you, the actor-player, take your make-up off and return home. Particularly here in the west, we get lost in the left side of our own brains and take life too seriously. We forget to play the various roles that this "I" enjoys playing.

Once we succumb to the "norms" of society, we end up whining in self-pity when we are beset by really difficult problems: "What can I do? I'm only human" the apologists cry. We enhance the consciousness of our inner poverty, belittling the great being that is within us. That is a crime and a sin. It totally misses the point. It misses the target completely.

Here then, my friend, is a truth without any cover or any hidden agenda. Are you ready to digest it with its total simplicity and illusive obviousness?

Therefore, I declare that:
You are a perfect being. You are light itself. There is nothing to struggle for, and nothing to defend. You do not in reality need any approval from others. Your body heals itself naturally. We are ill because our mental distortion of reality, interferes with our natural flow of life – Life as it was intended to be, the state of Homeostasis. A body in homeostasis has no disease.

So, Who is the "I" that resists movement and change? The "I" that can see, in its self-reflection, the nothingness of itself, can accept all of life unconditionally, can reconcile conceptually and practically the so-to-say "opposites". This "I" can accept totally its own vulnerability. Being vulnerable is the gentle acceptance of life, of oneself. So, what is there to fear? Vulnerability is strength in disguise, the invisible made visible in its opposite.

I am NOT a Human Being, I am a Human Becoming. Becoming what? That which I am, both something and nothing. Why? Because I am aware of "something" in me that I am in touch with, some invisible power that guides me, a source of creation and knowledge where fear and limitation does not exist, something infinite and nameless is guiding every step of my being toward developing and choosing my total expression as a being becoming.

On stage I am the name that I use, but I say there is only the play itself, the reality of that illusion, the truth of that lie. And "I", like you, am simply "I", utterly and simply nothing, (Ani Ha'Ayin – **אני האין**). Go figure that now.

Now that I know who this "I" is, the most important question is how to use it. And so, the real quest is this beautiful saying from the wise that I learned in my childhood, from Pirkei Avot, The Sayings of the Ancients 1:14. Hillel used to say:

אם אין אני לי, מי לי ? וכשאני לעצמי, מה אני ? ואם לא עכשו, אימתי ?
פרק א. פסוק י"ד פרקי אבות

If I am not for myself, who will be for me?
And if I am only for myself, what am I?
And if not now, when?

We can say. If I am not thinking for myself, who will think for me? Most people let others think for them. And if I am thinking only for myself, then WHAT am I? Or if I am not acting for myself, who will act for me? And if I act only for myself, then WHAT am I?

And if not now, When? If I do not think, speak and act NOW, when? This urgency can motivate us to think, speak and act NOW. Now, this present moment is the right time to think, speak and act. It is a call to end laziness, the greatest enemy of self-evolution.

We can heed to this sense of urgency, of the futile illusion of our limited concept of "time" and "space," and appreciate the NOWNESS, the preciousness of this present moment. "If not now, when?" addresses itself to this noble quest.

I would like to add to this sense of urgency by changing – adding one letter to the word אימתי Eimatai. The word אין (Ein) the negative. Reading it way, it means: If not now, there is no when. ואם לא עכשו – אין מתי ? A slight change of a letter can change the interpretation. Increasing this urgency can even motivate us to dare to explore, NOW, not later, no procrastination, no escape and no postponement.

Ponder on this practical wisdom and DARE to be yourself in "this" world. BE IN THE WORLD, BUT NOT OF IT. A gentle suggestion of living a life of a peace and practical wisdom.

"Their Way is Like That Of Animals"

שֶׁדַּרְכָּם כַּבְּהֵמוֹת

בָּכָה רַבִּי יוֹדָאִי. אָמַר לוֹ רַבִּי שִׁמְעוֹן: לָמָּה אַתָּה בּוֹכֶה?
אָמַר לוֹ: בּוֹכֶה אֲנִי (בְּלִבִּי):
אוֹי לִבְנֵי הָעוֹלָם שֶׁדַּרְכָּם כַּבְּהֵמוֹת וְאֵינָם יוֹדְעִים וְאֵינָם מִתְבּוֹנְנִים שֶׁטּוֹב לָהֶם שֶׁלֹּא נִבְרָאוּ.
אוֹי לָעוֹלָם כְּשֶׁהָאָדוֹן יֵצֵא מִמֶּנּוּ, שְׁמִי יוּכַל לְגַלּוֹת רָזִים? וּמִי יוֹדֵעַ אוֹתָם?
וּמִי יִתְבּוֹנֵן בְּדַרְכֵי הַתּוֹרָה?
שֶׁדַּרְכָּם כַּבְּהֵמוֹת (מִזְדַּוְּגִים בִּימוֹת הַחוֹל וְאֵינָם מִתְקַדְּשִׁים בַּזִּיווּג)
וְאֵינָם יוֹדְעִים וְאֵינָם מִתְבּוֹנְנִים (אֵין לָהֶם יְדִיעָה בְּתוֹרַת הַסּוֹד,
וְאֵינָם מְבִינִים בְּכַוָּנוֹת הַתּוֹרָה) שֶׁטּוֹב לָהֶם שֶׁלֹּא נִבְרָאוּ.

משנת הזוהר. תשבי-לחובר. כרך ב. חלק שלישי.
סדרה שניה – חיי אישות. דף תרל"ט.

Rabbi Yodai cried. Rabbi Shimon asked him: "Why are you crying?"

He said: I cry in my heart, because the world is in trouble,
when their way is like that of animals, and they do not know and understand that,
it would have been better for them if they were not born at all.

The world is in trouble when the MASTER of the UNIVERSE leaves it,
and his presence will be absent from this world.
And who can reveal the hidden secrets of the Universe?
And who will contemplate and understand the hidden ways of the TORAH?
—*From The Wisdom of the Zohar, by Tishby and Lachower, 2nd Volume, 3rd Section*

Kabbalah Articles and Stories

The Great Shift	15
Adam	19
The Street Violinist	26
Generating Positive and Creative Thoughts	27
Balance: The Middle Way of the Tree of Life	29
In the Beginning was the Dot	37
The Golden Letters	38
The Shield of the Beloved	46
The Rabbi and the Alchemist	52
When a Human is Born to this World	54
To Thee My God, Is My Passion	56
The "Presence of the Living Teacher" and the Emanation of Energy	60
"Maybe" and "Whatever"	66
What Kabbalah Is and Is Not	69
The Debate of the Two Twins	76
Personal Commentary on "Nothing"	83
The Gate Long Shut	87
The Awesome and Terrible Story of Rabbi Joseph De La Rheina	88

The Great Shift

THE PURPOSE OF the exercises in this book is to participate individually in what I call the great shift of consciousness. This practical work will assist you to explore within yourself the great paradox of being, in order to shift yourself from conceptual thinking, to original being.

Now, this great shift will occur when every human comes to understand that the existence of the world depends on him or her. That is a big responsibility, but it's possible to make that shift, little by little. But how?

We know that everyone is born for a purpose. We came to this world with a purpose, with work that we came to do. When you discover that purpose during your life, you will succeed in all that you do. However, unfortunately, the focus of most people's existence is physical satisfaction only, as it says in Isaiah, "eat and drink, for tomorrow we die."

Therefore, one of the good remedies that I suggest is to have the awareness to discover what you came here to do. You are a spiritual agent and you came for a mission. In that mission, you have to be focused; you have to have sharp observation of everything, especially of yourself – **always looking in the mirror, not through the window**. Because when you look out the window, you are looking outside of yourself for answers, instead of looking in the mirror to yourself. This work will assist everyone, no matter what your age is.

If you look at it, the problems we have now are because our relationships with one other are flawed. We think of the other as the enemy. But if, through this opposites work, you can develop from thinking of the other person as an enemy, to the other is my friend, the other is my beloved, the other is me – then the great shift will happen.

This great shift of consciousness can happen with sweetness. It can happen with calm practice. But if not, it will happen in spite of you, and with great suffering. So, we have two choices, two options here.

This practice of the opposites can help us advance in the evolution of this great shift. This great shift, as we call it, is shifting from the primitive way of thinking, to a higher way of thinking. In this shift, we are being introduced to the transition from human limited thinking to divine eternal thinking. These words may seem mysterious to the reader, but from our tradition, this is one of the main personal individual works, which we call Tikkun – restoration of one's self.

In kabbalistic principles, this is called **the shift from receiving to giving**. It means to shift away from the common attitude of "What's in it for me?" It means to shift away from the attitude we see rampant everywhere of "Me first, and to hell with you." It means the shift from shouting about human rights, to considering human responsibilities. It means to begin to produce more than you consume. It is the shift from constant receiving, to focus on giving.

This whole shift is finding a new center of balance – shifting from receiving to giving. This will help each individual to shift and to approach what we call essential being, without getting lost in the trap of conceptual thinking.

So, the great shift is shifting from only receiving and not giving, to starting to practice giving constantly. And if we can begin to practice this as a community, there will be no hatred and relationships will be better. We will consider the other with respect, respecting our parents and anyone that we meet.

Now, as we begin to work systematically with the apparent paradoxes, we can shift from the puzzle of the great paradox, to no paradox at all. That is a state of being, in total balance with yourself and others. It is a state of being in total balance, actually, with everyone and everything around you. It is the secret of accepting. It will perhaps assist you, the reader, in finding your purpose in this life.

If you can come to know your purpose, it will be good, not just for you, but for everyone. So, try to give from the attitude that you enjoy giving, not because you have to. To be there only to receive is purposeless, as the Kabbalah has spoken about many times.

In this book are various exercises and writings for your own personal work. It will work no matter how old you are, as it has nothing to do with age or personal history. This is a true private work with your being. These suggestions will assist you in making a shift, at least for yourself. And if you practice the exercises, you will feel that change in no time. But don't believe my words, instead consider and contemplate this, and don't believe it until you yourself have practiced and experienced the results for yourself. If you implement these suggestions, you may be amazed at what you discover.

The amazing thing is that this Tikkun, or restoration, is so simple, that if you begin to practice it right now, your life will totally change. The first thing is to respect every human being. The second is to think of the other as a potential friend. And the third is, try to give more than you receive. These are three simple keys that are not considered by most people, exactly because they are so simple. And these simple practices could change your life completely, so you can at least feel that you are happy in this world. So the question is, are you going to consider this now for yourself? The keys are here – Are you going to practice them?

"כָּל אָדָם צָרִיךְ לִרְאוֹת אֶת עַצְמוֹ בְּכָל רֶגַע
כְּאִלּוּ הַפְּעוּלָה שֶׁיַּעֲשֶׂה תַּכְרִיעַ אֶת הָעוֹלָם כֻּלּוֹ"
משנה תורה להרמב"ם הלכות תשובה ג. ד.

**"Everyone must regard oneself
as if every action one does affects the whole world"**
Maimonides, Mishnei Torah, Hilkhot Teshouva, 3.4

Note about The Great Shift

People call our kind humans. But from my experience, in my brief passage on this planet, I prefer not to dare to call ourselves humans, in essence. For history has proven the constant violence in all cultures and empires. Therefore, it is well known that people behave like animals. There is a difference – looking at most of the behavior, we call it humankind today, but it is not kind. Humanity utterly failed to find a form of government that can avoid wars and killing each other.

And according to the kabbalistic sources, the humans of today use the animalistic soul, the Nefesh Behemit (**נפש הבהמית**), and interfere in all the spiritual sources within them. So, instead of developing civilizations, in my short life on this planet, I can observe that they are human, but most of them are not kind.

One characteristic, which is abused by all, but is not recognized or acknowledged, is talking about life. I call this new disease "aboutism." It is the compulsive over-explanation of everything. And curing it is the practical remedy of our current human condition. True humans are trying to **be**, rather than being busy explaining or **talking about** "life", "spirituality", "God", "love", etc.

Most people talk about those great principles and don't dare to experience it in their realities. So, talking about does not mean knowing. If I had a western university education, I would have liked to write a thesis on how languages have insulted and even prevented human evolution, so that instead of producing a civilization, right now it is an anti-civilization.

And probably in the birth of most languages, they were formed to distort reality, to talk about it. In other words, they were set up to seek explanations for that which cannot be talked about, which is beyond words.

The shift is from the human animal to the human being. And I would add – the human being and becoming. Because we need to shift to that link with the one who created us, which is beyond name, beyond terms, beyond time, beyond space, etc., which I call in this book, "Nowhere."

Adam

KABBALAH SPEAKS ABOUT Adam, the human being. The tradition speaks of Adam HaRishon (the first man) (אדם הראשון) and Adam Kadmon (ancient man) (אדם קדמון) and Adam Elyon (higher man) (אדם עליון). But who and what is this Adam, the human being? Most people think that Adam just refers to any regular person, but the meaning is far beyond that. Adam is the essential being. Adam is not a title, it is a state of being, and you must earn it.

To understand, imagine you have a picture puzzle. You can't complete the whole picture until you fill in every part of it. So, we can understand Adam HaRishon, Adam Elyon and Adam Kadmon, as a big, big puzzle. And we know that each part of the puzzle is there in order to discover the whole picture. Now, each of us individual human beings are a little piece of the puzzle. We are the Adam of that part. We are little Adams, little human beings that have to be put together to find out what this Adam actually is.

Imagine this Adam Kadmon is the whole universe, the whole of existence. And that whole body, or whole house, is built of parts, of particles. These parts are important. For instance, if one of the pillars of a house does not stand in its place, the house will fall down. Understanding this, little by little, you can come to know the importance of who you are.

So, you are part of that great puzzle – but that realization is hidden and not revealed, yet it can be sensed, it can be personalized in each of us as a conscious capsule. And if you do that, you will always be good to the other, you will always seek to give instead of to take. This is why at Le Centre Du Silence Mime School, we always start and end every session of the summer mime training by saying "May it be for the benefit of all."

Your body is the body of Adam, but it is a micro-micro-micro-particle of that. There is an example I always give people: The mirror is Adam. Break the mirror, and you can still see your reflection, even in a piece of the mirror. If you take a little part of a broken mirror, you can still see yourself there, can't you?

In the mime workshops, I had my students do an exercise in which they would sit facing one another, looking into each other's eyes. I asked them what they saw. At first, they started philosophizing, but

I told them to stop that. I said, "Just tell me what you see, that's all." Then suddenly, someone said "I see my own reflection in her eyes." Then we developed it from there – reflection. In each particle, there is the reflection of the whole.

So, everyone is Adam, but in a minimal way. We are a kind of mini-Adam – because we all come from the big Adam, the big picture. As a result, when you understand this, you begin to give importance to the smallest of the smallest thing. You begin to discover that your eyes can see. That is obvious, isn't it? But as I mentioned many times, one Tikkun (restoration) of the eyes is to develop the inner eye, to understand from the heart. And I always asked my students, you listen from your ears, but do you listen from your spiritual ears? You listen with your physical ears, but do you really hear? And with our eyes, we photograph everything we see, without knowing it. So, if you see bad events or bad things or bad movies, it will come to haunt you. These are the obvious things.

Little by little, you have to realize that you are part of the puzzle. And so, I'm with you to discover my puzzle, which is the same actually. We are both the same picture. Without you, the world would not exist, it would be flawed. What I just said is true. The world is flawed without you. And that is why the attitude of separation is so dangerous, along with the negative thought and negative action, and the common attitude out there that the other is the enemy. Like a puzzle, it is not complete without all the pieces. That other person is just one little piece, but it's not complete without every single one.

But because of the obsession of viewing everything from the physical aspect only, when you see a person, you see only the physical. You see their nose, their clothes, and you think that is them, and as a result, you are totally confused.

In other words, our eyes exist, but they only see the physical. If you see a range of mountains before you, you see the mountains, but nobody sees the space between the mountains. We call it the negative space, because nobody notices it. But that empty space is where it is! It's where everything is. It's obvious, it doesn't need explanation. So, I call it the great puzzle. And the great puzzle is nowhere. Could you touch it? Could you touch your breath? No.

In Petihah, in the Zohar, there is a passage that speaks about the heart that understands – "בינה לבא ובה הלב מבין". So the heart is what understands, not the brain. This is why in Hebrew, the first letters of the words for brain (מוח), heart (לב) and liver (כבד) form the word King (מלכ Melekh). Because these are the three main centers of the universe.

So, if you have a heart and it's placed in the center of your body, it is a reflection of the big puzzle. And your heart is roughly the size of your fist, but imagine the heart of the whole Adam, the whole being of existence. Where is the heart of it? And you know that the heart you have in your chest is part of that heart of everything. This is why, I was walking with one of my students once who told me that they feel alone sometimes, and I said "Yes, you are all one."

This is why, when Adam was created, the messengers of the upper world became jealous. Because those angels can't manifest in physical form, and they have only one mission in the world, and that is it. The human being, however, exists in this world of physical duality and has to overcome it — Because of that, he or she can act and change the world. And what is changing the world? In our tradition, they say, restore yourself first, and then you can restore the other.

Therefore, fear is a dangerous emotion. If you are connected with that bigger picture, there is no fear. And all your needs and wants will be provided, because they are constantly linking to that big picture. It is a big puzzle. And so, your eyes are part of that big picture eye. But if you are not there, it causes the whole Adam not to be. When you begin to understand the importance of this, it can make you shiver, or cry without knowing why. It is a state of ecstatic awe (**יראת הרוממות**) when you breathe with the whole.

And so, every single person is important and has a role to fulfill as part of that whole. But nobody wants to do that. Instead, every particle of this Adam has the attitude that "I am King!", "**אני אמלוך**". "*I am King*" means I think I am governing the whole. That is true and also not true. Why? Because the part that wants to be the King is actually our negative tendency in disguise, that tendency to try to control the other, instead of serving for the good of all.

In my work, I expressed that with robotic movements — automatic physical movements, which are robotic and lack awareness. I showed how these get confused with human, organic movements, and we do them all the time. Seeing this can help us understand the difference between the real and the fake. But most people just go on and say "I am King." They want to control and rule over the other. And if you examine it, this expression of "I am King" relates only to the physical aspect. When you say that, actually you express total weakness, but you think it's power, you think it's strength.

This is why you have to have what we call in Hebrew "**ישוב הדעת**", the setting of intelligence. You have to have presence of mind, composure, equanimity, you have to be a balanced being, period. This is the state of a spiritual King, to rule over oneself, not over others.

That total picture that we are talking about is the perfect beingness. And we have part of it, but we don't realize it, because it's hidden, you can't talk about it. We give the metaphor of the puzzle and the particles. Quantum science is trying to explore that also, but this is the source of it. That is what Adam Kadmon is. But we did not yet become Adam, the human being. Because it's not a title, it's a state of being you have to earn, when you achieve the Midot, character traits, in a way that is complete.

And so, you have the form of the human being, and that's the physical manifestation of the part of the part of the part of the big picture. It is like the soup of the soup of the soup. You can call it macrocosm and microcosm. In the Hebrew language, the letter Yod (׳), which is a dot, is the microcosm of everything, and the letter Aleph (א), which stands for oneness, is the macrocosm of everything.

This is why when I said to many of my students, "You are beautiful," they thought I meant physical beauty. They would say "thanks for the compliment," but I told them it's not a compliment, it's reality. It's what makes you beautiful in and out. And you can sense that, and the physical can project that, and if so, you live in total harmony and balance. We explored that balance physically in BodySpeak™, and it is not difficult. But if you try to be balanced, you fall. That's the edge again. I can talk about these principles from now until eternity, but you have to become it, to feel it and sense it. That's the way the creation was meant to be, so that you can face this puzzle.

The puzzle I presented in my first mime performance, was that as I walked, I kept finding different doors everywhere that would not open. I wanted to go in, but the door was locked. So, what could I do? I knocked, but nothing happened. So many different doors, big doors, revolving doors. This was an introduction to the yes and no that we face all the time in life.

In that mime performance, there is a door, but I don't have a key. But each door has different keys, so I found myself looking everywhere to find the key. I tried different things. I tried to be polite and knock on the door, but nobody opens it. If someone did open the door, they would immediately push me back out. So, suddenly, I create a key out of nowhere, and I open the door, and another door, and another. And the last door was very small, like a little mousehole, but I created a little key and opened it, and I had to crawl to get through there.

Then I came to an immense space, and there was a big treasure chest there, and there was no key. But by now, I was conscious of how to find the keys. I shape the key from nowhere, and that is a key that opens all doors. Doing this, I opened the big treasure chest. And inside the storage chest was another smaller chest, and another one inside that, until I found the tiniest box. I opened it, and inside was a balloon, which I blew up, and then I stepped inside it and flew away.

This is the big Adam, one picture inside the other. This is a kabbalistic idea. This is like the human body. You have one body, built of many organs, and the organs are built of little cells[*]. And all of them operate naturally in perfect health. But then you have the technology to create commercials to tell people that they are sick, and that they need a bunch of drugs to survive, and people get sick and die just by that. That's what I realized in the beginning when I arrived here, that this really is an insane asylum.[**]

---

* See the article, "In the Beginning was the Dot"
** See the article, "Madness and Sanity on Broadway" in Last Word

Now, when you begin to realize that bigger picture, you are in a state of awe (יראת הרוממות), a higher uplifting awe, that state is ecstatic. When you realize that, you will be amazed that you can move your finger, amazed that your hand could reach to pick up a glass of water. When the ordinary movement becomes extraordinary, it means you are getting closer. For example, do you appreciate your knees? No, the knees are there, and you take it for granted that they know how to walk. This may seem simple and obvious, but I am sincere about this.

Are you aware of every posture that you do, of every movement that you make? You just did a miracle now, taking a certain posture. When you begin to feel that, not to think about it, but to experience it, you are surprised that you have lips that can speak, you are surprised that you have ears and they can hear. We are coming to the obvious movements here. That simplicity is the secret. That is why I had a whole practice I called OMSOL – obvious movements are the secret of longevity.*

We are talking about Adam, the human being, about the small picture and the big picture. So, is there some coordination between them? I call it the link. You know that you are part of the whole, yet you are the whole, in miniature form. If you experience that, then all the fears of the world, and all the needs and wants, will not exist for you. You will use that ego, you will use that knee, you will use all of that with that larger consciousness. It is a different attitude. When you have that link that I am talking about, you are taken care of.

What you will find is that people don't know what eyes are, what a nose is, what a knee is. Sure, it's a physical organ to see or to hear with, or to walk with – but people think the body is just a tool to go from point A to point B, and that's all. So all the movements become automatic, even walking. This is something we explored in BodySpeak™. But imagine that all these automatic movements and attitudes become conscious. Now, you can't do that all at once. As I say, you can't eat the whole elephant in one bite. You have to do it bite by bite, bit by bit.

Remember, you are not just part of the whole, you are the whole. This is the great puzzle. You are both. Because without you, the humanity cannot exist. But is every human on the planet operating from that state of being? No. We know that. But we can become that. That is the whole process of being and becoming, that I talk about often. That is why, in the 50 Gates of Wisdom article that I wrote, the first one is that we created ourselves, but we forgot how.** That appears confusing, but there is something behind it.

Now, in the Torah, when King Saul was chasing after David, trying to kill him, he ended up in the same cave where David was hiding, and David cut a piece of his kingly cloak. This was a hint that he would

---

* See the Defintuitions section
** See the 50 Gates of Wisdom in the book *From Ecstasy to Lunch*

be king in the future. This is a kabbalistic understanding, that what is happening on the surface in life is all symbols and messages for us to understand. But very few people understand in this way.

The Torah is built that way. Every story in the Torah is a reflection of the big story. And so, I told my students, we have the words "In the beginning, God created the heavens and the earth." It is not 'In the beginning', it is not 'God,' it is not 'heaven,' and it is not 'earth.' So they ask, "well what is it then?" They want you to explain it in a literal way.

In Hebrew, this world is called Olam (עולם), which is the same word for hidden, concealed (עלום) Alum, because this world hides the essence of things, so we can uncover it. But for that, you have to do some work, which is called Tikkun (תיקון), restoration. Relating to that, the great genius Rabbi Azekri, wrote the classic book, *Sepher Haredim, The Book of the Pious*, where he talked about the mitzvot, the deeds of restoration, to do with the different parts of the body – the hands, the legs, etc.

Those great Kabbalistic geniuses of our culture, Moses and Avraham, and all of them, they were that little part of the big Adam. That small part here knows the entire whole it is part of. And the kabbalists say that since each of them is a miniature of that whole, they give us another view, another angle to understand and explore from, and that deepens the mystery. Each of them explored this great mystery in a different way, but not from their ego-personality – from the whole.

Now, do you see that you are miracle?

The Aleph Stairway of Different Dimensions

The Street Violinist and the Bal Shem Tov

ONE DAY, a man came to the Bal Shem Tov, and began to speak harshly with him. "You crazy Hassid! You dance and sing, and meanwhile the world is crumbling! What are you thinking!?" The man carried on and on, "Aren't you aware? Don't you know you what's happening in the world?! Look at what is happening to the Jewish people. There are serious things happening. How can you dance and sing?!"

The Bal Shem Tov listened to him carefully, and he said, "Alright, I will give you an answer." And this is what he told the man:

"Once upon a time, there was a violinist, who came to the marketplace on an ordinary Tuesday. He placed his violin case before him. He opened it up, and taking out the violin, he began to play. He played beautifully. The music was lyrical, and had such a joyful cadence, and the melody soared as he played it.

And so, as he played, a few people began to assemble around him, and they put some money in his violin case. This attracted attention, and more people began to gather around them. And they began to clap their hands to the melody. Some of them even began to dance and sing. Soon, their joyful whirling attracted an even larger crowd. And so, it grew, until the whole marketplace stopped their business, and began to dance and sing together. They were all caught up in the music of this seemingly insignificant man, with his remarkable violin playing.

But then, a deaf person from the neighboring village came along. And he thought to himself, "Has the market gone crazy? Why is everyone dancing?" And he wondered to himself if it was a holiday. But no, it was surely not a holiday. So why were these people all dancing? Had they gone crazy?! What was going on?"

The Bal Shem Tov continued, and he said, "See, that is you. You don't hear the music. You are like one who is deaf. When you begin to hear, then you will know why the people dance, even in the midst of the chaos of the world."

Note: I was told this story by a friend who is a Hasidic Rabbi s.a.

Generating Positive and Creative Thoughts and Thoughts of Gratitude

PRACTICE:
Start by setting a special place and time, for a regular "<u>QUIET MOMENT</u>," to focus your positive thoughts and desires toward the benefit of all CREATION and all of humanity. Focus on these thoughts and repeat them to adopt them in your consciousness.

<u>GENERATING POSITIVE and CREATIVE THOUGHTS</u>

1. I am now relaxing all my physical and mental body to guide my positive thoughts toward all beings and all creation.
2. May all beings BE and BECOME at peace with oneself, others, and all beings.
3. May all beings guide their thoughts toward the basic good, and manifestation of all creative and good desires for the benefit of all beings.
4. I join mentally and spiritually all beings at this time that are focusing their good thoughts toward the good of all beings on this planet.
5. I know this is a very meaningful occasion to BEAM my benevolent thoughts toward all beings.
6. I dedicate myself to help every human being who needs help from me, and I practice this day as a good day to help someone in need, quietly and discreetly
7. The possibility is there to create a genuine contact with the people I meet today, by looking in their eyes when communicating and exchanging ideas, or enjoying a good time, without taking any breath for granted.
8. I am aware of my breath every moment, knowing that the source of all souls is ONE SOURCE.
9. I am aware what lessons I am learning today and how I manifest the learning into practicality.
10. Becoming aware of all my organs, I am witnessing the "miracle of life" that is occurring right this minute of my being here, fully aware and awake.

THOUGHTS OF GRATITUDE

11. I am thankful for the vibrant gift of life within me, giving me the opportunity to appreciate every thought and event in my life now, right now.
12. I am thankful for the returning of my soul this morning to its body place, to give me another opportunity to LIVE LIFE FULLY and CREATIVELY, to benefit others and myself included.
13. I am thankful for what I learn from everyone I meet, and earn the ability to see the positive aspects of everyone I meet.
14. I am grateful I can see, hear, feel, speak, walk and enjoy every breath in my life NOW.
15. I am grateful that I now emanate the positive thoughts of love, light, abundance, health, wealth, generosity, peace and profound gratitude to all humanity and all beings.
16. I am grateful for the gift of life and for the ability to be useful in a positive way in every life situation.
17. I am grateful for the inner power I was given, to use to increase awareness and kindness in every situation I am in, in this life.
18. I am grateful for the ability to use my thoughts creatively for the benefit of all concerned.
19. I am always grateful for the ability to choose and focus the thoughts that are kind, loving, and to always consider the "other", with every action in my life.
20. I know that thoughts are like passing birds. And I am careful to be constantly in this present moment, always, with every thought and action in my everyday life.

"Souls that recognize one another Congregate, those who don't…argue"
Anonymous

Balance:
The Middle Way of the Tree of Life

From The Torah to Kohelet to Maimonides (3)

WE OBSERVE ONE great unity, and one central line of focused thought, that is expressed with simplicity in the wisdom of King Solomon, and the Great Rambam (Maimonides). They show us how to be a balanced and harmonious being, living in both worlds, "this world," and "the next world" – That is, how to live in balance in both the limited world of duality, and the state of perfect oneness. To truly be lived, this balance must be both expressed in thought and manifested in action.

We see this perfect and balanced way of being expressed very clearly in Kohelet (Ecclesiastes) 7:15-18:

טו. אֶת־הַכֹּל רָאִיתִי בִּימֵי הֶבְלִי יֵשׁ צַדִּיק אֹבֵד בְּצִדְקוֹ וְיֵשׁ רָשָׁע מַאֲרִיךְ בְּרָעָתוֹ:
טז. אַל־תְּהִי צַדִּיק הַרְבֵּה וְאַל־תִּתְחַכַּם יוֹתֵר לָמָּה תִּשּׁוֹמֵם:
יז. אַל־תִּרְשַׁע הַרְבֵּה וְאַל־תְּהִי סָכָל לָמָּה תָמוּת בְּלֹא עִתֶּךָ:
יח. טוֹב אֲשֶׁר תֶּאֱחֹז בָּזֶה וְגַם־מִזֶּה אַל־תַּנַּח אֶת־יָדֶךָ כִּי־יְרֵא אֱלֹהִים יֵצֵא אֶת־כֻּלָּם:
קהלת ז. טו. טז, יז, יח.

15   All things have I seen in the days of my vanity; There is a just man who perishes in his righteousness, and there is a wicked man who prolongs his life in his wickedness.
16   Do not be too righteous, nor make yourself too wise; Why should you destroy yourself?
17   Do not be too wicked, nor be foolish; Why should you die before your time?
18   It is good that you should take hold of this, but do not withdraw your hand from that either; For he who fears God shall come forth from them all.
Kohelet (Ecclesiastes) 7:15-18.

Kohelet turns our attention to wisdom, not to be too just and righteous, but neither to be too wicked and foolish. Instead, we can find the middle way, to function from the **middle pillar of the Kabbalistic Tree of Life**, the **Balanced Way of Being** in this world.

The Rambam, Maimonides, elaborates in more detail about this balanced way of being. In the introduction to the *Mishna Avoth*, he points out the negative extremes on both sides, right and left, as well as the middle, balanced way of harmonious being.

Negative Left Extreme הפרזה לשלילה	**Middle Center Balanced Way** הדרך האמצעית המרכזית	**Negative Right Extreme** מיעוט לשלילה
תאוותנות Lust, Greediness, Intemperance, Envy, Lasciviousness.	פרישות Reclusion, Seclusion, Secrecy, Abstention, Discretion.	העדר הרגשת הנאה Lack of sensing pleasure.
פזרנות Extravagance, Wastefulness, Lavishness, Overspending.	נדיבות Generosity, Largeness, Benevolence, Openhandedness.	קמצנות Miserliness, Stinginess.
חירוף נפש Emotional Risks, Self-Sacrifice, Risk of life.	אומץ Courage, Nerve, Valor, Daring, Fearlessness. Prowess.	מורך לב Faint-heartedness, Cowardliness, Fear.
חוצפה Impudence, Effrontery, Presumption, Immodesty, Impertinence.	בדיחות Hilarity, Jest, Facetiousness, Humor.	טמטום Stupidity, Imbecility, Stupor.
גאוה Pride. Haughtiness. Conceit, Boasting, Vanity, Loftiness.	ענווה Humility, Modesty, Meekness, Lowliness.	שפלות רוח Modesty Humbleness, Meekness.
התהדרות Ornamentation, Self-aggrandizement, Self praise.	רצינות Seriousness, Solemnity, Profoundness.	שפלות Meanness, Baseness, Lousiness.
התיימרות Pompousness, Pretense. Arrogance.	הסתפקות במה שיש Satisfaction with what is, Living within one's means. Frugality, Temperance.	סגפנות Asceticism, Mortification.
רגזנות Bad-Temper, Anger. Easily angered over anything.	מתינות Moderation, Poise, Calm, Balanced Temperament, Centeredness.	קרירות המזג Cold energy, Chill, Frigidity, Frostiness, Cool-Tempered.
עזות מצח Insolence, Brazenness, Impudence, Daring in the negative direction.	ביישנות Shyness, Timidity, Bashfulness. "Conscious innocence". תמימות הדעת	רתיעה מופרזת מכל דבר Exaggerated tendency to recoil from everything.

This table illustrates these extremes, and it can serve as a practical tool in order to acquire these balanced traits. The traits, presented both in Hebrew and English, illustrate how common it is for humans to tend toward an extreme, edgy character.

Consider this as a map of how to cultivate balance. It can help us remember and learn how to be and become a balanced being. It shows us how to be in the "between," the middle way, the perfect way.

In his *Mishneh Torah, Sefer Habadah, Halacha 3*, Maimonides states clearly:

"The two extremes of each trait, each far removed from one another, do not reflect a proper path. It is not fitting that a man should behave in accordance with these extremes or instruct himself in their way."

"One may find that their nature tends towards one of these extremes and adapts easily to it. Or one may have learned one of the extremes and become used to acting according to it. If so, he should bring himself back to what is proper, and walk in the path of right. This is the straight path."

We can view this balanced way of being from many different angles.

Balance as a Physical Exercise
Balance can be experienced as a practical tool. At Le Centre Du Silence Mime School, students in the BodySpeak™ Summer Mime Workshop experience it, when they learn a practical exercise called "The Stick" exercise.

This exercise is one of the ten principles or components of the bodywork method I developed, called BodySpeak™. In it, we study the two edges of a staff. In reality, the edges exist only in our imagination, for it appears that there are two opposite edges, but actually it is only one stick. Students learn the awareness to focus on what they are doing at this moment, right now, and by doing so, how to prevent and avoid accidents. For when doing stick exercises, if one is not alert and aware, it is easy to get hit with one side of the stick.

"The Stick" exercise can illustrate this principle of being totally in balance within ourselves, on all levels and aspects of our being – mentally, physically and spiritually.

Playing with the two edges of the stick, and manipulating it ONLY from the center of it, one can learn how to practice physical, mental and spiritual balance, through the physical exercise itself. This helps the student to be sharply aware and totally present with the practice.

Working with "the Stick," we explore how to harmonize the paradox, the two opposites, using the center, which includes both of the edges. This idea comes from the structure of the Kabbalistic Tree of Life.

In the Tree of Life, there are three pillars, and three principle sephirot: Hesed is the right pillar, Gevurah is the left pillar, and Tiferet is the middle pillar of the whole system of the Tree of Life. So, we have the principle of the two opposites, and the middle that includes both edges, and harmonizes and reconciles them.

Students learn and experience this principle directly in the stick exercise. Later the student will be able to apply that principle in life and solve the hoax of the "paradox," which is a rampant conflict in human life today that perplexes people everywhere.

Avoiding Extremes
Balance: Maimonides and King Solomon both talk about balance and avoiding extremes. King Solomon says that in order to find balance, one should "hold on to the one opposite, without letting go of the other." When taken to the extreme, even good things become bad. Kindness (Hesed – Right side) is good, but it has to be balanced with strength (Gevurah – Left side). And strong judgment (another element of Gevurah) has to be sweetened with kindness, and balanced with Tiferet (the Center), which restores the edges.

King Solomon also says "Don't make yourself too wise. Why destroy yourself?" and at the same time "Don't be a fool and lose your life." Instead, take the middle path. This middle path is Tiferet, the reconciler and harmonizer of the right and left sides. Even if you are wise and great, balance yourself by realizing that you are both important and insignificant at the same time. Thus, you will learn the way of equanimity, and you can function from that balanced state in your creative life.

Instead of being swept to emotional extremes by life events, use the two essential guidelines below. View them as two nuggets of practical and active wisdom:

The first is: As you go about your everyday life, adopt the attitude that whatever is happening at this moment, allow it to pass, knowing that "גם זה יעבור" "This too shall pass."

The second is: Consider all that happens to you with the thought of: "This also is for the good" "גם זו לטובה" – Activating these two thoughts in various situations will assist you to overcome all difficulties, and you will discover the power of this very real moment of now.

The Balance of Rich and Poor
One of the traditional and classical examples is the instruction of Moses for the Israelites to contribute in order to build the temporary temple as a tent in the desert. There is a natural balance between the rich and the poor, and the equality of giving is indicated, saying,

"הֶעָשִׁיר לֹא־יַרְבֶּה וְהַדַּל לֹא יַמְעִיט" שמות ל. טו.
"The rich shall not give more, and the poor shall not give less than half a shekel...."
Exodus 30. 15

This simple and beautiful attitude of giving instructs us not to exaggerate that tendency for the rich to give more and for the poor to be unable to give. Instead, both are able to give in balance. When we heed to this balanced way of giving, we really feel the inner wealth of our essence of being, something which goes beyond physical having and not having.

The Hebrew Letter SHEEN as a Principle of Balance
Another way of seeing the principle of balance is by examining the Hebrew Letter SHEEN.

The Hebrew Letters are the building blocks of the creation of the universe. Each letter stores and contains within it certain spiritual powers, and serves as a special tool of practice, for exploring ourselves and the universe. They present a unique way of learning how to learn, think and be.

The Sheen (ש), which is the 21st letter of the sacred 22 Hebrew letters, teaches us the principle of balance which we have been discussing. The letter is composed of three lines, right, left, and center. Thus, Sheen (ש) relates to the right and left extremes, which are rampant in the human character, and indicates how we can come, intelligently and willingly, to choose and apply the balanced middle way.

Contained in this letter's code is the principle of Three. The Sheen (ש) is composed of three lines, flames, directions, symbolizing the inner dimensions of being. These are three ways, gates and levels. It is the three branches of the tree of Life – left pillar, middle pillar and right pillar – reaching high like the flames, purifying the conditioning of our lives. It can also be understood as the original three ways of learning, to be and become one with oneself, aligned with the whole of Creation.

Keep in mind, this is only touching on the surface of the surface of the profound study of this Hebrew letter. The deeper meanings of the Hebrew letters have been studied over thousands of years, by many unique and dedicated beings who prefer to stay unknown to this world.

A Learning Moment of Balance
I can also add a personal note about this balanced attitude that Kohelet and the Rambam taught us. There is a reason I have chosen to share this example with my committed students and others who read these words. They may realize that this possibility of balance does exist. It depends on the great gift of choice.

On the one hand, we can choose to go to extremes. Many people only change after going to the extreme edges physically, mentally, or through accidents and disasters. Ninety-nine percent

(99.9%) of humanity is doing this, because we are trapped in our conditioning and confused habits. On the other hand, we can choose to shift consciously to a right and balanced way of being and living.

I grew up in small and ancient village in Sefrou, Morocco, in a modest family with an ancient lineage of great sages. We lived the way of the Rambam's teachings by developing character through learning. Learning for me was mainly through osmosis and direct living, learned through the living examples of my parents and grandparents. We lived by these principles and focused on learning, in spite of the poverty and suffering we lived in under some repressive and abusive Muslim rulers.

In this way of learning, my parents and teachers never preached to me to do this or that. It was lived through examples and emulation. Learning was not through telling me words, or ordering me about what to do or not to do. The focus was on learning the essence wisdom and the tradition which had been transmitted for thousands of years.

One example lives clearly in my memory. My grandfather, my father, and my mother (three immediate transmitters of knowledge), never uttered a word until it was necessary. One of the sacred practices called "Fasting from words" "תענית דיבור" was practiced one day a week (and sometimes two days a week), plus some important times during the year. The habit of this practice was instilled within me, and I have found that through it, one earns great benefits in life.

Word Economy
The below childhood story illustrates this well.

"My grandfather once told me that we are born with a certain number of words in our "word bank." If one uses too many words (just like if one overspends their money), it empties our word bank account. We become overdrawn, and become mute. When we use words only when necessary, we practice word economy.

"Words are only one of the ways to communicate. 99% of our real communication occurs in silence, through body language."

"I highly recommend to practice one day of silence a week, to achieve the ability to speak less and do more, and produce more and consume less – practicing consistently the practical wisdom of the "Word Economy."

Growing up, traveling and experiencing life's challenges, I did not make a big deal of my suffering, or complain to anyone of what I was feeling or thinking, or share the experiences of any important turning point events in my life.

All I knew was that the seed of true and original knowledge was invested within me. I knew that I was profoundly living that, quietly, in a natural way, and experiencing life with my "Conscious Innocence." I thought that most people must know and live that way.

But no, the cultural shock hit me when I began teaching in the USA. I found out that it was unknown to my students, those elementary and natural ways of living harmoniously with yourself and others. That realization saddened me deeply.

Then I began learning about how people here lived, and found out that they must LEARN these balanced ways of living, because they did not learn it directly from their parents. Their parents may not have known how to transmit those values via their example, from their way of living and being.

What I witnessed in living in the USA is that tendency of many Americans, and the Western way of living in general, is to dwell constantly in the extremes. But doing so is actually a mask to cover up one's laziness, an excuse to escape reality. Or else it is lack of knowledge of how our brain works.

I understood then, the intricacies of the games people play, that cause them to create and deepen their conflicts, which in turn, causes diseases, mental imbalance, and physical illness.

So as a result, living in our extreme society, many of us, consciously or unconsciously, create problems where they do not exist. And that conflict deepens exponentially again from individuals to entire groups of people.

Tikkun
Those who know and become aware of these extremes can begin the process we call Tikkun – restoration and healing oneself and the world. This is becoming the being we were meant to be in the first place.

This is why I wrote these words, to bring to your awareness the practical teachings of Kohelet and Maimonides, that are rooted in the tradition of the Torah. These ideas are still relevant and very important in our very perplexed and confused times. So hopefully, you may also choose to walk and be in the middle way, and emanate that balance to all around you.

May you see the simple logic, obvious innocence and the light of profound understanding, to undertake the restoration of yourself first. So it is.

Samuel Ben-Or Avital

Thursday, Sept 1st, 2011. 1st day of ELUL, 5771.

כִּי־טוֹבָה חָכְמָה מִפְּנִינִים וְכָל־חֲפָצִים לֹא יִשְׁווּ־בָהּ: משלי ח. יא.
For wisdom is better than rubies;
and all the things that may be desired are not to be compared to it.
Proverbs 8. 11

The Mandala of EMET (Truth)

In the Beginning was the Dot

"**IN THE BEGINNING** there was the dot, and another dot and another one. They played and multiplied in space and time and became a **LINE.** And the line moved and became a **circle**, and the dot within the circle began to move, touching the walls of the circle, and bouncing strongly back and forth, from one wall of the circle to another; Thus energy was created.

And with this mighty movement was created new forms that shaped into a triangle, cells, organs, hearts, kidneys, and a whole life became visible and manifested.

And finally, the human organism emerged and uttered the words, and worlds, and wrote them in symbols, lines, circles, diagonal shapes, letters. And the symbols became reality, and concealed within each letter were the "**secret**" codes of Creation.

From the **Original Dot**, we call **The Source of all Life** and beings, coming and emerging "**out of nothing**" (**Yesh Me'Ayin**), the whole universe comes into being, and contains all beings and all that is becoming. And they begin to "Breathe."

And the **CREATOR, DESIGNER** saw the "**Great Design**", and called it "**good**" **Tov.**

So, our task now, as the created and creative human beings (as the **image, or Tzelem, of the Creator**) is to explore, decipher, recognize and use the **power** of the Creator, the Designer and sublime Animator of all the manifestations of existence; Our role is to align ourselves with that greater will. We call this **LIFE** (**Hayyim**) and **LIGHT** (**Or Elion**), and we also call it "**Good**." And we know that our role is to use that "Power" (**Koah)**, for the good and benefit of all living beings.

The Golden Letters – הָאוֹתִיּוֹת הַזּוֹהֲרוֹת

IN THE SHADOW of the great Atlas Mountains of Morocco, you will find a small village named Sefrou. This tiny village could easily be overlooked by the unaware observer. Yet the influence and inner traditions of Sefrou are greater than its physical size. As a center of the spiritual tradition of Kabbalah, Sefrou has produced many of the great rabbis, sages, and mystics of North Africa. This beloved village is called by its people, "Little Jerusalem."

The history of Sefrou is intertwined with the history of the Jewish people. Many inhabitants of Sefrou were exiled here from Spain. They fled from the inquisition, when King Ferdinand and Queen Isabella expelled all Jewish people from their country in 1492. Exiled throughout North Africa, they planted their cultural roots anew. They joined their Jewish brethren who had inhabited North Africa since the time of King Solomon as traders and merchants.

As a child, I grew up in this unique Jewish community. I lived with my family in a big three-story house that my grandfather had built. My grandfather lived on the ground floor, while the rest of my family lived on the upper floors.

I was deeply connected with my grandfather, a great hidden kabbalist called R. Eliyahu Ya'akov Abitbol. After school, I would rush to see him and help with his many crafts. I would help stomp grapes to make fragrant wine, or lend a hand in the shop where my father and grandfather made scented soaps. Everywhere Saba (grandfather) Eliyahu went, he carried with him an ancient copy of the Zohar, passed down through our family for many generations. The Zohar, the Book of Splendor, is the ancient Kabbalistic source book, which contains many of the inner secrets of creation and the Torah.

I would often find Saba Eliyahu out in the garden, just outside of the big house. His eyes sparkled with smiling wisdom. I learned from him in a way that was a natural as breathing. Saba's actions, his strong silences, his words and stories – all of these were full of meaning. He did not speak often and when he did, it was generally through a story or through hints that indicated to me how to find my own life answers. The inner meanings of his teachings unfolded in the silence between us, and in the sheer and vast and rich experience of living and being.

There, out in the garden, was a feeling beyond time and space. Words were not needed. Just a look or a glance was enough. Without a word, I could feel that my grandfather understood. There was no time, even when we were apart, that I did not feel my grandfather's presence with me.

One day, during my twelfth year, I arose at dawn. It was the first day of Rosh HaShanah, the Jewish New year. This was a very significant holiday, during an important year of my life, the year when I prepared for my Bar Mitzvah. The Bar Mitzvah is the rite of passage for a boy to enter into manhood and become a responsible member of the Jewish community. The morning was an unspoken symphony, soft rose and purple hues pierced by the stirring strains of the golden sun. The entire community gathered at the synagogue, where we spent the morning in intense prayer.

After returning home in the afternoon, I fell asleep, and found myself dreaming an amazing dream. In it, I saw myself holding a Great Shofar. (The Shofar is a ram's horn instrument, traditionally blown on Rosh Hashanah and Yom Kippur, which produces a primordial wailing sound. The piercing sound is meant to awake the people from their sleep, so they will restore their souls and plead for their sins to be forgiven.)

I blew into the Shofar. But instead of a sound, the holy letters of the Hebrew Aleph-Beit came flying out from the Shofar. They whirled and dancing in the air, like great golden eagles of light. I danced with them and it felt as if I was one of them. I noticed that the letters of my name, Sheen, Mem, Vav, Aleph and Lammed, **שמואל** were so bright, that I had to cover my face to protect my eyes from that powerful brilliance. I enjoyed being one with those flying letters. It was as if there was no time or space, just a sense of continuous being with that dance. After seeing these beautiful images, I awoke.

I couldn't wait to tell my grandfather about his marvelous vision. I leapt up and ran out to the garden, calling out "Saba!"
   My grandfather smiled at me with those knowing, sparkling eyes "Yes, Shemouel."
   "I had a dream about the Great Shofar," I cried out excitedly. I sat on a smooth stone beside my grandfather to tell him all that had occurred.

"My dear Shemouel," Saba said, "You have dreamed a story from the pages of the Zohar. It is said that a Great Shofar was sounded at the beginning of all Creation. But this Shofar did not produce a sound one can hear, but only a sound that one can see, the sound of a still Silent and small Voice. (Kol Demama Dakkah) קוֹל דְּמָמָה דַקָּה"

Then, my grandfather gently opened the pages of the ancient Zohar and read to me:

The Rav Hamnouna, the Venerable, commented on the verse "In the Beginning, God created the heavens and the earth," "בְּרֵאשִׁית, בָּרָא אֱלֹהִים, אֵת הַשָּׁמַיִם, וְאֵת הָאָרֶץ" (Bereshit/Genesis 1:1). This is what he said:

We find the first verse of scripture begins in an order that is reversed. BEITH [ב] (which is the second letter of the Alphabet) is found at the beginning. For BEITH is the first letter of the first word, BERE"SHEET [בְּרֵאשִׁית] (the word which means 'In the beginning'). It is also the first letter of the next word BARA [בָּרָא] (which means 'created'). Then ALEPH [א] (which is the first letter of the Alphabet) follows after. For ALEPH is the first letter of the word ELOHIM [אֱלֹהִים] (which means 'God') and the word ETH [אֵת], which comes after it. (So, the second letter appears first, and the first letter appears second. Why is this?)

The reason for this is because when Holy One, Blessed Be He was about to make the world, all the letters were still sealed in an embryonic state. For two thousand years, the Holy One contemplated and played with them. When he wanted to create the world, all the letters presented themselves before him, from the last letter Tav [ת], to the first letter Aleph [א].

The letter TAV [ת] advanced forward and pleaded, "Master of the Universe, may it please You to place me first in the creation of the world. For I am your seal and signature, formed by the word Truth [EMET אֱמֶת], and You are called by this very name of EMET [אֱמֶת]. It is well for the King to begin His work with the final letter of EMET [אֱמֶת] and to create the world with me."

The Holy One, Blessed Be He, said to her, "TAV [ת], you are worthy and deserving, but it is not proper that I begin the creation of the world with you. For you are destined to serve as a mark on the foreheads of the faithful ones (Ezekiel 9:4), who have kept the law from Aleph to Tav, who because of this mark, are free of death. Further, you form the conclusion of death [MAVET מָוֶת]. Hence, you are not to initiate the creation of the world."

The letter SHIN [ש] came and pleaded, "O Master of the Universe, may it please you to begin the world with me. I am the beginning of Your Name, SHADDAI [Almighty] [שַׁדַּי], and it is most fitting to create the world through Your Holy Name." He said in reply, "You are indeed worthy, you are good, you are true. But I may not begin the creation of the world through you, since you form part of the group of letters expressing forgery and lies, SHEKER [שֶׁקֶר], which are not able to exist unless the QOF [ק] and the RAYSH [ר] draw you into their company.

So we see that, in order to be believed, a lie must always include something true. For the SHIN [ש] is the letter of truth, that letter by which the Patriarchs communed with God. But QOF [ק] and RAYSH [ר] are letters belonging to the evil side, which attach themselves to SHIN, in order to stand firmly, thus forming a conspiracy, QESHER [קֶשֶׁר]. Having, heard this, SHIN [ש] departed.

The TZADI [צ] entered and said: "O, Master of the Universe, may it please You to create the world with me, for I am the sign of the righteous, TZADIKIM [צַדִּיקִים] and of Yourself, for you are called righteous. As it is written, "For the Lord is righteous, he loves righteousness" (Psalms 11:7). And so, it is right to create the world with me."

The Lord answered, "O TSADDE, you are TSADDIK [Just] and you signify righteousness. But you must be concealed. You should not be made be too revealed and visible, so you will not give the world cause for offense.

For you consist of the letter NUN [נ] with the letter YOD [י] attached to it, representing the male and female principles together. This is the mystery of the creation of the first man, who was created with two faces (male and female combined). In the same way, the NUN and the YOD in the TSADDE are turned back-to-back [צ], not face-to-face. One day I will turn your two faces to be face-to-face, but that will happen in another place." The TSADDE then departed."

The letter PEH [פ] presented herself and pleaded, "May it please You, Oh Master of the Universe, to create the world through me. You see that I signify Deliverance [PURKANA פּוּרְקָנָא and PEDUT פְּדוּת], which You vouchsafe for the world. And so, the world should be created through me. The Lord answered: "You are worthy. But you also represent transgression, PESHAH [פֶּשַׁע]. And you are shaped like a serpent, who has his head curled up within his body, symbolic of the guilty, who bends his head and extends his hand."

The letter AYIN [ע], was likewise refused as standing for iniquity, AVON [עָוֹן], despite her plea that she represented humility, ANAVAH [עֲנָוָה].

Then SAMEKH [ס] appeared and said, "O Master of the Universe, may it please You to create the world through me, for I represent upholding, SEMIKHA [סְמִיכָה] of the fallen. As it is written, "The Lord upholds all that fall" (Psalms 145:14). The Lord answered her, "This is the reason why you should remain in your place. For if you should leave it, what would be the fate of the fallen, since they are upheld by you?" She immediately departed.

The letter NUN [נ] entered and pleaded her merit as the initial letter in "awesome [NORA נוֹרָא] in praises" (Exodus 15:11), as well as in "comely [NAVAH נָאוָה] is praise for the righteous" (Psalms 33:1). The Lord said, "Oh NUN, return to your place, for it is for your sake, as representing the fallen, NOFELIM [נוֹפְלִים], that SAMEKH returned to her place. Therefore, remain with her for support. The NUN immediately returned to her place.

The letter MEM [מ] came up and said: "Master of the Universe, may it please You to create the world with me, as I begin the word King, MELEKH [מֶלֶךְ], and You are Named King. The Lord replied, "Truly, it is so, but I cannot employ you in the creation of the world, for the reason that the world requires a

King. Therefore, return to your place, along with the LAMED [ל] and the KAF [כ]. For the world must not be established without a King [מֶלֶךְ]."

At that moment, the letter KAF [כ] descended from the Throne of Glory [כִּסֵּא]. Two hundred thousand worlds began to shake, the throne trembled, and all the worlds quaked and were about to fall into ruins. The Holy One, blessed be His Name, said to her, "KHAF, what are you doing here? I will not create the world with you. Go back to your place, since you stand for extermination, KELAYAH [כְּלָיָה]. Return thus to your place and remain there." Immediately, she departed to her place.

The letter YOD [י] then presented herself and said, "May it please You, O Lord, to begin with me in the first place in the creation of the world, since I stand first in your Sacred Name. The Lord said to her, "It is sufficient for you that you are the channel of My Will. You must not be removed from my Name."

The letter TAYT [ט] came up and said: "O Master of the Universe, may it please You to place me at the head in the creation of the world, since through me You are called good, TOV [טוֹב] and upright, YASHAR [יָשָׁר]." The Lord said to her, "I will not create the world through you, because the goodness which you represent is hidden and concealed within you, as it is written, "O how abundant is your goodness, which you have stored up for those that fear you" (Psalms 31:20). The true good is not for "this world," it belongs in the world to come.

And furthermore, it is because your goodness is hidden within you, that the gates of the Temples sank into the ground, as it is written, "Sunk [TABE'U טָבְעוּ] into the ground are her gates" (Lamentations 2:9). Furthermore, when the letter HAYYT [ח] is at your side, you join to make sin, HET [חְטָא]. It is for that reason that these two letters are not found in the names of any of the tribes." She then departed immediately.

The letter ZAYIN [ז] presented herself and put forth her claim, saying "O Master of the Universe, may it please You to put me at the head of creation, since I represent the observance of the Shabbat. As it is written, "Remember [ZAKHOR זָכוֹר] the day of the Shabbat, to keep it holy (Ex. 20:8). The Lord replied, "I will not create the world through you, since you represent war. Your shape is like a sharp-pointed spear or lance" [זַיִן]. The ZAYIN immediately departed from his presence.

The letter VAV [ו] entered with her claim, saying, "O Lord of the World, may it please You to use me first in the creation of the world, inasmuch as I am one of the letters of Your Holy Name. The Lord said to her, "It is enough for you, VAV [ו], as well as the HAY [ה], that you are one of the four letters of My Name. You are part of the Mystery of My Name, engraved and impressed in My Name. Therefore, I will not give you the first place in the creation of the world."

Then the letter DALLET [ד] and the letter GIMEL [ג] appeared, and they put forth similar claims. The Lord gave them a similar reply, saying, "It is sufficient for you both to remain side by side together, since "the poor will not cease from the land" (Deut. 15:11), and they will need benevolence. For the DALLET signifies poverty, DALUT [דַּלּוּת] and the GHIMEL signifies beneficence, GEMUL [גְּמוּל]. Therefore, do not separate from each other. Let it be enough that one maintains the other."

The BEITH [ב] then entered and said, "O Lord of the World, may it please You to put me first in the creation of the world, since I represent the benedictions, BERACHOT [בְּרָכוֹת] offered to You on high and below. The Holy One, Blessed Be He, said to her, "Truly, WITH YOU I WILL CREATE THE WORLD, and you will form the beginning in the creation of the world" [בְּרֵאשִׁית בָּרָא].

The letter ALEPH [א] remained in her place without presenting herself. The Holy One, blessed be His Name, said to her, "ALEPH [אָלֶף], ALEPH [אָלֶף], why do you not come before me like the rest of the letters?" She answered, "Because I saw all the other letters leaving Your presence without any success. What, then, could I achieve there? And further, since you have already bestowed this great gift upon the BEITH [ב]. It is not proper of the Supreme King to take away a gift which He has made to His servant and give it to another."

The LORD said to her: "Oh ALEPH, ALEPH, although I will begin the creation of the world with BEITH [ב], you shall remain the FIRST of the letters. My unity will not be expressed except through you. All calculations, operations, and computations of the world will be based on you, and Unity will not be expressed, except by the letter ALEPH [א]."

Then the Blessed Creator of the World made higher world letters, of a large pattern, and lower world letters, of a small pattern. And so it is, that we have two words beginning with BEITH [ב]: BERESHEET BARA [בְּרֵאשִׁית בָּרָא] and then two words beginning with ALEPH [א], ELOHIM ETH [אֱלֹהִים אֵת]. They represent the higher-world letters and the lower-world letters. When the two operate together, above and below, ALL IS AS ONE."

After telling the story, Saba smiled down at me, "Shemouel, would you like to know what the Holy One, Blessed Be He did, when he wanted to send the letters down into this world from his Holy presence?" I nodded, yes.

"He blew His Great Shofar and all the Letters, Great and Small, flew out, like golden birds. The Great Letters flew up to be with Him, to amuse him before His Throne. The small letters flew out and journeyed downward and downward, from sphere to sphere, from dimension to dimension, from that which is pure, to that which is thick. Gradually, they became more and more visible, until they appeared in this world of limited dimensions, where they developed shape and form, so we may use them to store the code of creation as instruments of writing."

In my heart, I felt a deep longing to see the vision of the golden letters again, and to carry it with me, so I would never forget. "Saba, what can I do so I will never forget about the dream of the shofar?"

"The letters will give you the answer," my grandfather told me. "Every day that you live, you journey between the horizon of morning and the horizon of night. The Zohar says that if you look into the eastern sky each day at a certain moment of daybreak, you will see what look like letters in motion, formed by sparks from the letters of the Aleph-Beit, with which the Holy One, Blessed Be He, created the world. The letters are a part of you. If you look you will begin to see them in your own body and in everything, everywhere that you look."

Sitting there, beside my grandfather, I thought, "One day, my body will become all these letters and I will set them in motion for my people." I gazed up at my grandfather's weathered face. The day was growing late now, almost sunset, but I did not feel cold. Instead, I felt a warm presence, like the feeling of an inner sunlight. No words were needed here. The echo of the Shofar had stamped within my heart the mystery of the primal sound of silence, a trembling silent cry. I was filled with great awe of the Creator, and also an immense joy of being one, beyond all verbal description.

As the sun quietly turned its head to set over the small village of Sefrou, the dream still echoed strongly in my spirit. I knew now that it was not just a dream, but that that the holy letters would always be with me. I would never forget the vision of the dancing golden letters.

Note: The Story of the Letters of Creation, which my grandfather read to me is translated from the Zohar (The Book of Splendor) from the "Hakdamat Zohar" ("Introduction of the Zohar"). This version was translated and adapted into English by Samuel Ben-Or Avital.

"Every blade of grass has an angel bending over it saying, 'Grow.'"
—From the Talmud

MESSAGES FROM "NOWHERE"

My Dove in the Clefts of the Rock

Illustration By Zev Ben Mosheh Ha-Cohen

The Shield of the Beloved

IN THIS INTRODUCTION to what is called in Kabbalah "The Divine Mirror" or "The Diamond Within," I am addressing myself both to the one within who knows, and to the one within who is ignorant. I will try to speak a language that reaches everyone. There is nothing new here, it is very simple.

We begin with a symbol to put these ideas in focus. The symbol itself is a form of focusing the left side of the brain, so we can cross over to the right side, and then we can get the marriage of ourselves. Then we can understand what it is we're all about and what we're doing here.

On the way to forming the symbol called "The Shield of the Beloved" is a very simple symbol in the shape of an hour-glass.

There is a lower pyramid and an upper inverted pyramid, and a place of connection between them. In the Kabbalah, these two pyramids or triangles represent the "lower world" and the "upper world."

The lower world is the finite world, the world of matter, the physical, the tangible, the world that is known, the world of Being. It is where we are when we are born from nowhere to something.

The upper world is called the "Ein Sof," the world of the infinite, the unconscious, the world of the spirit, the unknown world, the world of Becoming.

Now each of these worlds, the lower and the upper, have ten stairs or steps, which are the stairs of ascending, of evolution.

The bottom three stairs of the lower pyramid represent the mineral, the vegetable, and the animal and human kingdoms, with their own different rungs and levels. Most of humanity, almost all, 99.9% of humanity are here on the third step.

The purpose of being here in this world is to ascend the ten steps of the lower pyramid of being, of learning to be, to the upper pyramid, the pyramid of becoming.

But you cannot ascend these steps directly. You must take an "invisible stairway," a spiraling stairway that is multi-dimensional, not like a ladder that you just walk up, but where you have to turn around and around and swirl and whirl in the air or in the understanding, to get from the space of one rung to another.

This inner, invisible, multi-dimensional stairway is the channel, the funneling process as it is called in the Kabbalah, the funnel through which ideas, manifestations of the upper world come to the lower world, to teach us, to show us this or that, inventions of scientists, and so on. Everything comes through this, it is the Passage, the birth canal, it is the "ladder of Jacob," the ladder of earth and heaven. It forms the tubes of communication from the lower world to the upper, from the upper world to the lower.

But the area where the upper part of the hour-glass unites with the lower part of the hour-glass is a very dangerous sphere, a cross road, a flame; It is very trying and very difficult. It has been called, "the dark night of the soul."

It is the revolving door of the Garden of Eden, and if you are unaware for even one minute, it is goodbye for now, and see you next incarnation.

We sometimes visit this place but can't get through it, it's so narrow, if our ego's too fat with all its extra baggage. We have to get thin for that.

Very few dare to try to get through, for this is all unknown to us, we are afraid. We whirl around in the world of the known, learning how to be, learning the physical primal things, learning how to eat and walk and make love and deal with this world, paying rent, dealing with stuff, with substance.

To get through that place where the upper meets the lower is to be cooked in the cauldron where the ego gets burned, though not to ashes. It is the alchemical "tannoor," the furnace. You have to be "cooked" to pass through there, to absorb that heat and get used to it.

You need a master's card, a VISA, to go through there, which means acquiring certain tools and mastering them. You have to master Visualization through repeated practice, first of all. You have to be able to quickly push the button into the world of inspiration and create, and you must have a realization of the Infinite being of light within you. If you don't have that, you can't pass through here.

You must have total Sanity, you must "walk Sane in the midst of madness" in this world that is gone off balance almost to the point of no return. You can't wait for he or she to love you and kiss you and all that, that's for lower level of humanity, and we're talking about ways and means so we can climb and spiral up to that sphere where we came from, which is our source. Once upon a time we were particles of light that got dropped from above to below. Somehow, we got the application to where to incarnate and got picked up by a man and woman in union and....phht... it got born. It forgets once upon a time it was light. It feels it is trapped in the physical organism, and forgets.

And that's the purpose. The lower triangle is the school of remembering, it's the cosmic theatre where all the egos come about and all the attractions of the polarities happen. It is a world of doubt, and we need the Sanity of certainty to pass beyond it. You can't pass through if you doubt.

That's a lot to ask of us primates on this planet, I know, but it's better to ask that than a raise from your boss. Here, you raise yourself, not your salary.

You must have total Awakening, total Awareness for your cosmic VISA. All these items you must get for yourself; Down here you write your own script, you author yourself, and do the lead acting, the activity of it, always with words in this world of words.

We talk and talk, but some of us learn to acquire the cosmic VISA. Then, we know how to swirl and to whirl and deal with this and that, and if we say "I love you," we know what's going on, we know who is this "I" and who is this "you" and what is this love, and what is this separation between "I" and "you", etc, etc.

If we say, "I am hungry," we know, "I am" is never hungry, the stomach is hungry. We can make distinctions. We learn how to transcend the male and female aspects, and all the polarities. Otherwise, there is no entrance, and no exit. Otherwise, we're stuck here for millions of years incarnating, coming back and coming back down here, where the cooking happens, all the relationships, all the petty things we do, the fathers and daughters and mothers and sons, the states and nations. If we get caught in the "cooking", we may not have the feast of passing through all this. And that passage through: the last supper happens here.

So, it is that some of us, focused units of consciousness, of light, depending on our inner velocity and voltage and degree of awareness and awakening, get SUCKED UP into the upper pyramid, perhaps unconsciously, accidentally, and we remember for an instant. And then maybe it happens again, we get SUCKED UP into that reservoir of knowledge of becoming, until we learn we can do that consciously, with practice, until we ourselves become channels of communication, teachers, artists, inventors, helpers of mankind.

That means we got used to the heat of the cooking, all the right ingredients, the water boiling just right, the cosmic recipe in the works... and something starts to happen that begins to make sense: we "crack the cosmic code" (the Hebrew letters). The ladder, the invisible stairway, gets shorter and shorter as we learn the routes, and the triangles merge, the upper infusing the lower, the lower becoming comfortable with the upper.

Here is the visibility of it, the center of being and becoming, the Jewel of the Kabbalah, the Shield of the Beloved.

This is the yin and the yang, the chakra of the heart, the state of total protection. You can walk on water if you want, or become a millionaire. You can overcome great difficulties in this sphere of certainty.

Until that can happen, you stay down here with the rest of humanity in the lower triangle, in the pyramid of limited time and space, with its arguments, divisions, philosophies and religions, most everyone pretending to know this or be that, always pretending, pretending to communicate, but talking without necessity with words that have no value.

There's no use pretending, that won't generate the voltage you need, the VISA. Human consciousness is a container of light, and you need the proper voltage and frequency to be sucked up there at will, although you do it every night while you sleep, and when you die. Sleep is actually the workshop of how to die. That merging of time and the timeless is the Jewel, and that is ALEPH.

The Kabbalah says that Aleph exists in all the letters of the alphabet, and all the letters exist in Aleph. Only in Aleph is there Unity, the One without a second. That is why Aleph is constructed with a diagonal line.

That oblique line (Vav) means in time and out of time together, as in the Divine Mirror, the invisibility of the upper reflected in the visibility of the lower. Aleph says we are already there, the upper world and the lower world are the same, as above so below. We are already enlightened. Aleph says we have to learn that, because we have forgotten, and we can stand the heat of it if we do not pretend.

But to ascend in the remembering of that enlightenment, we first have to acknowledge the hiddenness of our "endarkenment." Endarkenment is when the light first comes into the body, the cellular organism. Inside the body, all is dark. You can't realize the light until you understand the darkness, all that you hide, all that you think nobody sees, the negative side, the shadow. You have to dare to face that (as explored by some of you who worked "the Mask Session" in the Le Centre du Silence Workshops). That is endarkenment, which is also enlightenment. They are one and the same.

You are a human being, you are a human becoming. The journey takes you to the edge of nothingness. Go carefully. Be well prepared. And the sadness you meet on your way, remember to enjoy it. And that is what we call "time" and "space."

Originally published in the Invisible Stairway: Kabbalistic Meditations on the Hebrew Letters, available on Amazon.

כִּי-תַעֲבֹר בַּמַּיִם אִתְּךָ-אָנִי, וּבַנְּהָרוֹת לֹא יִשְׁטְפוּךָ: כִּי-תֵלֵךְ בְּמוֹ-אֵשׁ לֹא תִכָּוֶה, וְלֶהָבָה לֹא תִבְעַר-בָּךְ.
ישעיהו מ"ג. ב.

**When you pass through the waters, I will be with you,
and when you pass through the rivers, they shall not wash you away;
When you walk through the fire, you shall not be burned,
neither shall the flame kindle upon thee.**
Isaiah 43:2

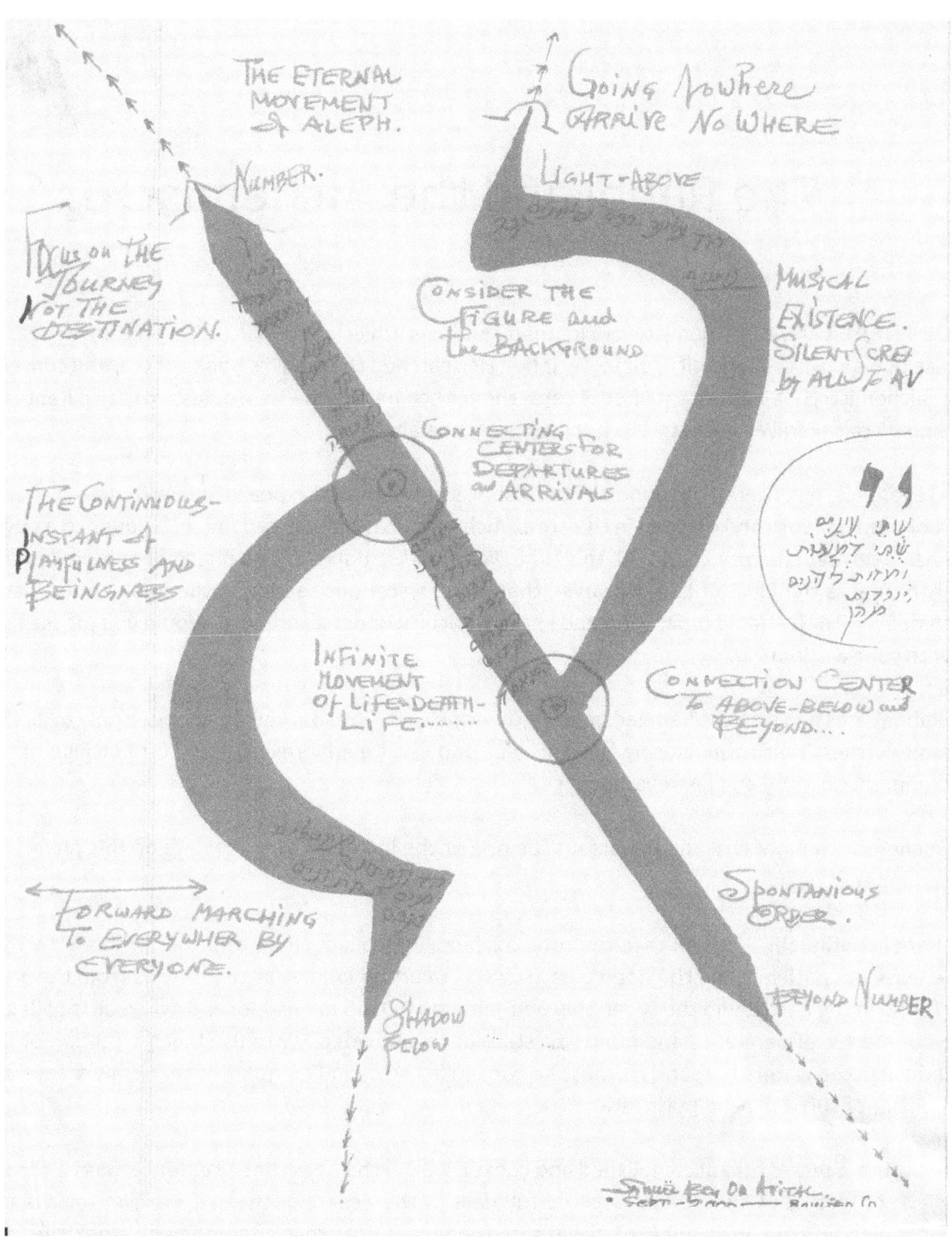

Aleph of Everywhere

The Rabbi and the Alchemist

ONCE THERE WAS an Alchemist, very learned and wise. While working in his laboratory, he reached a phase of his work that was difficult to decipher. He searched through his books of old, and consulted other alchemists, but was not satisfied. Then a thought came to him – he would go to see a Rabbi who was known to several alchemists as a luminary in Kabbalah.

With reverence, he entered the abode of the Rabbi, saluted him with peace and said, "Rabbi, in many years of study, theory and practice in the art of Alchemy, I have perfected my techniques to a degree that has been satisfactory to me. At this time, I am working on the last phase of the process that finally produces the Elixir of Life. However, there is a mysterious section in the book of instruction, which deals with the final preparation and I have difficulty understanding it. Would you please assist me with your wisdom?"

The Rabbi, caressing his beard, smiled gently to him and said, "My son, you do not need now to confuse yourself further. That formula is very clear to us and I will gladly reveal it to you because of your genuineness, sincerity and perseverance."

The Alchemist thought that the Rabbi must be one of the invisible living Masters on this planet, and he was eager to hear.

The Rabbi continued, "You can take the roots of humility, collect them together before dawn with some leaves of patience and the hope that grows all over the land. Add some twigs from the Torah, also found in the earth. Find the seven thirteen-petalled ROSES of wisdom and, when all is collected, use your mortar of penitence and grind to a state of fine powder. Try to use much affection of Love and add also the waters of fear. This must be cooked in the oven (Tannour) of thanksgiving and over the hot fire of suffering and purification."

"When this process is fully accomplished and cooked well in the heart of the essence, pass it through the sieve of truth and faith. Then fast two full days in the desert of the self, waiting for the third day's glowing horizon. Wait until the dawn star appears and, at that very moment, drink the influx of God's Light through the Elixir, and let the fluids of the rivers of Life flow in your veins and thus be illuminated in Him that blessed you with the holy dew."

"This is the formula that is known to us. It may seem invisible to some, but to the wise, this is the way and this is the REAL Elixir of Life. Peace be with you, my son."

"Take the Shalom of the Heart and give it to all you see and hear."

Aleph-Pele Cup

When a Human is Born to this World…

תָּנֵי בְּשֵׁם רַבִּי מֵאִיר, כְּשֶׁאָדָם בָּא לָעוֹלָם יָדָיו הֵן קְפוּצוֹת (סְתוּמוֹת), כְּלוֹמַר, כָּל הָעוֹלָם כֻּלּוֹ שֶׁלִּי הוּא, אֲנִי נוֹחֲלוֹ, וּכְשֶׁהוּא נִפְטָר מִן הָעוֹלָם יָדָיו פְּשׁוּטוֹת (פְּתוּחוֹת), כְּלוֹמַר, לֹא נָחַלְתִּי מִן הָעוֹלָם הַזֶּה כְּלוּם. קֹהֶלֶת רַבָּה ה. כ.

We studied in the name of Rabbi Meir,
That when a human is born to this world,
their hands are closed, meaning,
"All the world belongs to me, **I will inherit it**"
(I have something to give in this world – s.a.)**;**

And when the human leaves this world,
their hands are stretched open, meaning,
"I inherited nothing from this world"
(I have given everything I had in this life journey – s.a.).
Kohelet Rabbah 5.20

THIS NUGGET OF ancient wisdom, that I learned in my childhood, helped me to stay sane in "this world," to realize that actually nothing belongs to me, and nothing is permanent. It is still a guiding light, helping me maintain balance in my thinking and activities. It helps me keep a clear and healthy way of being, keeping sane and present in every movement in my life. It also assists me in constantly and consciously living, throughout my activities in "this world." And it is guidance for my students to practice for creative living.

Here is another suggestion that can allow you to live harmoniously without worries, if you practice it. True, there are some difficulties and challenges in practicing, but it can give you some hints as to who you are, and how to stay sane in the midst of madness. The following temperaments are for your contemplation and inspiration.

There are four temperaments within the Human Being.

הָאוֹמֵר שֶׁלִּי שֶׁלִּי וְשֶׁלְּךָ שֶׁלָּךְ, זוֹ מִדָּה בֵּינוֹנִית
וְיֵשׁ אוֹמְרִים זוֹ מִדַּת סְדוֹם,

**The one who says, what is mine is mine, and what is yours is yours,
is an average person, and some say, is the temperament of Sodom.**

שֶׁלִּי שֶׁלָּךְ וְשֶׁלְּךָ שֶׁלִּי, עַם הָאָרֶץ,

What is mine is yours and yours is mine, this is an uneducated person.

שֶׁלִּי שֶׁלָּךְ וְשֶׁלְּךָ שֶׁלָּךְ, חָסִיד,

What is mine is yours and yours is yours, this is a pious person.

שֶׁלְּךָ שֶׁלִּי וְשֶׁלִּי שֶׁלִּי, רָשָׁע:

What is yours is mine, and what is mine is mine. That is a wicked person.
The Ethics of the Fathers: Chapter 5. 13

לְךָ אֵלִי תְּשׁוּקָתִי
To Thee My God, Is My Passion

THIS IS A short version of a unique and ancient Piyut, a touching prayer-meditation that stayed with me all my life, that was sung in the evening of Yom Kippor.*

> "From your hand, everything comes,
> And from your hand, we give back what we receive."

Note: I have revised the old translation and terms of this poem, so you, the reader, can understand this spiritual dialogue between the created and the Creator.

The poet says to the Creator "To you are my hands." And so, if you move my hands, they are your hands. If you give me eyes, you look through my eyes. To you is my soul. This is not just poetic, but it creates that link. I chose this poem to express the constant link-connection of the Creator and the created everywhere, every moment, every second.

If the Creator is perfect, he created a perfect creation. So perfection is possible. This also refutes the negative meme that there is no perfection and that you are not perfect. True, you are not perfect, in that you interfere in using the body, or the thought, or the intelligence. In that way, you are not perfect. But in essence, you are perfect. When I say that, people will ask me, "What are you talking about? What essence?" The answer is: Well, beyond your definition of yourself.

If you can be friends with your essential self, there will be no second. That is why you are unique in the world. There is no one like you, there will never be anyone like you. It is true. I still say this to people who can understand it. Yes, you are unique. No one on earth has ever been like you. No one was like you, no one will be like you, no one is like you.

That is the greatest truth that all the fields of knowledge are trying to hide. They all put doubt in your life. They tell you that you are stupid, and if you are creative when you are young, they want to commit you, etc. There is that whole attitude out there of thinking the other has some lacking.

But why do we think of the other as lowly? If you are a real conscious created being, you even come to the conclusion that if another person needs help, they come first. But that consciousness is not there. That is why supposedly they have healthcare, but now it has become health-scare, where they scare you into thinking you are sick, instead of realizing your natural state of well-being. You were created to be healthy and the interference of others and yourself is what makes you unhealthy.

This is the point that comes from nowhere. But many people could sense that. I am totally confident there is that spiritual spark within every person that can relate to this. Now, this nowhere exists in everybody, but we don't dwell in it all the time. But that's where the great guidance is, if you need guidance.

TO THEE, MY GOD

לְךָ אֵלִי תְּשׁוּקָתִי,

To Thee, my God, is my passion,
it is You whom I desire and love
To You is my heart and my mind,
to You is my spirit and my soul
To You are my hands, to You are my
feet, and from You is my personality
To You is myself, to You is my blood
and my skin, along with my body

לְךָ אֵלִי תְּשׁוּקָתִי, בְּךָ חֶשְׁקִי וְאַהֲבָתִי
לְךָ לִבִּי וְכִלְיוֹתַי, לְךָ רוּחִי וְנִשְׁמָתִי
לְךָ יָדַי לְךָ רַגְלַי וּמִמְּךָ הִיא תְכוּנָתִי
לְךָ עַצְמִי לְךָ דָּמִי וְעוֹרִי עִם גְּוִיָּתִי

[Chorus:]
To You are my eyes and my thoughts,
and my shape and my form
To You is my spirit, to You is my
strength and my trust and my hope

פִּזְמוֹן:
לְךָ עֵינַי וְרַעְיוֹנַי וְצוּרָתִי וְתַבְנִיתִי
לְךָ רוּחִי לְךָ כֹּחִי וּמִבְטַחִי וְתִקְוָתִי

To You I shall yearn and shall not
quieten, until You shall illuminate my
darkness
To You I shall cry, to You I shall cling,
until I return unto my earth

לְךָ אֶהֱמֶה וְלֹא אֶדְמֶה עֲדֵי תָאִיר אֶת
אֲפֵלָתִי
לְךָ אֶזְעַק בְּךָ אֶדְבַּק עֲדֵי שׁוּבִי
לְאַדְמָתִי

To You is the Kingship, to You is the superiority, to You my praise shall befit
From You, aid comes at times of need, Be my aid at my time of need

And what am I, and what is my life, and what is my strength and my might?
As blowing chaff am, I driven away, and how shall You remember my wrongdoings?

[Chorus:]
To You are my eyes and my thoughts, and my shape and my form
To You is my spirit, to You is my strength and my trust and my hope

To You I shall yearn and shall not quieten, until You shall illuminate my darkness
To You I shall cry, to You I shall cling, until I return unto my earth
And the light which is hidden before You, shall be my protection and my shelter
And 'neath the shade of Thy wings, please give my place unto me
To Thee, My God, is my passion

By Rabbi Avraham Ibn Ezra

לְךָ מַלְכוּת לְךָ גֵּאוּת, לְךָ תְּאוֹת יִתְלָהֵת
לְךָ עֶזְרָה בְּעֵת צָרָה, הֱיֵה עֶזְרִי בְּצָרָתִי

וּמָה אֲנִי וּמָה חַיַּי וּמָה כֹּחִי וְעָצְמָתִי
כְּקַשׁ נִדָּף מְאֹד נֶהְדָּף וְאֵיךְ תִּזְכֹּר מְשׁוּגָתִי

פִּזְמוֹן:
לְךָ עֵינַי וְרַעְיוֹנַי וְצוּרָתִי וְתַבְנִיתִי
לְךָ רוּחִי לְךָ כֹּחִי וּמִבְטָחִי וְתִקְוָתִי

לְךָ אֶהֱמֶה וְלֹא אֶדֹּמֶה עֲדֵי תָאִיר אֶת אֲפֵלָתִי
לְךָ אֶזְעַק בְּךָ אֶדְבַּק עֲדֵי שׁוּבִי לְאַדְמָתִי
וְאוֹר גָּנוּז לְפָנֶיךָ יְהִי סִתְרִי וְסֻכָּתִי
וְתַחַת צֵל כְּנָפֶיךָ תְּנָה נָא אֶת מְחִצָּתִי.

לְךָ אֵלִי תְּשׁוּקָתִי

---

* This deeply personal Piyut, authored by the great Sephardic Rabbi Avraham Ibn Ezra, opens the Yom Kippur prayers among most Sephardic communities. Although some scholars throughout the ages have claimed that this text may have been written by Rabbi Yehuda Ha-Levi, most agree that it was crafted by the pen of Rabbi Ibn Ezra. Throughout the text, the author describes his innermost feelings, his pining for the Lord and for His closeness. The simplicity, precision, and sanity of his words leaves no doubt to deny that link of our essence-reality connection with the Creator. He thanks God for all he has received – beginning with his daily life and ending with his death. The author requests forgiveness from his God for all aberrations and sins he has committed. For the full text of this sacred song, see any Sephardic Siddur, Hebrew prayer book for the high holy days, Rosh Hoshanah and Yom Kippor.

Note:
The following verses contain some kabbalistic messages to apply
in order to live in balance with your Creator, yourself, and the other

נֵר יְהוָה נִשְׁמַת אָדָם חֹפֵשׂ כָּל־חַדְרֵי־בָטֶן: משלי כ. כז.

**The spirit of man is the candle of the Lord,
searching all the inward parts of the belly.**
Proverbs 20, 27

אַתָּה | סֵתֶר לִי מִצַּר תִּצְּרֵנִי רָנֵּי פַלֵּט תְּסוֹבְבֵנִי סֶלָה: תהלים לב. ז.

**You are my hiding place; you shall preserve me from trouble;
you shall surround me with songs of deliverance. Selah.**
Psalms 32. 7

כִּי־אַתָּה יְהוָה לְבָדָד לָבֶטַח תּוֹשִׁיבֵנִי: תהלים ד. ט.

I will both lie down and sleep in peace; for you alone make me, Lord, dwell in safety.
Psalms 4. 9

הַט־אָזְנְךָ לִי שְׁמַע אִמְרָתִי: תהלים יז. ו.

...incline your ear to me, and hear my speech.
Psalms 17. 6

טוּב טַעַם וָדַעַת לַמְּדֵנִי כִּי בְמִצְוֹתֶיךָ הֶאֱמָנְתִּי: תהלים קיט. סו.

Teach me good judgment and knowledge; for I have believed your commandments.
Psalms 118. 66

וַאֲנִי קִרֲבַת אֱלֹהִים לִי־טוֹב...תהלים עג. כח.

But for me it is good to be near Elohim...
Psalms 73. 28

וְהַבּוֹטֵחַ בַּיהוָה חֶסֶד יְסוֹבְבֶנּוּ: תהלים לב. י.

...but loving kindness shall surround him who trusts in Adonai.
Psalms 32. 10.

כִּי־טוֹב חַסְדְּךָ הַצִּילֵנִי: תהלים קט. כא.

Good and faithful as you are, rescue me.
Psalms 109:21

The "Presence of the Living Teacher" and the Emanation of Energy

THE MASTER-TEACHER EMANATES a certain quality of presence, whether the student is aware of this energy or not. This awareness can be experienced as a genuine energetic frequency, and is very balanced and accelerated.

The Teacher serves as a tuning fork, a "conscious sending-station," and has a definite influential vibration on all that is in their environment and in their immediate proximity. The student or anyone orbiting around in his or her presence is like a "receiving-station," a l'écoute, always at the state of listening, ready to receive that "presence" energy and its communication.

This experience is available at every moment now, and in full range of the human benevolent presence of the Master-Teacher.

This is a very important key to understand the phenomenon of the Master-Teacher encounter. This exchange between the Teacher-giver and the Student-receiver, happens in everyday relations, flowing harmoniously by the simple presence of the Teacher in teaching situations: meditating, talking, walking, sharing food, explaining great concepts of life with simple words, or by simply being silent and communicating without words, sensing the ordinary reality as an extraordinary experience. It is like sensing a merging with the universe, a union with all that is, a sense that "one is one and not two."

This giving-receiving energy functions on many levels, and it is like a circle of flow of practical wisdom, both silently, and with other means of communication. A teacher is also one who knows how to receive, and a student is also one who knows how to give.

This exchange of energy is based on no conditions and no reward basis. It is, and there is no "because" between the beings. This is a very subtle form of relationship that is built with care, kindness and love, and a purposeful and conscious direction.

This energy is always in relation to anyone who is consciously aware of this "Presence." By simply spending a valuable time in the presence of the Master, as the source of knowing and being, one experiences a sense of balance and spontaneously expands one's awareness. One learns many subtle aspects of knowledge by osmosis.

This experience is known as "Transmission," a state where the Master-Teacher pours the "knowledge," "light of understanding" to the physical proximity, the student, as the vessel awakes and is ready to receive, practice and embody that "knowledge."

This Transmission is also like a 1000-volt light bulb pouring more light into a 100-volt light bulb. The awareness and readiness of the 100-volt to receive from the 1000-volt bulb without being shattered to pieces requires a very definite state of being. It is a certain attitude of "conscious innocence,"[*] in order to be able to receive more "light" gradually without breaking to pieces. One must stay whole, expanding both the moment and making the space for more light, until they will be able to contain the 1000-volt degree of light, gradually.

So, meeting with the Master-Teacher is a momentous occasion to embrace, experience, and expand. It is a time to use the "teaching situation," to evolve in one's honest efforts, to use one's learning ability to move another step in the ladder of being and becoming. Doing so is activating the restoration of oneself and "others."

More About Teachers and Students:

Here are some nuggets of practical wisdom to ponder and practice.

THREE WAYS OF LEARNING

When my grandfather and I sat on a small smooth rock in his yard, after stamping the grapes rhythmically with my bare young feet, learning how to make wine, he told me that there are three basic ways of living and learning:

1. The first priority and purpose of life is to live to learn, absorbing like a sponge, sharpening and using your intelligence to learn as much as you can, with increased curiosity.

2. The second priority and purpose of life is living your learning, mastering the practicality of your learning.

3. The third priority and purpose of life is to tell a passionate story of your experience, so others can also learn and benefit from your brief existence on this earth.

---

[*] See the definition of "Conscious Innocence" in the *Defintuitions* section.

Over the years, I reflected on this profound wisdom many times. I adapted these three processes of learning to most of my activities. (See the article "What is BodySpeak™?" at BodySpeak.com about the three phases of learning I use in my work).

Teacher / Trickster

True teachers not only live the truth, they love the truth that they live, modestly living it on many levels. But in fact, that truth, for the students, is a lie until they investigate it for themselves. So the teacher plays out his or her own role – being simple, stupid, outrageous, a trickster, whatever, luring the students on, sometimes satisfying their expectations, sometimes frustrating them, always testing, measuring, so that the students will measure their own something-ness.

Even false teachers, with their half-truths, can unwittingly aid in the quest if the students learn to relax and not force the issue – if they learn that in all their struggles what they are looking for is already looking for them.

Student-Teacher – Mentor Relationship

Both teacher and student know. One remembers, and one has forgotten. When they get together, they remind one another.

More Than What You Think

It is said by our revered sages: "The more you think about teachers, the less you may learn".

One must learn how to learn. Your focus must be on LEARNING, not the teacher, or the book, or this or that. One can learn from everything. Life is our great teacher, if we learn HOW TO READ IT. So do not think of yourself when learning, focus on that which you learn and practice.

This teaching/learning situation environment can be manifested and offered to you by a guide, a genuine teacher, someone WHO KNOWS HOW TO KNOW, and one who has a natural wisdom to impart. This is by one who is willing to transmit knowledge to you, when you are "ready." That is when you know HOW to be a receptive vessel, willing to learn how to shape new ways and new forms for your life and yourself. That shaping new forms for your life is done by yourself and with yourself.

But if you think you "know," you don't need a teacher. (Remember that the most abused and misunderstood word in any language is "knowing.") With that attitude of "Been there, done that," one will never find an authentic teacher.

In a time in history that most negativities are defined as positive, it is a creative effort to search for a living authentic teacher. The fake teachers know very well how to introduce you to their teachings with "laughter," "kindness" and "happiness." They present a life of eternal happiness, and that is half of the problem. That is why when you come to real life and you have problems, it creates confusion.

It is a search for one who can guide you back to your essential, authentic and spiritual self, in a healthy and sane way. I consider that as a spiritual effort – that is, if you know what you really want to learn. And that requires one to first unlearn what you learned. That is a good introduction to rediscover your sane being in a perplexed and confused generation.

Finally, not everyone is interested in finding an authentic living teacher. For this, one needs to be accomplished in three things:

1. Understanding one thing from the other.
2. Having some knowledge in a few languages.
3. One needs to have developed and experienced understanding through intuition (However, false intuition can appear, in the form of ego or toxic thoughts. And that is why it is difficult to distinguish.)

These are important, because these teachers are primarily unknown and not heavily advertised. However, there have been great sages in the kabbalistic tradition in the past, whose work is documented in a code, and built into that code is how to practice and apply the teachings.

Many of us pass by authentic teachers and we don't notice them. Just as we breathe, but most don't know that the breath can heal.

Various new age traditions contain negative memes, that are obstacles to learning. And, with our innocent search, sometimes we don't notice them. But they appear authentic, while containing half-truths. (See the article, *The Spiritual Ratatouille* in the book "From Ecstasy to Lunch").

We need the ability to acknowledge the sanity in the midst of madness and act accordingly. This is also why it is so important to learn how to learn, by unlearning what you think you know.

Some people do not know how to be a student. They are mostly lazy and pretentious and their attitude of learning is superficial and just a way to pass the time. Learning must be playful and deep at the same time. Learning from someone who knows is really rare, unless you prepared yourself enough to be able to be called a student, and to attract the "teacher" you deserve.

Bon courage to you who is the caring true seeker of authentic wisdom.

And remember:

כָּל־הַנְּחָלִים הֹלְכִים אֶל־הַיָּם וְהַיָּם אֵינֶנּוּ מָלֵא אֶל־מְקוֹם שֶׁהַנְּחָלִים
הֹלְכִים שָׁם הֵם שָׁבִים לָלָכֶת: קהלת פרק א. ז.

"All the rivers run into the sea; yet the sea is not full;
to the place from where the rivers come,
there they return again"
Ecclesiastes 1. 7

Here are some more nuggets of practical wisdom to ponder and practice:

רַבָּן גַּמְלִיאֵל הָיָה אוֹמֵר,
עֲשֵׂה לְךָ רַב, וְהִסְתַּלֵּק מִן הַסָּפֵק, וְאַל תַּרְבֶּה לְעַשֵּׂר אֹמָדוֹת

"Provide yourself with a teacher;
be quit of doubt; and accustom not yourself
to give tithes by a conjectural estimate."
Rabban Gamliel – Sayings of the Fathers 1.16

רַבִּי יִשְׁמָעֵאל בְּנוֹ אוֹמֵר, הַלּוֹמֵד תּוֹרָה עַל מְנָת לְלַמֵּד, מַסְפִּיקִין בְּיָדוֹ לִלְמֹד וּלְלַמֵּד.
וְהַלּוֹמֵד עַל מְנָת לַעֲשׂוֹת, מַסְפִּיקִין בְּיָדוֹ לִלְמֹד וּלְלַמֵּד לִשְׁמֹר וְלַעֲשׂוֹת

"He who learns in order to teach,
Heaven will grant him the opportunity to both learn and to teach.

But he who learns in order to practice,
Heaven will grant him the opportunity to learn and to teach,
to observe and to practice."
Rabbi Yishmael – Sayings of the Fathers 4.6

שַׁמַּאי אוֹמֵר, עֲשֵׂה תוֹרָתְךָ קֶבַע. אֱמֹר מְעַט וַעֲשֵׂה הַרְבֵּה,
וֶהֱוֵי מְקַבֵּל אֶת כָּל הָאָדָם בְּסֵבֶר פָּנִים יָפוֹת

"Make a regular period for your study;
Say little and do much;
And receive every human being with a cheerful countenance."
Shammai – Sayings of the Fathers 1.15

בֶּן זוֹמָא אוֹמֵר, אֵיזֶהוּ חָכָם, הַלּוֹמֵד מִכָּל אָדָם,
שֶׁנֶּאֱמַר (תהלים קיט) מִכָּל מְלַמְּדַי הִשְׂכַּלְתִּי כִּי עֵדְוֹתֶיךָ שִׂיחָה לִי

Ben Zoma said "Who is Wise? The one who learns from everyone."
As it is said, "From all my teachers I have received understanding."
Pirkei Avot 4.1

And this last one can begin to convey to you the gentle urgency of becoming a good student of life. This will help you explore the "mysteries" of yourself, become the "mystery," and learn the art of BEING and BECOMING.

רַבִּי טַרְפוֹן אוֹמֵר, הַיּוֹם קָצָר וְהַמְּלָאכָה מְרֻבָּה,
וְהַפּוֹעֲלִים עֲצֵלִים, וְהַשָּׂכָר הַרְבֵּה, וּבַעַל הַבַּיִת דּוֹחֵק

"THE DAY IS SHORT, and THE WORK IS GREAT.
THE WORKERS ARE LAZY, and THE REWARD IS MUCH.
AND THE MASTER IS URGENT."
Rabbi Tarfon – Sayings of the Fathers 2.15

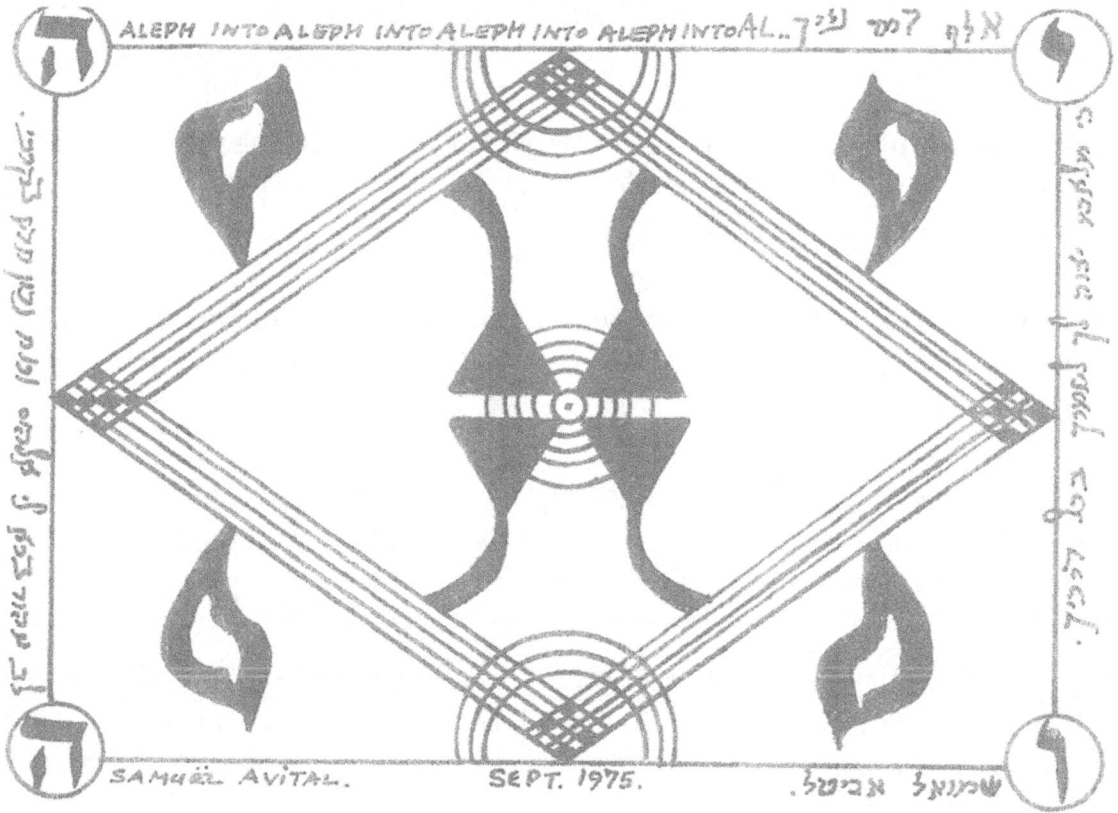

4 Corners Aleph

"Maybe" and "Whatever"

רַבִּי חִדְקָא הָיָה אוֹמְרָהּ בְּלָשׁוֹן אַחֶרֶת
הֱוֵי אוֹהֵב אֶת הַשֶּׁמָּא וְשָׂנֵא אֶת הַ"כְּמָה בְּכָךְ":
מסכת דרך ארץ זוטא פרק א.

**Rabbi Hidka used to say, in another way:
Love the "MAYBE" and hate the "WHATEVER".**
Talmud Masekhet Derek Eretz Zuta, Chapter 1, Verse 11

A story about **MAYBE** and **WHATEVER**.
and "**THIS TOO SHALL PASS**"
and "**THIS TOO IS FOR THE GOOD**"

ONCE, THERE WAS a peasant, living in a simple village, who had a beautiful horse. One day, the horse ran away. His neighbors were sad and expressed their concern. "Now you are without a horse" they said, "What bad luck." He said, "**Maybe**."

The next day, the horse came back, bringing with it another eight wild horses. The neighbors were very happy for him, saying "What good fortune. You will be so much more productive now that you have nine horses." He said, "**Maybe**."

The next day, his son attempted to train one of the wild horses, and fell, breaking his leg. The neighbors, again, expressed their sadness and concern. "What a bad situation. We are so sorry for you and your son." His response, again, was "**Maybe**."

But the next day the army came to recruit young men for the war. Because of the injury, his son was not able to go. His friends again were happy, knowing his son would be spared dying in the war. He again responded with the same magical word "**Maybe**," and concluded "**This too shall pass**" and "**This too is for the good**."*

Rabbi Hidka said "**Love the maybe and hate the whatever.**" This story illustrates what "**Maybe**" can teach us. "Maybe" has many possibilities, it leaves the door open. On the other hand, "**Whatever**" is a state of giving up easily. It involves jumping to conclusions about what is happening and reacting to it.

This suggests that when you realize the truth beyond judgement, continue with it. Insist on following the focus on what is. And don't use the word "Whatever" to cause you to release your focus.

As an example, say that someone has a friend who owes him $100. The borrower comes to thank him and return the money. But if he has an unfocused character and says "You can give me whatever," his friend may give him less back. He is not exact and as a result, he doesn't get his full amount of money back. So, people who use the word "whatever" are not persistent in achieving their goal exactly.

"**This too is for the good**." All that happens to us, we categorize as "good" or "bad," which is false. Therefore, one can say "This too is for the good." Something happens and we think it is terrible at the time, but it turns out to be for the good. And also, not everything that we think is good is actually good for us, anyway. It is just a result of our stupid, categorized decisions, which we only think are good for us.

There is also a subtle question here – why did God give us the freedom to choose? This has to do with decision-making. Because we don't know the divine calculations of this also is for the good (Divine calculations just means that which is beyond our limited human consciousness and linear "understanding".)

Do we really see clearly and understand everything that happens to us in life? Do we know that it is for the good? No, because that which we do not understand, we judge. So therefore, we are the ones who decide good and bad, by our language. You define it as good, therefore it is good, you define it as bad, therefore it is bad. We choose the words to define "understanding."

"**Whatever**." Many people say "Whatever." Whatever has the tune and the attitude of giving up and not following the plan of what you want to achieve. In other words, when you "jump to conclusions," and react instead of responding to what happens in life, you welcome ignorance. If you do that, you consciously invite ignorance, actually.

---

* Original story of the horses as told by Alan Watts. The addition of This too Shall Pass and This Also is for the Good by Samuel Avital.

When someone says "What do you want to do today?" and the person answers "Whatever," that is an escape of the now. Therefore it is not using your intelligence, and that is an insult.

This is why it is a journey between ignorance and knowledge. Ignorance is whatever and maybe is knowledge. Whatever welcomes ignorance, while maybe opens the doors to knowledge.

פִּתְחִי לִי פִּתְחָא כְּחִידוּדָא דְּמַחֲטָא — אֲנָא אַפְתַּח לָךְ תַּרְעִין עִלָּאִין
פירוש הסולם פרשת אמור. ספר הזוהר.

**"Open to me so much as the eye of a needle,
and I will open up to you the supreme gates."**
Zohar. Parashat Emor. Perush Hasoullam

אַף הוּא רָאָה גֻּלְגֹּלֶת אַחַת שֶׁצָּפָה עַל פְּנֵי הַמַּיִם אָמַר לָהּ עַל דְּאַטֵּפְתְּ אַטְפוּךְ
וְסוֹף מְטַיְּפַיִךְ יְטוּפוּן: פרקי אבות. פרק ב. ז.

**"Moreover he (Hillel) saw a skull floating on the surface of the water and he said to it:
Because you drowned others, they drowned you;
and those that drowned you will eventually be drowned."**
Pirkei Avot 1. 7

What Kabbalah Is and Is Not

"You can learn and inform yourself about the finger (a detail), but that does not mean you know the entire body (the whole)."

SINCE THE KABBALAH is becoming very popular these days – something that is very significant for the future of humanity and the Universe – it is very important to make a few things clear about this sacred, ancient and new knowledge, wisdom and exact science of the Cosmos. For Kabbalah contains the cosmic laws and the practical wisdom of natural balance, which can be harmoniously integrated, to become in tune and resonating with all creation.

Many great minds in history have orbited around the Kabbalah to learn about life and the "**mystery of our being here**." However, many of them have missed the target and gotten the wrong notion. They were not able to perceive what this enigmatic ancient knowledge has to offer and teach us – about our being, who we are, and what we are doing in "this world", and what our role is in life as a whole. Until now, sad to say, most of us humans have been using only one hemisphere of the brain to function and seek knowledge – which is a great limitation.

Kabbalah is both a great "**mystery**" and also very simple to understand; for it is a science and wisdom of the Cosmos. It is both simple and complicated, which seems to be a "**paradox**" to the ordinary person's mind. But when one begins to really know, it is not a paradox, it is simply an integration of both aspects of our being. However, since we humans have always been at war with ourselves, since the dawn of time, it is a difficult thing for us to interact with the oneness of the Creation.

Kabbalah is a science of actual learning, which means learning not just with words, and not just with the intellect, but with the full intelligence. This includes actual kinesthetic practices, which are very effective, but are generally not acceptable to the average human being today, because most people are completely immersed in "**playing the violin with one hand**."

This article was transcribed from a Public Talk in Boulder, Colorado. March 1989

Among other aspects of knowing, Kabbalah teaches one to **DARE TO BE** fully oneself without fear. Kabbalah teaches how the laws work of the Cosmos, and the creation, and "**this world**" we live in now – for us to manifest on all levels and dimensions of life, both visible and invisible.

These laws can be mastered and worked with, until one becomes "in tune" with them." This is done by specific practices of **Tikkunim = restorations**. This will lead to being and becoming who we were meant to be. One can then actually reach a stage of having the merit to be called "**human**."

There are some basics one needs to know before embarking on the journey of exploring Kabbalah:

First, you **must differentiate very clearly between information and knowledge**. In this day and age, the focus is on information, and most think that information is knowledge. One must be able to make a very clear distinction between these two things.

It is good to be informed, as a starting point, but knowledge is an experience that comes from working on yourself with a genuine Teacher. However, since there are many so-called "teachers", you must use your common sense of sanity and lucidity, to recognize and really find an authentic teacher, who can guide you properly. When you find an authentic teacher, be ready to engage deeply, without fear or mind-heart limitations.

One must know how to ask, and be in the true state of knowing how to be a "**student**." The "**Teacher**"[*] will recognize you, and when you make the true contact and connection, that's when you begin your great adventure. You will learn to know who you are, what is the genuine meaning of your life, why you are living, and how you can learn and apply the laws of the Universe, as the Kabbalah teaches.

A Few Thoughts About What Kabbalah Is Not

1. Kabbalah is not a philosophy or just an intellectual pursuit.
2. It can never be learned academically in an intellectual way.
3. It is not a religion.
4. It is not black magic. It has nothing to do with the occult and is not superstitious.
5. It does not have any Greek, Egyptian or any other non-Jewish cultural elements. It is not part of Christian, Rosicrucian, Masonic or any hermetic philosophies.
6. Kabbalah has nothing to do with "new-age" beliefs – historical or modern.
7. It has no connection to any Eastern religions.

---

[*] See the articles "Finding Your True Living Master Teacher" and "The "Presence" of the Teacher, and the Emanation of Energy", at BodySpeak.com

Kabbalah will never be understood until one begins to **know** the profound meaning of the terms: "**Human**," "**Jewish**," "**Light**," "**Love**," "**Life**," "**Vessel**," "**Tree of Life**," "**Spiritual**," "**Soul**," "**Self**," "**Time**," "**Space**," and, many other ideas. These contain within themselves, a complete understanding, and a specific relation to the whole of Creation. There are many more things to understand, but for now, these are essential and basic enough for one to come to some important realizations.

Now, in English, the word "**Jewish**" usually brings up a historical and cultural understanding of the Jewish people, including their experiences and contributions over the history of humanity. But in Hebrew, it means something else completely. The word "**Jewish**" is from the word **YEHUDI**, which comes from the tribe of **YEHUDA**, one of the 12 tribes of Israel. In Hebrew it simply means:

- **YEHUDI (יהודי)**(**Yod, Hay, Vav, Daleth**, and **Yod**) means **B E I N G**. The root word of **Yehudi** comes from the Hebrew verb, **Hay, Yod** and **Hay (היה)**, meaning: **TO BE.** We know that in "this world" humans have been habituated to think only with the logical side, and self-awareness of only the physical. This creates habits of mostly talking about being and not essentially being. This Yehudi is a stage of spiritual development of shifting from talking about being, to actually being.

- According to the Zohar, the verb also means **YIHUD (יחוד)**, meaning **Union,** or **To Be One**. It indicates the work of every **being,** to **unite** with the **Creator** of the Universe, with every thought and action. The possibility exists to "**UNITE all that is separated**," in every situation in life, and in all dimensions.

- Another aspect hinted at by this beautiful verb is **HODAYAH (הודיה)** (**Hay, Vav, Daleth, Yod, and Hay),** which means deep gratefulness for BEING. So, in Hebrew, the gratitude for BEING is already built in, within the word and letters of the verb of BEING.

- So, this word simply means TO BE. What to be? **To DARE to BE and BECOME** close to the Creator, and navigate life for the benefit of all. This is living "**this life**" of "**matter**" on earth, as it was meant to be in the "**First Place**"- **restoring** oneself to that state of complete perfection, **homeostasis**, right here on earth, and not after "**death**." Right here and now, no postponing.

This is a state of being consciously in the process of transition from being a human animal to divine human. The one who is spiritually aware can understand the spiritual state of being, which is the balance between duality and nonduality. This allows one to transition from the state of being a human animal, which is the state of 99% of humanity, to go from the state of duality, to that of essential being.

Through these **Tikkunim** = **Restorations**, one can purify the vessel to receive Kabbalistic insight about oneself and the Universe. The learning process becomes so different from what passes these days as "**education**." Here, one gains a completely different understanding of what information and knowledge are.

A Few Thoughts On What Kabbalah Is

1. Kabbalah is rooted within the Jewish tradition, but it is not a religion, it is a sacred science of the universe, both wise and practical. It was called "**The mother of all sciences**." Kabbalah in Hebrew, means **to receive**. To receive what? That is the ancient exploration, exploring the "**mystery**" of the human will, the purpose of Creation, and the process of being and becoming.

2. Kabbalah dwells with the essence of being. It is a code of becoming. It is an integration of thinking, using both right and left-brained ways of orientation, both "**inner and outer space-time**", integrating both the physical and spiritual aspects of who we are. This way we can use the duality and conflict to balance the opposites. For I call it a trap and a laziness on the person's part, not to accept both sides of the paradox and find congruency between them.

    As one studies with an authentic Kabbalistic teacher, one can learn to use both hemispheres and beyond. One can develop the ability to go beyond the thinker and the thought, and get to that space I call "Nowhere." I consider the perfect art and science of Kabbalah as a **Cosmic Computer** that can reveal all the "**mysteries**" of life, on all dimensions, in a practical and logical manner.

3. Are you willing to study the original languages, Hebrew or Aramaic, to go deep in the study of the Kabbalah? This means to drink from the source-waters and not the stream. For you must know that most translations are treacherous in transmitting the authentic message. When you want to study Shakespeare, clearly you must learn it in English. Or if you study Molière, it must be in the original French. The translations can be good, but it is like drinking from watered down soup – the learning gets diluted and becomes more superficial.

4. You can read any book on Kabbalah and be informed to a certain degree. But if you do not have access to, or cannot build for yourself the proper background in the original language in which it was written, you will never understand the totality of its "**secrets**" or "**mysteries**." Book learning can be good information to **inform** yourself to a certain degree, but you must go deeper to understand. Kabbalah is full with codes, both simple and complex, and computations, among other things. In learning, it is recommended to drink from the source, rather than from diluted vessels or streams.

    Kabbalah is a unique spiritual language, that has to be learned in order to access this source of wisdom and spiritual health of being. It is a total language which has infinite styles of spiritual instructions, that is neglected by academia. It is a unique language, like music, in which you must learn the musical notes in order to play.

5. In teaching certain *BodySpeak*™ exercises, I say "**You can learn about the finger, but that does not mean you know the whole body.**" One does not know the whole body by knowing only a finger. Unfortunately, in the shallow "culture" we live in these days, many people learn one tiny part of knowledge and pretend to know the whole.

6. Kabbalah contains the metaphysical understandings underlying the commandments (Mitzvot), and stories in the Torah, given by the Creator to the Jewish people at Mt. Sinai. The stories are there to keep the tradition alive and safely stored across thousands of years. The Kabbalist however, understands and dares to go beyond the "**stories**," through a specific system of study, including Tikkunim (deeds of restoration).

   These bring one closer to the Creator – working with the laws of the universe to restore one's personal world and the whole world. In this way, the student of Kabbalah learns to use all (or most of) one's faculties of intelligence and thinking. This means the constant application of what one learns, in order to be and become with genuine knowledge.

7. Kabbalah is actually more than a subject of learning, it is really an exact science. It embraces a whole system of practices that revive the life of the spirit that is concealed within the body of the stories in the Torah, and other sacred writings. Within every letter and word, and between the lines and spaces, lie the laws of Creation. It reveals how to live in both worlds with total harmony, developing one's spiritual evolution, and restoring oneself and the universe at the same time, right here and now.

8. Kabbalah offers a very profound and proven system of meditation that enables the student to achieve the state of beyond, being close to the Creator – to achieve the perfect union with the one that uttered the word and the world came into existence. Perfection is possible for the genuine student of Kabbalah.

9. The **613 Mitzvot of the Torah** are the deeds that one practices with focused **intention** = **Kavanah**, in order to orbit more around the Presence of The Creator, and merge with that oneness with the whole beingness of all life. These are the restorations, **Tikkunim**. Through them, one learns to integrate the personal universe within us all, with the outer universe that seems to us as a separate reality.

10. The more one develops this **healthy**, **logical**, **intuitive** and **sane** attitude of learning, the more one gets closer to the authentic and proper way to study this sacred science of the Kabbalah. For it is widely known that, without the proper preparation and an attitude of "**Conscious Innocence**,"[*] Kabbalah can be really "dangerous", and even harmful for a person's health and life.

11. There is a vast literature about Kabbalah in many languages. Authentic books on Kabbalah and its practices have been translated, to help inform one to some degree. While this information does exist, it does not offer any actual experience and practical wisdom to use in life, which is needed so you can know who you are, what is the meaning of your life and all Creation, and what your purpose is being in "this world."

---

[*] See more about **Conscious innocence** in the book *From Ecstasy To Lunch*, and the Defintuitions section in *The BodySpeak Manual*.

In order to enter the experience of knowing Kabbalah, one has to graduate the logical only understanding of the world, which is the cause of the limitation. Trying to understand logically only will put you in the muddy river, and you will not understand it. You have to find a balance between understanding information and actual experience.

12. When these profound questions of self-examination really begin to dwell within your thoughts in an urgent way – And when you really ask deeply what is the purpose of your being here, and what is the purpose of creation – And when your soul yearns and cries out for you to search profoundly – And when you yearn for that perfect state of being – When all of this happens, then you will find your **living teacher**. Then you begin on the meaningful journey toward discovering yourself. At that point, you can truly begin to make a difference in your life and the lives of "others."

13. The **Book of the Zohar**, the **Sefer Yetzirah**, and others, gives us a glimpse of the various deeper interpretations of the Torah. In them, Kabbalists have explored deeply and recorded their teachings in a specific way to learn and practice. However a "**guide**" is necessary for you to learn how to explore this knowledge yourself. This knowledge has been kept very closely concealed for thousands of years, but it is available today for those ones who are ready for it. And it will only be open when one approaches it for a specific purpose – to help us change this world into a harmonious and balanced state of being and living. Your "**Guide**" in this might be your spiritual environment itself, until you learn **how to walk by yourself** in the "**ocean of wisdom and great wonder**."

One of the most important aspects of Kabbalah study, is to learn to use one's thoughts consciously, with a benevolent direction, and to transform one's negative inclinations into a positive, creative source of the good. The student of Kabbalah must fully understand and practice focused and intentional thought for the benefit of "others" and oneself.

When we learn **to love the** "**other**" **MORE than oneself**, we connect with the **Power Source** of the **Creator**, and act with the same benevolence, humility and mercy of the Creator.

So, my friend, with our focused, directed and intentional thoughts, we **can** learn to align ourselves with that sacred energy, and attract ourselves to what we simply call, "**LIGHT**" (אור Orr in Hebrew). We actively mold and shape our personal, mental, spiritual and physical reality, **to manifest the good in** "**this world**."

This aspect of Kabbalah study and practice is a very powerful and creative process, to observe silently and discreetly, and to use for the benefit of all beings, in all worlds of the soul's existence.

So, Kabbalah is a vast body of knowledge, both concealed and revealed, and a practical science of wisdom that one can learn easily, both intuitively and logically. Kabbalah is available today to those who are honestly ready and seeking authentic knowledge in "**this world and beyond**."

The Aleph Circularity

The Debate of the Two Twins in their Mother's Womb

THE REVIVAL OF the Dead: Inevitable, or Unacceptable?

This story* is translated and adapted from the book Gesher HaHayim, The Bridge of Life. It is a look on life as a bridge that connects the two sides of life. The book shows us how a Jewish person with faith, Emunah אמונה, sees this world, and the passage of life. This life is viewed within the mirror of Torah and divine account.

The story gives us an example that relates to the belief in תחיית המתים, the revival of the dead, one of the 13 principles of the Jewish life. It is illustrated with this story of the two twins within the belly of their mother.

A human being comes out from the belly of their individual mother, to the belly of the earth, which is the mother of all life. The person comes from the earth, and to the earth they return. This is the mother earth. They will suckle and eat from it all the days that they live in the belly of the earth. But we find that this life is only a bridge, that connects between two different ways of original life. It connects the two sides of one's life, the life of the past, and the life of the future.

Now, even though both of these edges are original life, they are separated, and are totally different from each other. But they have one common purpose: They both influence the future. One side of the bridge, from which "life" comes, is the exit from the mother's womb, which we call "birth" Leda

---

* Translation, introduction, and commentary by Samuel Ben-Or Avital.
The original story is from the book: **Gesher HaHayim** (The Bridge of Life). Part 3
Published in Hebrew, Jerusalem, Israel 1960 (5720), By Harav Yehiel Michael Tokshinkski.

See the article "When a human is born to this world"

See the article in the "Café Salon Philosophique" section in www.bodyspeak.com called:
"Death: Inevitable, or Unacceptable?"

לידה and "life" Hayyim חיים. At the other, is the return to the earth, which we call "death" Mavet מות. During this process, this journey of passing between the two, a person doesn't feel anything besides the essence of their life now. And they don't have any sense or any notion of the true life, beyond this existence here.

One doesn't have any awareness at all of the two sides of this journey. And they don't have any clue that what they see now as the long future before them, they will later perceive as a short passage. It appears to one as if this passage is all their world, what they perceive now, without past, and without future.

Now, during the time that a person passes, being an embryo in the womb of their mother, their head is between their knees. Their mouth is closed. They are fed through their belly, from the nourishment that is given to them through the umbilical cord. These early months are actually a very excellent and clear life. And during this process of human "development," there is no doubt that one sees the whole world then, only from the inner fluid space of the womb.

For a baby, with all its being, far from the worries of life, the sense of time seems very, very long. To them, this period, seems so long, perhaps too long. Now, when it comes to the idea that beyond the space of the mother's belly, there is a much greater period of "long life," the baby cannot even imagine this.

This is illustrated by the story of these two twin brothers. The story goes that they were together in the belly. And they were investigating, and asking each other the question, "What will happen to us after we go out from this womb?"

Now, these two twin brothers don't have any notion or sense at all of what is going to happen to them. They don't have a clue of what they are going to experience. For there is nothing they can see or hear of the world outside the womb. They have no sense of it at all.

Now, when we imagine these two twin brothers, one of them is more innocent. He believes in the tradition that there is a future "life," after leaving the womb.

The second one is more intelligent. This intelligent one doesn't believe this at all. He doesn't see it in his imagination, and truly, he doesn't perceive anything but "this world," this moment that he senses now.

Now, the two of them were discussing and arguing between them, about what their future would be, and what's going to happen to them. For, the one twin believes there is no end to life. And the one thinks there certainly is.

But truly, neither of them has any notion of their future life on the earth. For, they don't have any sense of time, or of the future. Their time here, enclosed in the womb, just seems too long to consider anything else, forced to accept the elements they perceive around them now.

Now, when they come out from the belly of their mother, they will be born to a new life, to a larger world than the space of the womb. And afterwards, they will eat through the mouth, and see far away with their eyes, and they will hear with their ears. And they will have legs on which they can walk upright. They will travel far upon the great globe of the whole earth, that has waters, rivers, mountains, and the sky, and green growing trees. And they will have above them the heavens and the moon and the stars.

The innocent one believes that there is indeed a life beyond the womb. But the intelligent twin believes only in what he perceives now. And so – how much will he mock the innocent one for his beliefs?

Now, this intelligent twin cannot believe what the innocent twin says. Because his senses do not reveal that future to him. He only senses what exists now. Now, the mouth is closed, and they eat from the umbilical cord, and their heads are between their legs, in embryonic form. He does not believe at all what his brother says. "Nonsense!" he tells him, "Only an innocent stupid person would believe these things that you say." He really cannot understand why his brother would believe this story.

So, the smart one continues to mock his brother, and to laugh at him, because he is so stupid. He doesn't understand. He thinks that there is life after birth.

The intelligent twin can see that they are now in the world of the womb, where they can eat and drink from what comes to them. It is clear to him that if one leaves this world and disconnects from this place, they will fall from the womb into the deep abyss, from which they will never return again. It will be as if they do not exist anymore. There is only this moment and this place for life.

But, while they were talking, the womb started to open up, and the innocent twin began to slip and fall outside. Now, the brother that was still in his mother's belly was completely shocked at the disaster that had befallen his brother. He was worrying how his brother could have fallen, and panicking over the terrible fate that had happened to him. Where had he gone? He began to cry and complain "Oh my brother! Where are you?! How come you fell down the abyss, with all your purity and stupidity?" And meanwhile, the contractions of birth were like an earth-quake around him, as the mother went through the birth-pains.

So, he bemoaned what happened to his brother. And this twin, still inside the womb, heard his brother crying, after falling from the womb into the abyss. And he began to mourn his brother. "Aiaiaiai!

What a great tragedy. His soul has disappeared." And during this time still in the belly, he complained grievously about the death of his poor brother.

But then, from outside the womb, he heard the happiness and joy of the people, singing and saying "Mazal Tov, good destiny. What a wonderful boy is being born to us!"

Now, it began to become clear that all the days of his life that had passed, were actually only a passage to life, to larger, more open spaces. Beyond this was a much greater and totally different world. So, also, when the time comes, we will see that this life is only a passage, to a life that is much larger, more shining, and full of greater life. This is something we do not even begin to sense from the life of this world. For here, we are almost like prisoners, caught in the colorful frames and limited perception of this world.

And so, if the difference between the world of the belly and "our world here," is great, the difference between our world here, and the world to come, is greater beyond measure. When the soul gets out of this limited frame, beyond the space of the belly of the earth, the view will be different. It will be clear then that all that we see is so very small, in comparison with the greatness and expansiveness of the world the soul will experience then.

So, in this life, it is like we are in the space of the belly. Here, we can at least perceive the place of our world, and we have certain measures with which to comprehend it. But, in comparison to the great spaces and reality of creation, our earth, in all its greatness, is like nothing. This is already the case when we compare our world to the great space of the sky that we see, which contains all the stars and planets, and heavenly bodies, which are counted not only to the millions upon millions, but to the trillions and beyond. Their distance is immeasurable, far past our perception. Even traveling at the speed of light, there are millions upon millions of kilometers that must be crossed, until the day comes when the light of a star or planet is revealed to us. Now, the Creator created the sky and the infinite, and we cannot even begin to fathom their greatness, or to measure all of this, as it is beyond our perception.

And all of this greatness beyond measure only corresponds to the first Rakia, or firmament, of the heavens. And there are some who say there are great worlds and great spaces far beyond this.

Now, for the smart brother that was left in the belly, he could not even begin to imagine, in any way, that when his brother fell from the womb, he didn't die. The opposite, rather, he came out from the small, limited space of the world of the belly, to a great and large world. Because, during the life of the embryo, even if he somehow possessed the wisdom of a grown person, it would still be impossible for him to perceive in his imagination that he would be with his twin again, after he too, leaves the womb.

Even if a person exists here on the earth, and already understands the reality that this is a life of passage, how can he understand how he will exist there, in that amazing, beautiful, unknowable future life? For just as the baby in the womb cannot perceive this world, it is impossible for any human to perceive the life of soul, after it leaves the body.

On earth, a person's sinews and bones and flesh are critical for their life existence. And when the person returns to their own essential source, we see no more life in that flesh. So, our situation is so similar to that of the intelligent twin, who was so confused within the belly of this mother, about whether life could exist beyond the womb that he knew.

What we see is that, just as the exit from the belly is the birth of the body, so the exit from the body is the birth of the soul, the Neshama נשמה. As it says, "הַיִּלוֹדִים לָמוּת, וְהַמֵּתִים לְהֵחָיוֹת", "The ones who are born are destined to die, and the ones who have died are destined to live" (Pirkei Avot 4:22). For, as soon as a person is born into the world, he begins to count his days toward death. And "טוֹב יוֹם הַמָּוֶת, מִיּוֹם הִוָּלְדוֹ" "the day of death is better than the day of birth" (Kohelet/Ecclesiastes 7:1).

One spends eight or nine months in the belly, from pregnancy to birth. And then one comes to the earth and lives eighty or ninety years on the earth, which is the pregnancy to his or her divine birth. The life in the belly is like an entryway, a corridor before a meeting room. It is limited and exists at a lower degree, compared to the life on earth. And so, too, we exit the limited world, to one that is more unlimited.

And so, birth, life, and death, teach us this understanding. For, though they seem like three separate things, they are actually part of one journey. And by connecting with our understanding of one of them, we can understand all three of them. For, if there was no past or future, we would not have this present moment.

In summary, the three births are:

1. The birth to the belly of the mother.
2. The birth from the belly of the mother, to the life of the body.
3. The birth from the life of the body, to the life beyond.

During each passage, we are contained by a certain vessel, a certain space, that we pass through. And this vessel that we pass through, is actually the tool or instrument that prepares us and brings us to the next phase of life. The belly of the mother is the first passage, which grows us and prepares us for the next phase of life. And all of these phases together, bring us to the life of the essence.

So, the birth from the belly of the mother, teaches us about all three of these passages. And if so, birth, life, and death, give us the possibility to understand these three passages of our journey of life.

Thus, we find, as we said before, that this life is only a bridge, that connects between two different ways of original life. It connects the two sides of life, the life of the past, and the life of the future. And what is "between" is this present, constant moment of living.

I would add that during this journey, we have to be present, through being here, now. This can give us the feeling of walking on a tight-rope. The constant awareness of the presence, from the point of departure, through every step, is extremely necessary, in order to pass through life harmoniously. It makes us aware of the constant sense of balance. And through it, we will be able to face any situation that may seem challenging or difficult.

In this way, we are constantly prepared for what is to come next. Thus, what I always asked my students – Life is now in session. Are you present?

The strength of Judaism, in difficult times, can be summed up in two magic words full of Emunah: "Hakol Letova" "הכל לטובה", "Everything is for the good." Yes, everything that happens to us is, at the end of the day, for the good. For we reposition, and even when we lose our way momentarily, we are guided. Even if the road is a bit longer, we are not afraid of a long way with eternity.

From the Book Hesed LeAvraham
by the Great Kabbalist Rabbi Avraham Azoulay

(Note: The above quote was probably intended to minimize the Jewish trauma of exile and suffering through history.

Hebrew Letter Wings

Illustration By Zev Ben Mosheh Ha-Cohen

Personal Commentary on "Nothing" from "Nowhere"

Note: This commentary demands a certain background and contains some kabbalistic terms that are not known to the general public. In this book, some of the articles, like this one, are not linear. Therefore, they may address your right creative brain. So please read carefully and if you don't understand, just continue, and you will understand later, as you go. And if you understand it, lucky you.

Personal Commentary on "Nothing"

I once read a book by a French writer, who spoke about how Jewish thinking goes beyond normal thinking. And you will find that the Biblical books, and writings of the Prophets and the Kabbalists, are all coded. This is because humanity was and still is "living" in a very limited energy frequency, using just the left brain.

However, now we are in that great "JUMPING OF THE WAY" – קפיצת הדרך (a term used by prophets and Kabbalists) – which is now activated, in order to SHIFT to the next higher spiritual evolution. And this is something that is sensed and perceived by very few as of now.

This jumping of the way is the gate to future realities. It has to do with shifting from this "time" to the "beyond time."

It is TO SHIFT FROM THAT LIMITED ENERGY DIMENSION, as the Bible speaks about in the Book of Bereshit (Genesis). Before Bereshit, there was no time and space. In Bereshit is the verse "It was evening and it was morning, day one" "וַיְהִי-עֶרֶב וַיְהִי-בֹקֶר, יוֹם אֶחָד" (Genesis 1:5). Time was beginning to be perceived. Then we begin to count, etc. Now this "Nowhere" that we speak about is beyond time and space, beyond normal consciousness. That which is inconceivable at this time in human consciousness.

This shift is to learn how to learn. It is what I call to enter "The Speed of Thought" – which is much faster than the speed of light. In Kabbalah it is named the HALAL PANOUY חלל פנוי = The Empty Space."

The "Empty Space" that was spoken about in the Zohar, is the original state of "GAN EDEN," the Garden of Eden.

This state is the one in which the "OR HAGANUZ," the Original concealed light of EDEN was stored – until humanity wakes up from the slumber of duality – of yes and no, you and me, etc. Because that is the lowest state of being. And that lower state of evolution is the one we have been experiencing here for some thousands of years on the earth.

I think THIS IS THE TIME, that humanity is going through that radical change, which to some will be very painful, and for those who are spiritually ready, they can "JUMP THE WAY," to SHIFT and ascend to that state we call "Eden."

However, that is a state of being which many humans will totally reject. Because some are still in that limited state of consciousness that we call the lowest level of the lowest level of "ASSIYAH," the lowest world of the four worlds of Kabbalah. That is the world of doing, the material level, which created conflict and war, and rejection of each other. It is also called "ALMA DESHIKRA," which in Aramaic means, "The World of Lies."

This is the great shift, the great return of civilization. And humanity has been going through this shift through suffering, through wars, etc., in order to purify the limitation of the duality of materialistic consciousness. Because that materialistic way of seeing the world is very limited, and it limits our understanding.

Therefore, the process of this shift in consciousness is constantly being manifested through human suffering. You see it in world events and life events, in the cruelty of humans to each other, through many things that we have trouble understanding. It is actually a process of purification happening throughout all cultures. I used the metaphor of cooking to my students. That "cooking" that we go through is the process of shifting to the nowhere state.

This does not mean that I am against duality. This duality is necessary at this time in human evolution. At that "future time," humanity will learn and become conscious, in order to unite the heart with the brain, and consider it in every situation. As of now, everything is measured with the left brain and judged either from the brain overthinking or the over-emotion of the heart. In the future, we will unite the two and act in balance.

I call it the great shift, or the great return. David Passig, the renowned Israeli Futurist, speaks about this, from another angle, in his books. As a Futurist, he observes the story of the changing consciousness through the history of humanity (through the study of patterns in societal systems across history.)

In the Kabbalah, we call this process, Teshuvah Shelemah (תְּשׁוּבָה שְׁלֵמָה), full and total returning to the "source" of being. And, that source is beyond our limited linear thinking. Because in the future, we will see everything from the whole, not just the particular, as we do now. And as a result, decisions will be better and easier.

So, those beings who are aware of this dimension beyond the duality of limitations, must use our intelligence to discriminate beyond thought, and graduate to the other higher dimensions of Yetzirah, Beriah, and to the ATZILUT frequencies, which are the higher worlds in Kabbalah.

Because, in the four worlds of Kabbalah: Yetzirah, Beriah, and Atzilut are the higher levels of existence, while Assiyah is the lowest. And according to some kabbalistic sources, we are actually living in the world of Assiyah, which is the physical material manifestation, and is the lowest of the worlds. Assiyah is called the world of making. It is the lowest of the lower levels, and as mentioned above, it is also referred to as Almah Deshikrah, the "world of lies."

Now, these four kabbalistic worlds are in actuality one, visible and perceived to those who use both hemispheres of the brain to "understand."

But our focus as humans has been on the physical aspect only. For example, in a conversation, the teacher asks the student "Do you want light?" She says "Yes." He says "Well, open the window so the light can come in." Or he says "Open the book, so you can get some information." Now, what is he talking about? Does he just mean to open the physical windows? No.

Similarly, the prophet Ezekiel was told to "eat this scroll." It is a metaphor. Should he really eat the scroll? How can you eat a scroll? It's not food. But there must be some kind of food that is not physical, the food for the soul. Just as "being cooked" is one way of understanding the human process of evolution. (*See the story of "The Rabbi and the Alchemist" in the Kabbalah section for more understanding*).

You will find that there are many examples like this available everywhere, happening every day, to everyone in the world, but we pass them by. This is because of the great sin, that we do not know how to listen. It is why some teachers keep repeating the teaching again and again, because the students don't listen. So that repetition is necessary.

I call it the great shift.* And this can actually be practiced every day by those who know the "secrets" of sleep, including why we sleep. Generally, we know this function of sleep regenerates the whole system, totally new. But the spiritual dimension, according to Kabbalah, is that sleep is a rehearsal

---
* Refer to the article, "The Great Shift" in the Opening Articles Section
Note: See the Article "Who I am Who Says I Am Nothing" in the Introduction

how to die. Those who know the secrets of sleep can practice every night, to go to that state beyond logic or reason. That state is something which is not accepted today, and that's why we judge each other and don't know how to get along with each other.

Now, these massive changes in consciousness have been available always, to those who have a glimpse of that consciousness "beyond the limited reality" of the lower dimension. And those shifts are happening <u>RIGHT NOW,</u> for those who are aware of these higher frequencies, beyond words and imaging, perceiving beyond perceiving.

The idea is to understand the new consciousness, beyond "understanding." And I call that state…. "Nowhere."

So, welcome to "Nowhere."

The Gate Long Shut

by Rabbi Solomon Ibn Gavirol[*]

THIS IS A song of the great Sephardic poet that we sang in Morocco, which has become a "prayer." We sang it in the Andalusian music, along with his other poems. This is a spiritual love song.

The Gate Long Shut	שַׁעַר אֲשֶׁר נִסְגַּר / ר׳ שלמה אבן גבירול
The gate long shut— Get up and throw it wide; The stag long fled— Send him to my side.	שַׁעַר אֲשֶׁר נִסְגַּר קוּמָה פְּתָחֵהוּ וּצְבִי אֲשֶׁר בָּרַח אֵלַי שְׁלָחֵהוּ
When one day you come To lie between my breasts, That day your scent Will cling to me like wine."	לְיוֹם בּוֹאֲךָ עָדַי לָלִין בְּבֵין שָׁדַי שָׁם רֵיחֲךָ הַטּוֹב עָלַי תְּנִיחֵהוּ
Lovely bride, what shape has your beloved that you say to me A ruddy face, and lovely eyes? A handsome man to see?"	מַה זֶּה דְּמוּת דּוֹדֵךְ כַּלָּה יְפֵה־פִיָּה כִּי תֹאמְרִי אֵלַי שָׁלְחָה וְקָחֵהוּ
"Aye, that's my friend! Aye that's my love! Anoint that one for me!"	הַהוּא יְפֵה עַיִן אָדֹם וְטוֹב רֳאִי רֵעִי וְדוֹדִי זֶה קוּמָה מְשָׁחֵהוּ

translation: Scheindlin, Carmi

---

[*] Rabbi Solomon Ibn Gabirol was born (c. 1022) in Galaga and died in Valencia (c.1055, possibly as late as 1070), living most of his life in Saragossa. Both poet and philosopher, he began publishing while still in his teens. He is considered the first Hebrew poet to introduce Spanish-Arabic styles of the Golden Age into synagogue poetry.

The Awesome and Terrible Story of Rabbi Joseph De La Rheina

THIS IS A great and terrible story about Joseph De La Rheina, who was a great and wise man, and an adept in mysticism. He lived in Safed, may it speedily be rebuilt, in the Galilee. It came it pass, that he made up his mind to bring about the Redemption, and to cause the rule of evil to pass away from the land.

Joseph De La Rheina had five disciples, who stayed with him day and night, and obeyed him in every particular. They were also adept in mysticism, which they had learned from him.

He said to them: "My sons, I have taken it upon myself to search and to inquire by means of the wisdom which G-d has granted me. For it is not good for us to waste our time without avail, and the Lord has not graced me with this wisdom in vain – but only to give joy to our Creator, and to cause the spirit of impurity and idol worship to pass from the earth, and to bring about the coming of our Messiah, who will deliver us from our enemies."

All the five disciples answered together, saying, "Our master, teacher and Rabbi, we are ready to do whatever you command and whatever you desire, for G-d is with you, and we are your servants and disciples. So, do whatever you see fit."

He said to them, "If so, do this. Purify yourselves and change your garments. Be prepared in three days' time. Do not approach a woman, and prepare food for the way, for on the third day, we shall go out into the field. And we shall not return to our houses until every man in Israel receives his inheritance in the land of Israel, by the aid of Him who does great deeds, who is Almighty. For, he gives strength to the weary. His right hand is glorious in power."

When the disciples heard the words of their Rabbi, they hastened to rise, and to put on clean garments. They purified themselves. And they took in their hands, food for the way, bread which they themselves had made in purity, and no woman had touched. They came to him on the third day, and he was standing alone in his *Beit ha-Midrash*, the house of study. He had sanctified and purified himself and was in solitary meditation, sitting with his head between his knees.

When they entered, he lifted his head and said to them: "Come my sons, blessed of G-d. And may the graciousness of the Lord be upon us. May it be his will, that the *Schechinah* should rest upon our deeds, and that the Holy One, blessed be He, should consent to our doing, and help us, that we may honor His Name." And they answered, "Amen! May G-d agree to our desire and grant us success."

• • •

After these words, Rabbi Joseph took all kinds of spices, and the ink-stand of a scribe was girded on his loins, and he said to them: "Come, let us go." They set out, and came to Meron, to the tomb of Rabbi Shimeon bar Yohai. They bowed down and prayed by his tomb. They spent the night there, and all that night they remained awake, except for a little fitful sleep.

And it came to pass, towards morning, before the rising of the dawn, Rabbi Joseph fell asleep and Rabbi Shimeon bar Yohai and his son, Rabbi Elazar, came to him in a dream. They said to him: "Why do you take on a burden which is too great for you, and in which you cannot succeed? And even if your intention is desirable, and even if you do succeed, nevertheless, take great heed for your soul." He said to them, "G-d knows my intention, and He desires the heart, and He will help me for the sake of His great Name." And they said to him, "May the Lord, your G-d, accept you."

In the morning, they went to the city of Tiberias, and walked in the fields. They then entered the city, which is full of trees, and sat there all that day, and did not cease from their study and fasting, and did not look upon any man or beast, but only at the birds of heaven. They occupied themselves in composing Names of G-d from verses of Scripture, and said "Prayers for the Unification of the Name," in holiness and great awe.

Every morning, they would go and immerse themselves in the Lake of Kinneret twenty-six times consecutively, according to the numerical value of the four-lettered Name of G-d (and every immersion was directed towards a certain 'Prayer for the Unification of the Name,' and a certain combination of letters from a verse in Scripture, which formed a Name). In this way, they spent three consecutive days in fasting, and at night, they did not eat either meat or fish, or drink wine or ale.

Towards evening, at the time of the Afternoon Service, Rabbi Joseph would rise with his disciples and recite the Afternoon Service in a pleasant voice, and with great devotion, while his eyes were closed. When they reached the Benediction *Shema Kolenu* (Hear our Voice), they would say *Anenu* (a special prayer said on fast days). They would mention the Great Name (the Tetragrammaton), and they prayed a lengthy prayer, asking all the angels to help them. At the end, he invoked Elijah to come to him at once, when he was awake to speak with him, and to give him instruction about what to do in order to carry out his enterprise. At the end of his prayer, they fell on their faces, and said the prayer which is said at this time.

• • •

Immediately after they had fallen on their faces, Elijah came running, and suddenly appeared to them. Elijah said, "Now, I have come, how can I help you? And what did you demand so insistently in your prayers?" Rabbi Joseph rose to his feet, he and his disciples, and they bowed down with their faces to the ground, and said: "Peace be to our master, the chariot of Israel and its horsemen, true prophet, holy one of God, bringer of good tidings, who causes us to hear of salvation. Let it not appear evil in your eyes, that I insisted that you come to me. For it is revealed and known before God, that not in my honor and for my sake have I troubled you. I am only zealous for the honor of the Holy One, Blessed Be He, and his *Schechinah (the divine presence)*. And you are worthy of being zealous for the Lord of Hosts, for such is your quality. Therefore, listen to my entreaty, and show me how I can conquer the forces of evil and strengthen and make great the forces of holiness."

Then, Elijah the Prophet answered, and said to him: "Know then, that the thing you wish to do is too heavy for you, and you will not succeed. Because of the transgression of Israel, the forces of Samael and his followers have become very strong, and you will not be able to overcome them. For an additional quantity of purity, holiness, and great asceticism, and separation from the affairs of the world is needed, and more penances and immersions must be carried out. For you will not be able to withstand the forces of evil without these. Perhaps the forces of evil will attack you and harm you. But know that your intention is desirable, and if you carry it out, happy are you, and happy is your lot. But my counsel is – abandon this enterprise, lest Samael and his followers harm you and you will not be able to overcome them."

Then Rabbi Joseph answered and said: "My lord, do not weaken my hand. Strengthen me, give me might, for I have sworn that I shall not return to my house until I bring the *Schechinah (the divine presence)* out into the light, and raise it from the dust. And you also, blessed of God, help us and teach us what to do. And I promise to carry out anything my master will command his servant. For I am ready and willing to give my life to die for the honor of the Holy One, blessed be He, and his *Schechinah*. Only answer us, and tell us what to do, for we depend on you."

When Elijah heard that R. Joseph was ready to die for the honor of the Holy One, blessed be He, and his *Schechinah*, he said to him: "Why shall I continue to speak to you? If you succeed in withstanding Samael and his followers, and observe what I command you today, happy are you, and your portion is goodly, and your fate is pleasant. Now, this is the thing that you and your disciples must do. Dwell in the field, far from where people live, as you have done up until now. Let there be neither man or beast with you. Stay there 21 days, and do not eat except at nighttime. Let your food be bread and water only, and do not eat until you are satisfied, only enough to keep you alive. Every night, eat less and less, until you are accustomed to eating very small quantities. And accustom yourselves to smell spices, so that the matter of which you are formed should be purified and cleansed. You will then be able to bear the heavenly angels that I shall bring down to you to speak with you. And every day, make twenty-one immersions, according to the numerical value of 'Ehyeh' ('I am that I am.' Exodus 3:14). After twenty-one days, make a break, and then undertake to fast three days and three nights consecutively. And every day, make twenty-one immersions. On the third day, at the time of the Afternoon services, mention the great name of G-d of forty-two letters, with all its combinations, and mention the Great Name which comes from the verse: "the Seraphs were standing above," when you know how it is vocalized, and its sources. When you do this, be covered with your Tallit and wearing your Tefilin, and cover your faces, and by mentioning the Holy Names, invoke Sandalphon the Angel, and his followers, to come to you."

"When they appear, strengthen yourselves by smelling the spices, for great fear, weakness, and trembling will fall upon you. And at once, throw yourselves upon the earth and say very loudly 'Blessed be the name of His glorious kingdom, forever and ever.' Immediately, Sandalphon and his followers will ask you why you did this. When he speaks to you, because of the great noise, from the might of his speech, your spirit will leave you, and you will remain without strength. You will be, as it were, stricken dumb, and will not be able to answer him, because of your great fear and weakness. Therefore, have pure frankincense ready to smell, and beg the angel, with every entreaty, to hold you and give you strength to speak. He will tell you that which will strengthen you, and give you courage to speak. And he will tell you what you must do, for he guards the way and the path, to prevent Samael from entering the holy places. He knows Samael's tricks and where he can strengthen himself, and what his strength depends on, so that you can fight against him. May G-d find pleasure in you, and grant you peace."

• • •

Immediately after Elijah went on his way, Rabbi Joseph and his disciples together girded themselves with strength and sanctified themselves. They did all that Elijah had told them, and did not leave out anything that he had commanded. They did not cease from studying, either by day, or by night, and did not think of things of this world, only of principles of faith, and of the work of the Celestial Chariot, so that they almost cast off their material bodies. After they had completed the aforementioned days, according to the commands of Elijah, immediately at the time of the Afternoon Services, Rabbi Joseph and his disciples arose in fear and awe, put on their *Tallit* and *Tefilin*, and covered their heads. They said the Afternoon Prayer with great devotion, and said the prayer *Anenu* ('Answer us' – a special prayer said on fast days). And instead of saying the name of God, as it is usually pronounced, they said it as it is written and vocalized, with the correct tune.

Then they finished the prayer, and fell on their faces to the ground, while covered with *Tallit* and *Tefilin*. And at once, they rose and said the Confession over their sins, and the sins of the whole house of Israel. After this, they cried with all their might, "Answer us, God of the Celestial Chariot," and they made an invocation with the forty-two lettered Name, which comes out of the verse: "And the seraphs were standing above Him." Then they invoked the angel Sandalphon, with all his followers, to appear before them, by the might of the Holy Names.

When they had concluded their words, the heavens opened, and suddenly Sandalphon, and all his train, came to them: A chariot of fire, and horses of fire, a great camp, and burning flames filled the earth. There was a great noise that did not cease, and Rabbi Joseph trembled with a great trembling, and no spirit was left in him or his disciples. They fell on their faces, and their hearts stopped beating, and trembling seized them. But they strengthened themselves and smelled of the pure frankincense, which was in their hands. Their spirit returned, but still awe, trembling and weakness, remained on them, so that they could not speak. When the angel Sandalphon and his camp came to them, he said, "What do you want man, who is dust and worms? How dare you to rouse the holy angels! Do you not pay heed to your little worth? Return home, lest my host attack you and burn you with their fiery breath.'

Rabbi Joseph answered in a voice that was low and broken, because of his great weakness. And there was great awe and trembling in all his body, and its organs. He said: "My lord, holy angel of God, what can your servant speak before you? Behold I am without spirit, like the dead, because of my great fear of you, and awe and trembling have fallen on me. For I fear this great fire, and I cannot answer my lord, only if in your kindness, you give me strength to permit me to speak before my master."

• • •

When the angel heard his words, he touched him, and said: "Rise and speak your words. See, I hold you fast." When the angel touched him, he rose and was strengthened, and he took his shoes off of his feet. But his disciples still buried their heads in the ground, and could not rise. Rabbi Joseph replied and said: "Peace be to you. May there be peace in your coming, and peace be to your holy camp. I beg you to give me strength and force, and help me to fulfill my desire. For, not for my honor, or for the honor my father's house, am I doing this thing, but for the glory of the living God, the King of Kings, to whom alone belongs the kingdom. You, holy one, and your holy hosts, have consented with me to fight against Amalek and its prince. Show me the way to make the kingdom of iniquity pass from the earth, how I can bring Samael down from his abode, and how I can raise holy hosts to strengthen the Highest of the High, as it was in days of old."

Then the Angel answered R. Joseph, saying: "Indeed, your words are good and acceptable. May God be with you, for this is the longing of all the hosts of angels and seraphs, who sit and await the revenge of God, the revenge of the holy *Schechinah*, who because of our transgressions is humbled and lowered to the depths. But know, son of man, all you have done until now is nothing. And if you know to what heights Samael and his camp have risen, you would not intervene in this matter, for who can overcome him, but the Almighty himself, until the appointed time of His word comes? And behold, I have come to you for the sake of His great name, that you spoke, but what can I do for you? For we cannot fathom or know wherein lies the great power of Samael and his camp, and on what his rise and fall depends, except for the great angel Akatriel, and his hosts, who, were it not for them, Samael would enter, and would have the strength to destroy Israel.

I have only enough power to guard certain holy paths in the 'World of Making,' through which the prayers of Israel pass. And I guard the prayers until I hand them over to those angels. They know, and will be able to tell you what the power of Samael depends upon. But who can stand before those powerful angels? You will not be able to bear the great vision and awesome sight, and the fire which consumes fire. If you were terrified of angels of a lower order, how will you be able to stand before these? With regard to the penances and other ascetic practices you undertook, you will have to perform far more. But my advice is, leave this matter, and you will receive your reward. But to tell the truth, if you could carry out the matter in the right way, your reward is very great, and if so, who can be compared to you."

Rabbi Joseph answered and said: "I am young, and of little value, and know that I am unworthy of doing this thing. For, who am I, to come before the King? But I know that God does not despise a broken and lowly heart, for He has not despised nor abhorred the lowness of the poor (Psalms 22:25). And I have made up my mind to sacrifice my life and my spirit for the Sanctification of the Holy One, blessed be He, and His *Schechinah*, to unite Him in perfect unity with the *Schechinah*. I will do all that is required and will make my spirit, and my flesh and blood, a sacrifice before the Holy One, blessed be He, and His *Schechinah*. And therefore, ministering angel, holy one of the Lord, show me what I must do to bring down Akatriel and Metatron. What penance and purifications must I add, and by what Names shall I invoke them? For I said 'let me die,' now that I have seen the Angels, the holy ones of the Supreme Being, may I have everlasting life because of this."

Then the angel continued and said: "Hear my words, and may God be with you. If you do this and God commands you, you will be able to stand. And may it be His will that you carry out your desire. Do all that you have done up to now with regard to immersions and fasts, and guard the purity of your thought. Do so for 40 days, and do not let your thoughts stray from the Principles of the Faith, even for a moment, either by day or night. Every day, lessen the quantity of food that you eat, until you are accustomed to sustain yourselves on small amounts. And add a little to the quantity of spices you smell, for this is the chief thing that sustains the spirit.

After 40 days, make mention of the Name of seventy-two letters, with all its mystical intentions, vocalization, and sources, as is known to you, and with this Name, you will invoke these two great and mighty angels. Before you invoke them, pray and beg God that he should help you and give you strength to bear the awe-inspiring sight and the great fire, so that you do not die. Afterwards, entreat these angels to come to you for the sake of His great Name. Strengthen yourself as you did now, and ask them to support you, that you may speak. For they are great and powerful angels, and they know the ways of Samael and how you will be able to bring him down. Now, strengthen yourself for the sake of our people, and for the cities of Our G-d, and may the Lord guard you from all evil. May He guard your soul." Then the Angel of the Lord returned to heaven in a whirlwind. But the disciples still lay powerless on the ground, because of their great fear and awe.

• • •

After the angel Sandalphon and his camp had gone, the disciples rose and R. Joseph said to them, "My sons, blessed of G-d, strengthen yourselves and we will hasten to do all the angel has commanded us." They replied, "We are prepared. And happy are we that we have seen visions of G-d and have heard the angels' words, although we lay on the ground. Now, all that you do, we shall do." And he said, "Blessed are you of G-d."

Then, they arose and went through the desert to a certain mountain near Meron, and they found a cave there, and dwelt in it. They spent the forty days in holiness and purity, as they had been commanded. All these days, they did not look upon either man or beast. After they had completed the forty days, they went out to the desert, in the place where the river Kishon passes, near its source. For there, they used to immerse themselves, all forty days. They prepared themselves to say the Afternoon Services. They said the prayer *Anenu* (a special prayer for fast days), and they prayed to God concerning their enterprise, with great entreaties and with weeping. Then they made a circle in the earth and entered it, and each one gave a hand to his fellow, so that they were all holding hands in a circle. After they had fallen on their faces, they cried out to the Lord, and they pronounced the Name of seventy-two letters, and invoked the angel Akatriel and his camp, and the angel Metatron and his camp.

It came to pass, when they uttered the Great Name, the earth trembled. There was thunder and lightning. The heavens opened, and the angels, together with their followers, descended and wished to attack Rabbi Joseph and his disciples. But their hands did not separate. And they strengthened themselves with Mystical Intentions, by pronouncing certain Names, known to them, in their minds, but not by speech, for the power of speech had been taken from them. And they all fell on the earth, but their hands remained joined firmly.

The angels began to reprove them angrily, and asking how could they make use of the King's scepter, and how had they thought of such a thing? "You, who are flesh and blood, dust and worms, how could you think of invoking an angel?!"

When Rabbi Joseph saw this great vision, fear and awe fell on him, from the sound of thunder, and the great fire. There were charioteers of fire, and horses of fire, angels and seraphs, and their hosts. The whole earth was filled with a wind and a whirlwind, that broke mountains and cleft rocks. And the great fury of the angels, who wished to harm him, made Rabbi Joseph and his disciples fall asleep on the earth. There was no spirit left in them, and they could not reply to the angels, for they were terrified of them.

• • •

Then the angel Metatron touched him and said, "Speak you dust and worms. Why did you make us hasten to come? Why did you not think of the honor of your Maker?" When the angel touched him, he opened his mouth and spoke quietly, because of his great weakness, and his eyes could not see: "What can this lowly servant speak before holy and pure angels? I am like a lifeless stone and my spirit and soul leave me." Then the angel Akatriel also stretched out his hand and touched him, and said, "Look, strengthen yourself, and say what you wish."

Rabbi Joseph strengthened himself and opened his mouth, and said: "God knows that I have not done all these things rebelliously, but only for the glory of the Holy One, Blessed Be He, and His *Schechinah*, to raise the *Schechinah* from the dust, where it lies because of our transgressions. And now, you sublime angels, this commandment is for you. This action will not bring glory to me. For you it is worthy to be zealous for the Lord of Hosts. Therefore, please, Ministering Angels, because of His great Name, on whom all creatures depend, both heavenly, and earthly, give honor to His Name, and reveal what is the power of Samael and his camp, so that I can bring him down."

The angels answered together: "You have asked a very difficult thing. For if you only knew how strong, and mighty, and uncontrollable he has become, because of the manifold transgressions of Israel. And no one knows him, but us, for we guard the Higher Way from the hosts of Samael. But he is very mighty and none can bring him down. For he has made his nest among the stars, and there is his abode. He is surrounded by three partitions, because of the sins of Israel. He is very powerful, and you will not be able to overcome him without the Holy One blessed be He, until the appointed time comes, when His promise is fulfilled."

But Rabbi Joseph still continued to speak: "I have already risked my life for the glory of the Holy One blessed be He, and his *Schechinah*. And after I saw the holy hosts, and yet was delivered, I trust in the loving-kindness of the Lord, that He will help me, and I shall be able to carry out your pure words, rightly. Whatever you tell me to do, I will be very heedful to do."

The angels answered and said: "Hear the word of God, Joseph. Up until now, it has been known to Him, who spoke, and the world was created, that your thought is desirable. But the appointed time has not yet arrived, and it has already been decreed that you cannot awaken or stir up love, until it pleases. And now, as a result of your knowledge and wisdom, and the hidden mysteries with which the Rock of Ages has graced you, and because of these, and because of His great Name, we are compelled to instruct you in the way you should go. But know that you will not be able to overcome him, and therefore, do not enter a place you are unworthy of entering, and do not go any further. But if you insist on continuing, using His great Name, we will tell you what to do. And to tell the truth, if you succeed, how goodly is your portion, and how pleasant is your fate."

Rabbi Joseph answered and said: "Supreme holy beings, your words are goodly and reasonable, but my heart is inflamed when I see the *Schechinah* laid low, and I am very zealous for Zion. So, may God do what is good in His sight. And even though he slays me, I shall hope for Him. I shall not turn away my thought from him. And you, angels of the Supreme One, strengthen me with your utterance, and it shall be for a memorial to me. I shall not turn to the right or to the left, and I shall trust in His great Name, that He will not be a snare unto me."

• • •

Afterwards, Akatriel the angel opened, and said: "Know then, that on one side opposite me, Samael has two mighty partitions. One is an iron wall, which reaches from earth to heaven, and the other is the great Ocean." Then the Angel Metatron replied that on his side, opposite him, Samael had a great mountain of snow, whose summit reached the heaven. "Now, pay heed to all we say to you, and gird yourself with strength. For you will have to bring low these three partitions, and destroy them, in order to ascend Mount Seir, and judge the Mountain of Esau.

"This is what you must do. When you leave this place, go towards Mt. Seir. We will be there before you, on the top of Mt. Seir, and whatever you do at the bottom of the mountain, according to our instructions, we will do at the summit. Your spirit will be with us at the summit, and whatever you do below, your spirit will do above. Therefore, be very careful not to leave out any of the things we tell you."

"When you arrive at Mt. Seir, be careful in matters of holiness, and eat little, and be in the Prayers of Unification that you have made up until now. For your souls have already been lifted up high, so that you are almost angels, and you have almost forgotten the ways of the world. Keep steadfast in this. Do not let your thoughts wander from the Principles of Faith for even one moment."

"There, on the way, a great pack of black dogs will come upon you. They are the bands of Samael, who he will send to confuse your thoughts. But do not be afraid, and pronounce a certain Name, and then they will run away. From there, climb up the mountain, and you will see a great mountain of snow, whose summit reaches heaven, where there is no way to turn aside, either to the right or to the left.

Then, pronounce the Name that comes out of the verse: 'You have brought us to treasures of snow,' that is known to you, with its combinations and correct vocalization. From this, the mountain will move from its place. Finally, pronounce the name that comes from the verse: 'It snows in Zalmon' (Psalms 68:15), with its combinations and vocalization. And the mountain will vanish entirely."

"Go on with these Mystical Intentions, and do not let your thoughts stray, until you come to the other partition of the Ocean, whose waves will rise to the heaven. Pronounce the Names that come out of the Psalm: 'Ascribe unto the Lord, O you sons of might,' with the Names of G-d that come from it, in their right spelling, vocalization, and source. Then the sea will dry up, and you will pass through on dry land."

"Continue, and you will find a great wall, which reaches from heaven to earth. Take a knife in your hand, and write on it the Name that comes from the verse 'A sword to the Lord and to Gideon,' with its correct vocalization. Cut the iron, and make a door and enter. But take heed to hold the door until you and your disciples go through, so that it should not close. Because after you have gone through the door, it will close again."

"Then, continue until you reach Mt. Seir. At that moment, we will throw Samael from his place, and he will be handed to you. Let the Four Lettered Name be ready in your hands, written and engraved on a lead tray. And further, let there be ready in your hands another tray, and engrave on it the Name that comes from the verse (Zachariah 5) 'And he said "This is wickedness! And he cast her down in the midst of the measure, and he cast the weight of lead upon the mouth thereof," and write the Name that comes from this verse with its correct vocalization and source. Then you may walk as you please on Mt. Seir, and there you will find the wicked Samael and his wife Lilith. Search for them, for they will hide from you in a certain ruin. You will find them in the form of two black dogs, male and female."

"Approach them and do not be afraid of them. Put the tray with the Four-Lettered-Name on the male dog, and put the second tray on the female. Immediately put a chain around their necks and the trays on them. They will follow you, with all their train. Then you will have succeeded in doing the will of God, and you will bring him to judgment on Mt. Seir, that you passed. There, a great horn will be blown, and the Messiah will reveal himself, and will make the spirit of impurity pass from the earth, and the Holy One blessed be He, will slaughter him before the Tzaddikim. The complete Redemption will come, and the Kingdom will be God's."

"If you do this thing in the right way, happy are you, and how good is your portion, and how pleasant is your fate. But be careful to have the proper thoughts in your mind the whole time, and do not let your mind stray for even a moment. Moreover, take heed that when Samael and his mate are in your hands, and they cry and beg you to give them something to eat or drink, so that they will not die, do not listen to them. Do not give them anything. If they make their voices kindly, pay no heed to them. Be very careful of this, and also of the mystical intentions. For even when he is in your hands, you need to guard yourself very greatly. Be careful and do not leave out anything we have said. May God be with you, and may he guard your feet, so that they do not fall into a snare!"

• • •

After this, the two angels went up in a whirlwind to heaven, and R. Joseph watched, while he kneeled and bowed. But his disciples still lay on their faces, and could not lift up their heads, until the angels went up. After the angels had gone up, they also rose with great joy. Then Rabbi Joseph and his disciples hastened to arise, and arranged the Orders of the Names, and the Names of God that the angels had commanded, and the two lead trays. And they set out on the way to Mt. Seir.

On the way, packs of black dogs came upon them and surrounded them from every side. But when they pronounced the Name that the angels had told them, the dogs scattered and fled, and they saw them no more. After they had walked for another day, towards evening, they found a great mountain of snow whose summit reached the heaven. Again, they pronounced the Names they had been commanded. At first it moved from its place, and then it vanished entirely.

• • •

They slept there that night. In the morning, they rose early, and walked another two days. On the third day, at dawn, they saw the great sea stretching out before them. A storm raged and the waves reached heaven. At once, they pronounced the Names they had prepared, and passed through the sea on dry land.

And at noon, they reached the iron wall, whose top reached heaven. R. Joseph took the knife, on which he had written the Name, and cut into the iron, the thickness of which was ten centimeters, and made an opening in it. They held the doorway open until all the five disciples had passed. But while they were going through, the last of the pupils let his thoughts stray, and the door slipped from R. Joseph's hands. It closed on the foot of the disciple, who was caught in it. He cried out, "Save me Rabbi and teacher, for my foot has been caught."

At once, R. Joseph took out the knife and cut around his leg, and he went through the door. Then, the door returned to its place.

Then, they climbed up to Mr. Seir, and they walked there until evening. There, they found a valley, in which there were a number of ruins, and he heard the sound of dogs barking. They entered the ruin, and found two very large dogs, male and female, hiding there. When they approached, the dogs jumped at them, trying to swallow them.

Now, the trays were in R. Joseph's hands. At once, realizing that the dogs were Samael and Lilith, he stretched out his right hand and put the tray around the neck of the male dog, and the second one around the neck of the female. His disciples had ropes in their hands, and they bound them, with the trays on them.

As soon as Samael and Lilith saw that evil had come upon them, they put off the form of dogs, and put on their true forms – the form of people. They had wings, and their eyes were like burning fires. They begged and entreated Rabbi Joseph to give them food and water, that they might live. They said to him, "You are our master. We, and all our camp, are bound and imprisoned in your hand, and all our strength is gone. Do to us as seems good to you, only, give us something that we may live. For we have been cast down from our true place, where we enjoyed the light of the Schechinah, behind the Celestial Screen. Why should we die now? Give us food, so we may live until we reach Mt. Seir." But Rabbi Joseph refused, as he had been commanded, and did not want to give them anything.

As they were walking on the way, Rabbi Joseph and his disciples were happy, and they rejoiced, and their faces were full of light. Meanwhile Samael and Lilith and all their followers were weeping as they walked. Rabbi Joseph too rejoiced, and he began to feel proud. He said, "Who would believe our news? For all said that we would never succeed. Behold, this day, the heaven will rejoice, and the earth will be glad, and among the nations it will be said that the Lord reigns."

Then, Samael said, "I knew that you would win, and nothing would be too much for you." He and his camp wept bitterly, and he said, "My lord, why do you fear me, and all my followers? We no longer have any strength. We are yours to do with us what you wish. But give us, we pray you, something to support our spirits, so that we may continue to live until we reach Mt. Seir."

Rabbi Joseph answered, and said: "I shall give you nothing, as I have been commanded."

• • •

When they neared Mt. Seir, Rabbi Joseph took a small quantity of frankincense to smell, and Samael said, "If you don't give me food, give me a small quantity of frankincense to smell." Rabbi Joseph stretched out his hand and gave him a little of the frankincense that was in his hand. But Samael took a spark of fire from his mouth, and burned the frankincense while it was still in Rabbi Joseph's hand. The smoke entered the nostrils of Samael, and he burst asunder the ropes and chains, and threw off the leaden trays. He and his hosts arose, and they attacked the disciples of Rabbi Joseph. Two of them died from the sound of the cry of Samael and his hosts, and two of them were harmed and became mad. Rabbi Joseph was left with one disciple.

Rabbi Joseph was tired and weary and puzzled, for he did not know that by giving the frankincense, he had given his soul, and he had offered incense to Samael. For the power of holiness in the leaden trays was lost because of the incense, because he had not paid heed to the words of the angels.

At that moment, all the mountain was filled with smoke. There was darkness and gloom, and a Heavenly Echo was heard, saying, "Woe to you Joseph, and woe to your soul. For you did not pay heed to what you were commanded, and you worshipped idols and offered incense to Samael. Now he pursues you, and will drive you out of this world and the next."

The disciple who remained with Rabbi Joseph was weary and weak. He had almost reached the gates of death, so he sat down to rest for about two hours under a tree. Afterwards, they buried the two disciples who had died. Then, Rabbi Joseph went with the one disciple to return. The appearance of their faces was greatly changed. It had become green and very weak. An evil spirit entered into the two others, and they fled. No one knew where they went, until a month later, when they reached the town of Safed and died, because of the sorrows the evil spirits inflicted upon them.

After this, Rabbi Joseph reached the town of Zidon. He dwelled there, and he strayed from the true way. When he saw that his counsel was not carried out, and especially after hearing the Heavenly Echo, he despaired of the world to come, and made a covenant with Lilith. He handed himself over to her, and made himself impure with all the impurities of the world. He even used the Names and mysteries he knew for evil purposes. He asked evil spirits to bring him whoever he wished every night. He used to bring the wife of a certain prince almost every night and return her every morning.

When the prince became aware of this, he sent for his magicians and made them guards in his house. He ordered them to stop the powers of evil from taking his wife. They sat and watched. That night, the evil spirits came by the command of R. Joseph. The magicians were immediately aware of this and forced them to reveal the meaning of the whole matter. The spirits said that they were the messengers of R. Joseph, who dwelt in Zidon.

At once, the prince sent one of his generals to the prince of Zidon with gifts and letters. He told him that he should bring R. Joseph alive, so that he might take revenge upon him by torture. R. Joseph saw that evil had come upon him, for it became known to him through the spirits, who returned to him before the letter reached the Prince of Zidon. When he saw this, he went and threw himself into the sea and died.

And I, the fifth disciple, remain alone. I lie on a bed of sickness all my days. There is no cure for my trouble. All my body burns with the fever, and I have no peace from the evil spirits. I have written down this story as a memorial. May God have mercy upon me and say to my sorrows – it is enough! These are the words of the disciple, Judah Meir, who took part in this great enterprise of R. Joseph De La Rheina.

From the book "The Gates of Holiness" by Rabbi Chayim Vital

English Translation, from The Stories of Eliyahu HaNavi
by Yisroel Ya'akov Klapholtz
A Terrible Story of R. Josef de la Rheine

Mime Articles

Practical Happiness	105
Advice to a Young Mime Artist	107
Artistic Zero	109
Beyond Opposites	113
Mime – The Silent Outcry	116
On Being Alert	121
On Being an Artist	125
Spiritualizing the Art of Mime	131
The Harmonious Cell	138
The Poetry of Activity	141

Mime Poster of Samuel, Boulder, Colorado 1971

Practical Happiness

The Journey from Thought to Action

THROUGH THE STUDY of mime, I learned to integrate creative techniques from theater, dance, music, and writing into a single productive and functional unit. Standard practice in the theater is that separate individuals perform different tasks: An author writes a play, the director directs it, the actors interpret it, the composer composes the score, and the dancer dances it.

While studying in Paris with Etienne Decroux, Marcel Marceau and Jean-Louis-Barrault, I discovered that in mime, there are no authors to write the scripts. I had to be my own author, actor, director, and composer. This proved to be a challenging effort. I had to integrate all of these specializations and become my own complete mini-theater.

As I developed my craft, I experienced a sense of elation in being able to use all of my abilities. I guided myself, without depending on the written words of another author, and without speaking words that were not of my own creation. I became the instrument of my inner voice. By directing my creations myself, I was the one who had to see the crucial details and the total vision simultaneously. To interpret the vision with integrity, my own philosophy had to be well integrated.

To think one thing and to do another, in essence to split one's expressions, is very dangerous, because it creates conflicts and problems where they should not exist. I had to eliminate this conflict, or risk becoming creatively stagnant. In the silence of a mime performance, the audience can readily sense this dichotomy.

My belief is that human beings naturally desire to behave honestly in thought and action. The life struggle sometimes gets in the way, however, and the mind devises deceptive survival strategies. But the body retains its innocence and reveals the deception with subtle indications. The conflict between mind and body is eliminated when the two work together.

In mime performance, the conflict is sometimes resolved by introducing the value of "heightening," or contrast; the body slouches, head hangs low, the face grins absurdly.

The audience recognizes the disparity and laughs. Humorous contrast or amplification can have the same effect in everyday life, resolving conflict and dispelling tension.

In my career I have met many thinkers who think and doers who do, but in a very fragmented manner. It is as if there is a junk shop with a merchant who has apparently unrelated items to sell. An integrated thinker walks into the shop, asks for nails, leather, glue, cloth, hammer… and produces a pair of shoes.

Non-integration and the splitting between mind and body are rampant in our society. The condition develops when people lack the confidence to think for themselves and then rely on guidance and approval from external authorities in order to function. The splitting between mind and body happens automatically when someone tries to behave according to a script written by someone else.

This is precisely why the discipline of mime became for me such an invaluable practice. Writing my own script became routine! I had to eradicate every inclination to laziness or dishonesty on the spot, making no compromises. My sense of responsibility increased in proportion to my passion for living. I became more decisive, closing the gap between thought and action. My art became one with my life. I achieved a state which may best be described as *practical* happiness. I then attempted to show others how they could achieve the same fulfillment.

> **All wisdom can be stated in two lines:**
> **What is done for you, allow it to be done.**
> **What you must do yourself, make sure you do it.**
> —*Anonymous*

Advice to A Young Mime Artist

SO, MY DEAR friend, you have decided to explore this marvelous art of mime – a territory unknown to many – and presumably your decision is motivated by sincerity and the honesty of your being.

If your motives are profound enough, that is, if they are not limited by time and space, this path will be full of great surprises and will unveil before you that which is considered the "invisible world" beyond. With this in mind, let us see if you are well-equipped. Let us see if you have the guidelines to lead you to success – which is to know yourself.

The art of mime, magical in many ways, is the ultimate language of silence, a universal language in itself, which will give you access to the most hidden places of your being, places where you are one with all creation. It is, my friend, an adventure that will fulfill you totally – when the time is ripe, and as long as your honesty and sincerity remain unfettered.

As an adventurer, you must know that the path drawn on the map is not the same as the real path. The map is only an indicator of where to go. It is only an instrument to lead you onward.

The instrument with which you play this art-venture is your own body, and, as an instrument, it has to be tuned. It is the house in which you live, breathe and move.

First, it must be exercised through the physical training in order to know the possibilities of movement, and to develop a certain discipline. This is of primary importance. The body-vehicle must be properly maintained, so that it functions with the precision and fluidity of a smoothly running organism. In this way, its performance will be harmonious in response to your simple command.

Through exercises designed to keep the body tuned, you will learn about motion and stillness, a work that must be given to the student by a master of the art. This is a phase which, you will agree, demands patience and endurance. It will test your strength, and eventually guide you to the next phases.

True enough, this work may take some time, perhaps a long time of perseverance, devotion, single-mindedness, and steadiness of purpose. Above all, it will require the proper application of your time.

While you are in this physical phase of the training, begin to sharpen and develop your faculty of observation. It will help you immensely later on. Observe around you the rhythms of things visible and invisible. Observe yourself, your actions and your thoughts. In so doing, you will begin to become aware of your psychic side, the hidden one in you, and your thought-processes. These will guide you to yet another level of awareness and self-organization.

This increased awareness will be very important along the way, enhancing your ability to formulate thoughts and to materialize them, to bring them from the realm of the invisible, into the visible, for your future audience to see and appreciate.

FROM CRAFT TO ART

The above steps will prepare you for entering a very desirable state of receptivity. You are mastering the instrument and training it to listen to your orders. You guide it to move in this or that direction, to express the specific idea that wishes to be born from you. As you do this, little by little you will find a newly awakened consciousness of movement, that is no longer random or wishy-washy. At this point you cross from the field of craftsmanship, into the realm of artistry.

A new world, a new dimension of the artist is gradually opening before you. By listening deeply to that hidden self, inside you, you begin to feel an urge to create. You discover how to formulate in space the dreams which you wish to bring to life, and to materialize thoughts into action. It is through the performance that the invisible is made visible. And this presents another test – the test of communicating to the audience what you have learned.

Stop now for a moment, my young one, and consider how much time and effort will have to be invested in you, by you, and towards you, in traveling this road. Ask yourself again if you are willing to embark on this non-time/non-space journey, the art-path of mime. Remain silent for a moment, and become still within yourself, reflecting deeply.

If the first thought to come into your mind is a positive answer, then by that urging alone, and that inner knowing and self-determination, you actually have your travel visa. You may enter the land of mime travelers, those explorers of the unknown.

Note: This article was published in Paris in 1961 and translated into English later and I am placing it here because it seems to me to be timeless to every aspiring artist.

The Artistic Zero

Images from the Void

EVERYTHING THAT HAPPENS at Le Centre du Silence is done to bring about radical changes in our *way of thinking*. Many people think with words, but few think in movement and vision. Instead of thinking in words, learn to think in images. Every moment is a new moment. We cannot hold onto the thought or image of one moment ago, because this is a new moment.

Nothing that happens here is accidental. This is true not only of *what* is said and done, but also of the *way* in which it takes place. A teacher is a reminder. If he speaks harshly, there is a purpose for it. He can hint, but he must not point the way, otherwise he stifles the imagination. A true teacher provides a nourishing environment in which the imagination may flourish.

Each of us comes here as a vessel, ready to be filled, ready to receive, ready to become pregnant with the seed of what mime is about... We eat the food that is offered according to our hunger. And the knowledge is digested, according to our need. Thus, as a teacher, I consider myself as a waiter.

When people gather together, they carry luggage with them: thoughts, fears, personal history. One cannot write on a sheet of paper that is already written on. First, it must be erased. There is much that must be unlearned. On a blank, white sheet, you can write anew.

The cosmos is pouring into us and through us continually. The body is the receiver of light and life. What is it to receive? I can pour water into an empty glass, not into a full one. If I shake the glass as I pour, much water spills out. The glass is filled only when it is held still. We too will receive, and hold all that the cosmos is pouring into us, when we remain empty and still. When we resist receiving, we create chaos.

What makes us resist receiving? Usually, the body will not listen to what it is told to do. Comfortable secure habits keep us from giving time and space to something new. "I'm used to it," you say. If you are heading for a fall and your ego gets involved in trying to stop you, you will get hurt. If you relax instead, the body will take care of itself. You can't live without the ego, but sometimes it is out of place. Keep the ego from interfering when it is not needed.

The body doesn't listen to what we tell it to do, because of the thought. The body can be occupied with only one thing at a time. Any thought distracts. The thought of panic, for example, tells the body to panic; without that thought, it would simply obey. We are always afraid of breaking our bones, or hurting our flesh, or our egos. By not trusting our bodies, we allow fear to exist in us. When there is no thought of fear, there is no fear. When you find out what you are afraid of, the fear can be released. (See the article "Fear Does Not Exist")

We think our thoughts are our own. Where do they come from? The ego yells, "*I* have an idea! *I* want to perform! *I* want to eat this and this and this!" But really, there is no *I*. On the day you accept totally that you are nothing (no thing), that day you are "enlightened." That day, you start to work.

To empty ourselves, we go to "artistic zero." In the zero posture, we do nothing at all. It is a standing meditation. There is a plumb line from the heavens that passes through the top of the skull, down the spine, through the just-kissing heels, and on down into the center of the earth. In "artistic zero," we stand, sensing this plumb line, breathing normally. Our eyes are focused beyond the horizon. The caravan of thoughts goes on, but we pay no attention to it. Zero is an erect state of total relaxation. It is the origin of all movement – the place of still, empty listening.

Even when standing still and empty in zero, there is movement in the body. If you let this movement take your weight in any direction, you will reach a point beyond which you will fall. This is your limit, your Edge.

Each and every person is limited in different ways. Only when you know your own limits exactly, will you know what it means to go beyond them. Then, you can find the unlimited. When you go beyond your limit, you free your spirit. Limitations are doors to the unknown. Know them intimately.

Stand in "artistic zero" and lean until you reach your edge. Now lean further still... Discover what is beyond the limit...A single step! That's all! That step stops the fall. The step is the beginning of something new – the next movement.

Beyond the limit is the land of the unknown, the void. Don't be afraid of it. Fear is just a limit, like any other. When you go beyond fear, there is a sudden calm. When you go to the void, it disappears, because you have filled it. Before taking the next step, always find "artistic zero," even if it's only for an instant. The void is endless. That which has an end is subject to gravity; that which has no end is not. There will always be a step, an image, an idea to stop us from falling, if we trust "artistic zero."

Do you dare to ask the question? The way you ask a question determines how you find the answer. There are ideas in the world outside our minds. To perceive them, we must seek total lucidity. Learn to ask the question with your whole body. See with your pelvis, smell with your eyes, swallow with your nose. For this work, we must become consciously mad.

Life is a study of illusions. Mime seeks to insert some truth into the illusions, by reflecting them. When you are in the land of the void and an image enters you from somewhere in the cosmos, let it occupy you totally. The image must be clear in every detail, before the body can reflect it. If it is just a feeling, it is not enough. Behind every movement, there must be a spirit. Then, expression occurs.

The right time to begin anything is when there is silence. The right time to act, move or speak is when there is silence. We must place ourselves in the receptive state. If we forget, the teacher is there to remind us. The intention is to release fear. We are working for total lucidity and for freedom of the imagination. Therefore artistic zero is a tool in our lives.

Flyer of First Mime Workshop, Boulder CO, 1971

Beyond Opposites

'There is an illusion of separateness in the world.'
—Samuel Avital

THERE ARE A multitude of dualities in this world. For everything that exists, its opposite also exists. We call this the Law of Polarity. All opposites exist simultaneously. Without father there would be no mother, without morning, no evening, without light, no dark. Polarity means having both positive and negative. Without summer, there is no winter, without hard, no soft, without tension, no relaxation, without motion, no stillness. After inhaling comes exhaling, after contraction, expansion. That's how the whole universe was born.

We really cannot perceive things unless we separate them. We divide and we divide, and the more we divide, the more there is the positive and negative. We are here and we want to be there. There comes a time when the dividing process stops. Division precedes uniting. There is a Oneness, one consciousness, underlying all things: One root, one beginning. Different manifestations, but one essence. We come to know that essence, that center, in silence.

Each of us has his own center, which is like the center of a circle. It is the place where we know who we are. It is the place we go out from, and return to, identical with the Center of all things, the One. When you condense yourself down to your center, you become a dot. When you get into an airplane, you are a dot in a plane; when the plane flies off, it becomes a dot in space. Then you are a dot in a dot in space.

Artists and mystics want to go directly to that center of things. When you work *from* that place, you are solid as a rock. It no longer matters if a critic tells you that you are not good. It doesn't apply. To do mime, to do art, there must be intention. The intention must be to stay in the center of silence

In our mime work, we train the body and waken the spirit. We strive to see the world perfectly, as one whole manifesting in many forms. The body has its own intelligence; When you meet a tiger, for example, freeze! Allow the animal in you to be, allow the I/you relationship. When the two animals recognize each other, maybe the tiger won't find you appetizing, and you won't get eaten. If you do get eaten, then you become part of that living being, and life goes on. By knowing the separateness, we know the One.

Life is a study of illusions. In mime, we seek to insert some truth into the illusions. A person reveals what they are by the movements they make. It is impossible to lie. People make many unconscious movements. In mime, we learn to see these movements, to reflect them. The truth of the stage takes what is not seen in life – like holding a pencil to write, or brushing your teeth – and makes it seen. It shows the invisible through the visible. We learn to write the dot in space.

We also learn how to listen to sounds, how to dissect words. We take words to the laboratory and dissect them. Invisible, for instance, means to be *in* the *visibility*. Likewise, insane means to be *in* the *sanity*. We can do this with any word, and the true meaning of that word reveals itself. Understanding means that when you are *under*, then you can *stand*. Remember means to put the *members*, the parts, back together. Just as we study the separateness of things, in order to reunite them, so we also take words apart, to understand what they really are. Words are symbols. Actually, they are symbols of symbols of symbols. Words stand for things and ideas. Things and ideas are symbols of the real world, the Center, the One.

An important part of our work is learning to be harmonious with opposites, or, as we say, "becoming lovers of paradox." This is indeed difficult, but unless we do it, we cannot enter the palace of true art. We are all limited beings, but we have to reach for the unlimited. Effort requires effortlessness. At the edge of ugliness, there is beauty.

In our mime work, we learn to embody the paradox in thought and action. For example, we have to stay very relaxed in order to be in a state of alertness. We have to express weakness, using our strength. Our point of reference, the body, is a structure made of both the hard and the soft. It has the appearance of permanence, but actually, it will die.

This is a paradox we can play on easily. If someone hurts you, play the opposite, say thank you. Break the logic of life, and laughter or crying results spontaneously. That is when education happens. If a bullet hits you, don't die. Pull it out, throw it back at the gunslinger, and watch it hit him! Accept the paradox, perform it, and then you are over it.

When you are in love, you cannot perform love. You can't express fear if you are still afraid. When you are still living an emotion, you cannot perform it. You can only express that from which you are detached.

In theater, there is the performer, the performed, and the performance. In thinking, there is the thinker, the thought, and the expression of the thought. These three are one. When we realize this, then we know totality. The paradox here is that the expression of totality happens through separation.

That which appears still, is essentially in motion, and that which appears to be moving is, in essence, still. The sun moves across the sky every day, but we don't notice its motion. We only see it now, above that tree, and then later, above that mountain. Each time, it appears still. We can't tell where the motion originates. A whirling dervish turns in a continual spiral, never wavering for an instant, but there is a profound stillness at his center that keeps him on one spot.

There are many other examples of this paradox in everyday life; the hub of a wheel turning, the calm before a storm, the eye of a hurricane, the frames of a film. When a person sits perfectly still in meditation, the blood continues to course through his body, and breath fills and empties his lungs. Time is the fluid in which all this motion takes place.

There is no stillness on this earth. But in art, painting and sculpture, time is arrested. Moments are captured in space. These moments are the spaces in between. It is the work of the mime artist to perceive them. He is the sculptor of space, the shaper of forms. His medium is space and time, and his paradox is that he must work simultaneously in the moment and in the timeless.

The mime artist knows that he shares the same space and the same consciousness with all other beings. He knows that negative space reveals the shape of an object, and he sculpts the space accordingly. He captures an emotion or thought in a freeze. He knows that just the suggestion of a thing is exciting. The hint of a kiss is exciting, not the kiss itself. He uses a minimum of movement, to achieve a maximum of expression. His work shows the marriage of subject and object.

In order to know the architect, you have to know the architecture. For the mime artist, the work becomes more and more important to him, until finally it becomes more important than himself. Then he becomes a symbol for his work, just as words are symbols for thoughts. The true mime artist must know the illusion of separateness so intimately, that he ceases to be separate. When he sees the One, he is free to reflect all the forms of duality in this world.

> **"True words aren't eloquent; eloquent words aren't true.**
> **Wise men don't need to prove their point;**
> **Men who need to prove their point aren't wise."**
> —*Tao Te Ching #81*

Mime – The Silent Outcry

THERE IS A story that my grandfather, a great Hebrew Kabbalist, once told me: "When a child is born, he is given a certain number of words to use in his lifetime. Every word you speak counts out of the total. Therefore, if you speak too much, one day, you may find yourself mute. And so, be economical with your words." This story has become the guiding staff in my life and teachings.

Many people think silence is a lack of noise, that silence merely means not talking. Experience in this field has caused me to think otherwise. There is a Kabbalistic idea that words are inadequate to express the essence of being. And so, only in silence can the expression of self be fully communicated. Thus, being and becoming expresses itself in action, through movement.

Without silence, there is no self-realization. Silence IS the realization. It is a non-point of reference. It is a state of being from which you can go, and to which you can return. There is a silence that is awesome, but not everyone can reach that center of silence. Our whole aim is to reach that, through specific work and understanding. Because in that center of silence, everything can happen. Visualize this center as a dot in the circle. You can think, and your thought just materializes before your eyes. Mime performance can illustrate this for us. The mime artist is able to visualize an image, a situation, and to immediately create it in their performance.

It is said that the great sin of mankind is egoism, doing things only for oneself. When a performer is doing things only for themselves, the audience feels it. That's the difference you see in performances. When you see a mime perform, you are either elevated to the heights, or put down to the depths. Sometimes a performance might be good technically, but it is totally empty.

We have many technicians in this age of technology, but they are not in touch with the invisible wires that live inside them. That technician/scientist who is separated from the experiment will never know anything. As soon as he gets involved with the experiment, then he becomes a mystic. But he has the right to also be a scientist. If he will embrace the other side, he will become whole. Until then, he will explore the world from "outside" and he will be out of the experiment. The mime artist is the experiment itself, the experimenter, and the laboratory. On this triangle of manifestation, our high ideal is built.

The artist in a community must live that sense of community. This artist, by reflecting the conditions and situations of man, acts as the prophet, actually the focal point, mirroring that community or society. When, in life, the unconscious is being pushed away and neglected, when the essence is being denied, the artist comes to expose it to our awareness. Then we cry, we laugh, we release tension, and we open the heart to new change.

The relationship of society toward the artist is similar to the relationship of the body toward the soul. If artistic expression tends toward mediocrity, this is a symptom of a state of decline in the world in which we live, and we have to act in such a way as to heal it. The artist, as a healer, will have to face the situation and behave accordingly. Art conceived in the absence of spiritual purity is not art. It may pass for art, but it is something else.

We are trying to teach the whole being – not just the physical, but also the psychical being. Then, thinking, which is analytical, and feeling, which is the essence of being, merge into a oneness of expression. Mime is an art in which intuition and intellect become one. We always seek to perpetuate and encourage the living totality of that being to express itself creatively in this artform. This is the ideal that we work for, and one that is being practiced – Now. Here.

שִׁמְעוֹן בְּנוֹ (שֶׁל רַבָּן גַּמְלִיאֵל) אוֹמֵר: כָּל יָמַי גָּדַלְתִּי בֵּין הַחֲכָמִים,
וְלֹא מָצָאתִי לַגּוּף טוֹב אֶלָּא שְׁתִיקָה.
פרקי אבות א. י"ז
**"All my days I have grown up among the wise,
and I have found no better service than silence."
—*Sayings of Fathers 1. 17***

מַהִי אוּמָּנוּתוֹ שֶׁל אָדָם שֶׁאֵין לְמַעְלָה הֵימֶנָּה ? שׁ ת י ק ה.
**"What is the most highly valued an art to do and to practice?
S I L E N C E."
—*Talmud, Masekhet Holin, page 89***

**"The only response to a fool's over-philosophizing,
in a simple word, is Silence."
—*Samuel Avital, 1971***

holy workspace • **the centre of silence** • jump into yourself • symphony of being • mind-body harmony • essence of yourself • dot in space • drop in the sea • think movement • still as a mountain • a l'italienne • the body cannot lie • slower than that • timing the space • spacing the time • blah blah blah • the tragedy of focus • you are the text • joke number 36½ • **burn, but not to ashes** • suicide, but don't die • swim but don't drown • listen to your body • **thank you for being here** • center yourself • **from ecstacy to lunch** • **the one who** • relax in it • unarchy • freak in • everyday movement • 2 stones get stoned • find your axe • line of work • **alert like a cat** • **claying around** • out of it • **be your own mirror** • sharpen your sword • **send a telegram** • **perfection in action** • brick by brick • build a mold • measure your energy • **verbal fast** • **day of silence** • fingers of the feet • jump into the fire • go mad with it • be sincere with it • such mastery! • **be a whole in the detail and the detail in the whole** • always come back to zero • it was not projected • no leader, no follower • don't panic • **the genesis of the self** • one breath class • thought to action • no philosophy • do the unexpected • no mediocre movement • do not manipulate • moving mandala • digest the food • take a picture • be sincere with it • instrument • it must project • be with yourself here • the body as a brush • a pinpoint of light • **to be and not to be** • tubes of vision • tubes of communication • dancing diaphragm • a circle inside itself • **echo of a whisper** • crystallized thought • **serve the idea** • it can be seen • be true to yourself • penetrate space • explore the space • cut through space • don't rape the space • it is known • **you are unique** • names are cloaks • think with your body • **organized panic** • confront the situation • move into space • challenge yourself • try not to try • don't act it • what is, is • silent acting • stand still and be • attention not tension • **shower on fire** • mark each new thought • dancing dots • think child • psychic surgery • immediate reflection • moo like a cow • see as for the first time • **turn the negative to positive** • do you have a passport • do you have your balls • the marriage of Mr. and Mrs. Lips • don't be too nice with yourself • let your body teach you the movement • **application is a dear time** • are you leading the movement or is the movement leading you? • **the leader of a group must be hidden** • the circle is everywhere • **a relaxed hand is the most beautiful** • **what is learned must be digested** • mime taught me how to live • the workshop is not here • your pelvis is in outer space • we are after the essence and the essence is after us • **laboratory of the self** • jump in and swim into it • **awareness prevents accidents** • write the text with your body • you don't make love, it makes you • we have only this one body • **not revolution, evolution** • a mime must know his spine, vertebrae by vertebrae • whatever your understanding • we can tell a person's progress by his control of the eyes • nothing would exist without parallels • it is not to make people laugh • **a circular movement is the most pleasing** • **the worker is hidden in the workspace** • give it the proper amount of energy • show the little unawarenesses of Man • get in a group and work individually • **performer, performing, performance are one** • dialogue with the earth • we are not in prison here • put your consciousness to the part of the body you are working • don't be anyone but yourself

MESSAGES FROM "NOWHERE"

• eyes into the horizon • act with the body • **collective orgasm** • **a leaf in the wind** • sing your death • lubricate the joints • squeeze an egg • pass through death • **curtains of silence** • **organic sound** • hug the universe • exquisite clarity • weight 50-50 • **75-25** • **empty the cup** • heels kissing • inner work • be with it • **be your own mirror** • auto-suggestion • **visualize the whole** • **carry the thought** • **face the situation** • fantasy in space • **empty the words** • **verbal labyrinth** • **speak to the point** • it's not to go out, it's to come back • first you become a craftsman, then artist, then a magician • **in the midst of agony, there is hope** • thought plus movement equals action • don't translate words into movement • you do it until it is doing you, then back to center • in transitions use crescendo of rhythm from one space to another • it takes alot of strength to be an old man • invisibility makes sound, the void creates space • if you are afraid of something—do it • pressed together like wheat • a moving letter in space • enter the space of a tone • one yes remembered itself • *laboratory—process of integration, assimilation, experimentation, expansion, becoming, visualization* • *see the line of your own body* • **they space out—we space in** • show confusion, but don't be confused • there are many shades between black and white • do it like doing it to yourself • mark each new thought and the end of each thought • the great fox in the night speaks to me • transform pressure into challenge • keep the extremes, but stay in the center • **a mime needs no mirror—a mime is the mirror** • learn to love without attachment • let your inner brilliance shine through • we are not working to make people laugh • enthusiasm of the moment • **point between yes and no**

• **no unneccessary movement** • **point of departure, center of return** • never be angry with your body • take the class with you • take the movement to its limit • take a picture of yourself in the attitude • the process here is one of absorption • try to see things said simply • know how to be in the other person's space • does your hand shape the objects or the objects shape your hand? • it is not to be a magician of the stick but to see what the stick can teach us • write the exercise with your body • if you want the space for you, you should give it to another first • the drunk can teach us a lot about life • do the illogical, the unexpected for a laugh • **relaxation—a conscious readiness to respond** • let your breathing lead you • find the animal in you • **is the movement doing you?** • be true to the action • let the movement be seen • **we are cells in the body** • **we are in the process of refining the instrument** • go mad with it—become what you are doing • put your energy in the center • prostitution of the art form • leave words behind when you come into this space • it is time to be with yourself—nothing would exist without the circle • **the dot that is yourself** • don't do it, let it be done to you • **the magician of space** • **everything is connected** • motion in neutrality • be imperialist • **embrace the opposites** • expect the unexpected • forget about technique • **edge of gravity** • **grasp the void** • stuttering of movement • **poet of space—P.O.S.** • stuttering of the eyes • **voyage pour l'inconnu** • don't anticipate • dog breathing • motion, not emotion • enjoy the process • state of mind • let go • transcend yourself • **rewind the film** • see yourself doing it • be here • pour yourself • **posture of openness** • hiss like a snake • humm like a bee

• expectations
without theme • work in the
possible space • one foot chasing the other
• be colorful with boredom • don't swim in the
philosophy • **vigorously, not violently** • the body is a
heavy feather • let the weight lead you • be concerned, but
don't worry • **the body is a container** • there is a dying in the laugh •
don't be tickled by the audience • **being faithful to the curve** • discreet
readiness, invisible awareness • close your eyes when you exercise • don't
kill the experience • psychic/spiritual body massage • **suggestion of the
dancing hands** • if you go too far, you restrict your movement • if you really
follow the echo it will go into infinity • to be aware of space is to be aware of
yourself • it appears free, but it should have an order • **slower than you think,
slower than you are—it is there but it is not there** • **put the words in the bank** •
nothing exists outside of this space • the work of the feet is hidden • feelings,
moods, thoughts are colors • **be detached, but not indifferent** • say yes with the
whole body • **go with your intuition** • do exercises with a beginner's mind • you
are a cell in the group • **to the point—measure your words** • Om—**Mushkil
Gusha—Nasrudin** • **be at peace with paradox** • make image real through detail
• **close your eyes and be** • thoughts are multi-dimensional parallels • a
fixation is a prolonged freezing • you are doing it for yourself, even if the
whole world doesn't understand • if the eyes are moving, you are not
doing it • holy workspace • **the centre of silence** • jump into yourself
• symphony of being • mind-body harmony • essence of
yourself • dot in space • drop in the sea • think movement •
still as a mountain • a l'italienne • the body cannot
lie • slower than that • timing the space •
spacing the time • blah blah blah •
such mastery!

Circle Teachings Terms of BodySpeak, 1975

On Being Alert

*"Movement is vibration, the total being of everything.
An intelligent being talks, an emotional being sings, a total being moves."*
Samuel Avital

ANIMALS DON'T THINK, they move. Their actions are instinctive, and they have an ability to stay still. They have an immediacy of response. They are naturally graceful and harmonious with nature. Animals know how to heal themselves; When wounded or sick, they withdraw and stop eating, licking their wounds. Unlike man, it is the needs of the animals that motivate them, not their desires. Animals have many ways of communicating with one another. Their senses are sharp, particularly the sense of smell. An animal stays alert, because its degree of awareness determines its survival. The alternative to alertness is death.

Men have these same abilities, but don't choose to use most of them. For instance, instinct speaks first within every person, no matter the situation, but the pushy exaggerated intellect starts thinking. It talks us out of following our intuitions. We rarely sit still as animals do, or respond to situations immediately. Our bodies are naturally graceful, but we lose touch with them. When something hurts, we complain loudly and run to the doctor. We talk incessantly to one another, rarely listen, and thus effectively block other natural means of communication. Our senses are dulled by lack of use. Although man has consciousness of his own death, which animals do not, he rarely behaves with the moment-to-moment alertness that knowledge demands.

The intellect loves to dominate. Its domination clouds the expression of our natural abilities. If you learn to turn the intellect off, these abilities reassert themselves, one by one. When you follow your true instinct, for example, your actions usually succeed. Each of us has experienced the sharpening of our senses, when we sit very quietly and focus our attention. Sounds we usually never notice emerge, filling the space: birds, crickets, wind, water. Subtle scents suddenly become noticeable, like moss, rich soil, the hair of a friend. We can feel thoughts and emotions from other people as clearly as if they were visible objects. Little by little, many people are now reawakening to both their innate ability to heal themselves and to experience ways of communicating other than talking.

It is the same with movement. When you think about doing a movement, your mind is not still, and the body does not do the movement correctly. But if both the mind, and any area of the body not involved in the movement, are still, while remaining alert and awake, the movement can take place while "you" stay in the center of silence. This is the difference between *thinking* alert and *being* alert.

Being alert, and moving without thinking, are two important animal characteristics. We can study these traits, if we wish to clearly understand the "animal in us," and integrate that naturalness of movement into our own motions. Every animal has its own essence. Similarities to certain animals often appear in the way people behave: "That big ape!" a woman might say about a large, clumsy man. Or "She wriggled up to me, just like a snake!" All the animal characteristics exist in man. Man can run, jump, leap, and make sounds, just as animals do. Apparently, the only thing man can't do is fly.

When we study animals, many of our attitudes and blocks, such as fear, insecurity, or games, are revealed. You can't fool an animal. The animal senses your fear immediately and reacts by taking a stance and preparing to attack. A mother bear freezes dead still when she first spots you. If you meet her gaze without panic, she will take her cub and withdraw silently into the woods. You can approach any animal, if you control your thoughts to the degree of purity, where you see the sameness between yourself and the animal. Love the animal and you will find that place of oneness between you. When you find that place of oneness, you learn the essence of the animal. It becomes your teacher in that moment. You learn its movement and its vibration, and you see its characteristics in yourself.

In order to experience the animal characteristics and to sharpen up our awareness, we do many exercises in our workshop at Le Centre du Silence Mime School. One is called "The Cat." In doing it, catness can pervade your being. Another, "The Phoenix," condenses the lifespan of this remarkable bird into a few minutes. When the moment of its death approaches, the phoenix gathers palm fronds, arranges them around itself, and burns up in them. Out of the ashes arises a little phoenix. In this exercise, you become a bird, you fly! You transcend the barrier of gravity between animal and man, and you experience a many-faceted legend on the physical level.

Other exercises develop individual senses like smell, sound, and touch. Can you recognize your friend with your eyes closed, using only your nose? Does every centimeter of your skin touch with the same sensitivity your fingers have? Alertness, flexibility, balance, and grace are just a few of the results of all these exercises. The exercises develop strength throughout the body, and awaken every muscle and blood vessel. They provide a practice for staying in the center of silence, while executing very precise movements.

In yet another exercise, each student chooses an animal he or she is sympathetic with, such as a cat, a bird, an elephant, a raccoon, etc. The characteristics of that animal are transposed into the body. The student temporarily "becomes" that animal, following its behavior in its own setting. If you choose to be a bird, you hunt for worms, build a nest, sing to protect your territory, and fly. We don't imitate the animal, but we find the sympathetic place between animals and men, and explore it.

The body is the medium through which we learn what the animal has to teach us. The exercises lead the student to find inner resources, that reveal to him his own inherent abilities of expression. When you allow yourself to "become" an animal, your body acts on a gut level which your intellect would otherwise never allow "you" to "stoop" to. Your natural behavior on this level reveals a whole new unexplored world, which is your own most natural means of expression. It is a delightful and totally absorbing exploration of self.

Following this development of the actual animal work, the student discovers how to use this understanding of animal nature. The animal movement informs the human movement. We learn to transpose animal characteristics into human characteristics. Performing a slothful person, and performing a sloth in a jungle, are two very different things. Performing inadequacy and being inadequate are not the same thing either. You have to be articulate enough to show inadequacy with adequacy, or slothfulness with keenness.

With this skill, the student is able to deepen the meaning of each movement he makes, because he brings it out of a primordial place within himself. He is in touch with the total being of everything, and he can perform the totality of being.

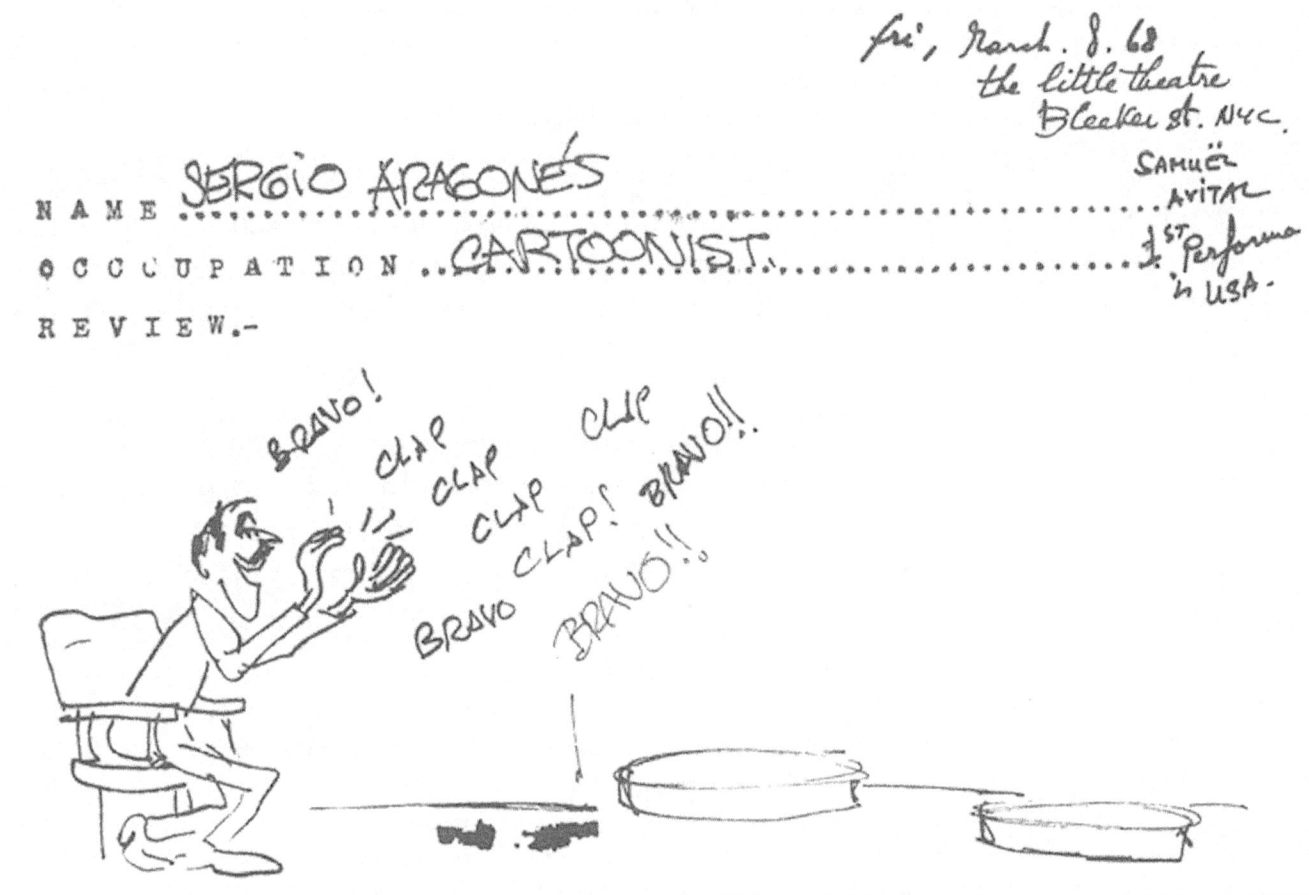

Samuel's First New York Performance in The Little Theater

Through the Eyes of Sergio Aragones

On Being an Artist

WHAT IS AN artist? What does one need, in order to be an artist? The person must have something inside them that needs to come out and be expressed. But how does one do that? First, the artist must have tools to work with. We must be concerned with practicalities. It is necessary to master the tools, before beginning to create.

What kind of person is the artist? The artist is someone who observes the world around them, and explores their feelings about the situations they encounter. When the artist applies their tools to express what they experienced, they transform it into something unique. In order to do this, the artist must work from the heart.

Each one of us is an artist, if we think of ourselves in that way. The way of the artist can be how we apply ourselves to whatever we do, whether it be carpentry or cooking. In some African societies, it is taken for granted that each person is an artist. This is different from western society, where the artist is considered as someone who is somehow uniquely removed from everyday life. Therefore, the modern artist enjoys both the privileges and pain of being thought of as special, elite.

Let's consider for a moment what art is. When I speak of art, I don't mean something buried in museums, or heard only in symphony halls. It is the art that has to reach all. Since everyone is a potential artist, everyone has to give their own effort for the betterment of this perplexed time we live in. That is an important point, because that is the ultimate purpose of being an artist.

Nature is an art in itself. Nature and the elements cook and shake and chew up the trees and the minerals and turn them into such things as nuggets of gold. That's a natural process, but it happens over a very long, long period of time. Now the alchemist, or the artist, can assist nature, using his mental attitude and conscious focus. You can make gold from lead right in your own laboratory. That's possible. The same work that nature does in a few thousand years, you can do within a few months in your own lab. And there is an analogy to yourself here, too – realizing that you can constantly transform into the brilliancy of illumination and golden attitude of being.

Museums are the cemeteries of culture, my friends. And the community in which there is no artist is dead. Where there is a community which is responsive and alive, you will find the artist there. If that state of being ceases to be, the artist must move on to a new community.

The artist counteracts negative forces in a society, by being truthful. Can you say that you love the truth, and are not afraid of it? It is not easy, is it? We are all afraid of the truth. The artist simply magnifies the truth, in order to wake up the community, whenever it is necessary.

Imagine yourself as a little-big boat on a huge ocean. There you are in your little-big boat, and all you know is the water all around you. All you are concerned with is your boat, and being careful not to fall into the water. But, one day you are able to go up in a helicopter, and you look down and see this little boat in the middle of the ocean. Suddenly, you see it very differently.

Seeing from the boat point of view is reasonable and rational, but seeing from the helicopter, you see the whole picture. From the helicopter, you know the uselessness of being in the boat. But how joyful will you be, if you only look at yourself from that higher vantage point? How different does the world look from a view that is greater than your little boat. Do you look at yourself only with the normal reasonableness and rationality, from only one side of yourself? That is the boat. Doing that, you limit yourself.

After all this, when you return to the boat again, you will never be the same, because of what you have seen. You have gained a new perspective on yourself and your place in this universe.

This is what the living artist must do at all times. He must be in his little-big boat (his own life), but he must also must be able to take the larger view of things from the helicopter. This way, he can be aware of the entire ocean. So, the artist lives differently. He sees from the helicopter *and* from the boat.

To explore this, here is an exercise you can try. It is so simple, yet because of that, very few people will do it. This is why simplicity is one of the great secrets. The exercise is, sometime go lie on the grass, and just look at the sky. Just look, and see. That's all there is to it. This is so simple, yet if you try it, you may make some discoveries. But just see, without thinking.

Now, the artist uses his tools to express that inner self for the benefit of all humanity, not just for himself. At the same time, the artist must be on guard against being taken advantage of commercially. If you think that the end-purpose to being an artist is to make money, then you are stupid. Sure, there are practical considerations. You have to eat. But you must find a creative solution to that problem. That is why, for example, there are painters now banding together to exhibit their own works, so they can avoid dealing with the profit-makers and those who pander to commercialism. This is a creative and practical solution.

When the arts become politicized, it's the end of art and of creativity. In Russia, for instance, there are writers who are paid – a good life, pretty girls, cars – to write what the government tells them to write. In ancient times, the kings sometimes didn't like real prophets. They liked false prophets, because false prophets tell you what you want to hear – and they don't tell you what you don't want to hear.

Of course, you want your work to be seen and brought to life, but concern yourself with your art. It's not a job. There's a difference between a job and work. That's why there are so many jobless people. Because it's not work, it's a job. You only do it to eat. But when you are an artist who works, you "eat" the work. The work feeds you in a certain way.

If you want to sell your craft, that's selfish. But if you want to make sense, people will come to you. This doesn't mean that we shouldn't help the artist. To help the artist means go to her activities, see and share her views. Learn what she is doing and enhance that. Make opportunities for art to be made and consistently supported in the community. Create the ability in that community to make art live.

Do you believe that you have a soul? Or does your soul have you? You are a soul that happens to have a body! God created you. Therefore, when you create, it is the God in you that is responsible. As an artist, you must be able to observe, and give form to what you observe, in order to share your vision with others.

What is the path to becoming an artist? One must know how to be a student. One must work as an apprentice. But there is no such thing as an apprentice in America today. Mediocrity is accepted as the norm. Most people want quick results. To be an artist, one must learn to invest oneself in the work at hand, and not to expect instant results.[*]

There is an old proverb that says: "The day is short, and the work is great. The rewards are many, and the workers are lazy, and, the Master is urgent." To be urgent doesn't mean to hurry up and get things done. It means to do things thoroughly, and with intention, in a consciously urgent way.

There are three kinds of students: Those who jump at the touch of the whip, those who jump at the sound of the whip, and those who jump at the mere sight of it. I know there is potential in the student when I can call him or her "stupid," and it is not regarded as an insult. If the student is emotionally attached to the word "stupid," then that student is attached to ego, and blocks their own learning.

In becoming an artist, you have to master the craft. If it is your body, your spine must be kept flexible. You have to do things consciously. You have to know how to walk consciously. You have to teach the body to become an instrument, to listen to you wherever and whenever.

---

[*] See the Article, the 3 Pillars of Becoming an Artist at www.bodyspeak.com

Whether the instrument is the body, the piano, or anything else, you have to learn the craft, so well that you know it in the dark. After that, the next phase is being an apprentice. As an apprentice, you learn the craft, but you learn it in a direct way. In America today, it's very difficult to get an apprenticeship – unless you want to be a plumber. We're going through very heavy changes. The old ways are disappearing.

The body is the instrument of the mime, the dancer, the clown. This is the instrument we have. Everyone knows how to walk, but how many people walk consciously? Everyone has feelings, yet how many feel truly? It's very important, while we are being trained, to be consciously artistic about what we do. To make a meal is an art. To sit is an art. And it's beautiful. And as a true student, actually you must be a walking question mark.

There is a cloud in our consciousness. We have to acknowledge that, to shatter it, to banish it. It's not going to be done by itself. That's why the artist is important. The artist is already a creation of God. We're already perfect. We're already created. What we do is an art. We must become receptive to The Unknown, The Unseen. The artist must do an inner search for his essential source. We duplicate that precious gift of life which God has given us to bring out. That spiritual code program is already in our DNA, and the artist just brings it out. In the case of mime, this is through essential movements, which allow the human body to express the ungraspable reality.

The thing is, you have to allow creativity to come in. But in society, as soon as that creativity manifests, you are shunned or sent to the mental hospital. So, your creativity is being killed since the day you are born. Do you understand this? The moment you say, "Mommy, I hear voices. I have seen the invisible" – the response is, "We had better take him to the mental hospital."

To be an artist, one who has vision, is to be consciously mad and to get paid for it. And those who are locked in mental hospitals are potential creators. And the society that locks them up, locks up its own truth and its own humanity and its own love. It's a greedy society. I have worked with the mentally ill, and I have proven with my art that they are potential creators.

To be consciously mad is to know the reality of what's going on today in the world. Even in the spiritual quest these days, everyone is jumping from group to group to find out where they fit in. By jumping from stream to stream, you scatter your energy. It's not focused. If you want to be a painter, be a painter. Learn how to design. Take your time.

Charlie Chaplin took a few years to make a single film. Are you popularity-oriented? Do you want immediate results and instant illumination? Or are you interested in the end result, in the finished product? Everything is changing, and it's so beautiful. Yet we grumble. We think only of how the changes affect us, and our product, and we skip the moment. That's a crime.

In Hebrew, the word for sin means missing the target, missing the point. We miss the point in many ways. We want to do something, but we don't do it. Intuition says to do this, and we don't listen, and we miss the point, and we're somewhere in the pit. When your heart tells you something, then stick with it! Stick with it, without becoming limited.

What's your focus? To become a Picasso? Well, you can take five incarnations to do that. Or you can do it, if you invest yourself properly, and you're surrounded by people who can teach you, and you talk with artists, and read, and learn, and keep yourself open. You can be anything you want. You are already everything you want.

The artist needs time to focus, and when the artist is focused, don't interrupt him. When you are working within yourself, you don't want to be bothered at that moment.

We don't know what is the process of creating. We create in silence. So, if you visit the studio with the painter who is painting, you have to be consciously invisible. It's not a time for socializing. At that moment, the artist is in the womb. In the womb, things work on the inside. If you choose to be with me, then you will see the artist working constantly, focusing. You are "nothing" there, during that time. Later we can sit and drink tea.

You can learn from an artist, and you can learn from anything. You can learn from everything! And if you find a teacher, well, then you're lucky.

Black and White, From the first American Mime Festival in La Crosse Wisconsin July 1974

Photograph by Bill Ray, From January 1975 Smithsonian Magazine

Spiritualizing the Art of Mime

WE KNOW FROM experience that the root of every art is spirit, just as the root of all creation is spiritual. Art today emphasizes the material, egoistic aspects of the being. So, it can lead to ephemeral success, but it doesn't last, because it's not rooted in the heart. When a person is illuminated in understanding of the universe, they begin to practice an art. For instance, when a Zen master sits in meditation, then paints a beautiful circle, he doesn't do it to exhibit it in a museum. No, he does it as an exercise in balance, to express that perfection within himself. That is a natural thing.

Therefore, if you have a tendency to be an artist, there already exists within you a declaration and a hope, to balance your own character and that of the culture in which you live. The state of balance is when there is no denial of matter and spirit. In other words, matter is important, because the body expresses the spirit within. And it is the spirit which motivates the matter to move.

Now, the word spiritual has been prostituted during the generations of man, and the concept has been applied by different religions in a very decadent way. It was not understood properly, because a religious man may or may not be spiritual, and a spiritual person may or may not be religious.

As an artist, if my goal is to reach the infinite, I have to deal with the finite. I have to use that finite in me to realize the in-finite in me, and that's why I'm an artist. That's why the tendency toward becoming an artist, springs from soul-consciousness. It springs forth when that which is hidden in us, wants to express outside ourselves. It happens when we are ready to express that part of ourselves in an organized and meaningful way. The outer expression is motivated from that high point within.

The art of mime, as every other art today, concentrates on the technique and form of the art. This might be okay, except that in doing so, the student may become hypnotized by the matter rather than what it expresses. They may become concerned only with the creation, rather than the Creator. But in fact, he or she, rightfully should be equally concerned with both.

If one gets caught up in the momentum of the training and it causes them to be hypnotized by the technology of the art, that person loses the essence of the art, and finds themselves to be just a performer. Then they are just someone who has good technique, and who works and makes a living.

But the artist is the one who addresses themselves to, and guides themselves toward, the balance of their two aspects. This is using the body as the instrument with which to express that which is within.

We use the visible to express the invisible. And simultaneously, when we begin to use the art properly, we have to address ourselves to this duality which we live in: yes and no, spirit and matter, and so on. There is nothing bad about the technology of learning an art. We have to teach the body to perform consciously. Then it can express, in a rational way, that which is irrational. It might seem like a paradox, but that's what the artist is concerned with. The artist is a being who is a synthesizer of right and left, of matter and spirit, of technique and expression, and so on. Unification of the spirit and matter, as an art form, calls to the person who is concerned with this work, to open themselves to greater dimensions of living and being. It requires a certain alertness to this duality of the work, in order to fully express the self. And that has to come from a soul-consciousness.

The soul is the same in each of us. The artist is concerned with awakening that inner aspect, that is beyond the personality, and bringing it to express itself. There is a saying that illustrates the state of the artist: "I was a hidden treasure and I longed to be known, so I created the world that I might be known." There is the force in us that we call soul. It is that unifying power, which I call the motivating force of the artist. It is there to guide us, and the potential to express that which is hidden is very rich.

This is not an easy task for the artist, however. In fact, a very courageous attitude is demanded, actually self-demanded, of the artist. You can learn technique, but you see where technology is today. It is technology without soul. The artist is also a restorer, who seeks to restore that which has been damaged by the generations of man. So, the goal is not that easy, but it is lofty. It's not burdensome, because if you discipline your body and you learn the keys and techniques of how to express it, you bring it to a very high level. It becomes an instrument, so that the soul force can really explode out from it, from the inner flame.

As an artist, you must look for balance, and work on it every second, and every minute. If the artist develops this attitude, then the spirit in the artist, the energetic aspect of activating the body, is able to express itself. Bring the flame of the spirit to perform this art of mime. Come with the consciousness that you are expressing the spirit and the soul, that inner power from within yourself. Then you can communicate something and fulfill the role of the artist. Then you can even the balance between yes and no.

The kabbalah says that the tree of life has three pillars. In the human system, there is the right side and the left side (male and female), and the middle pillar. This middle column is the place of transcendence beyond the right and left, between opposites, between yes and no. That's the place I call the center of silence. It is the place in which the artist should function. So, when I say Le Centre Du Silence, I don't mean Le Centre du Silence Mime School in Colorado. I gave it that name for a purpose, to express the essence of that idea.

Every true artist brings something to the whole community of the art. Every artist has to redefine his or her universe consciously. Everyone should do this, but especially the artist. By being here all the time, the artist is able to project far off from this moment, while he or she is *in* this moment.

When the mime performs, he or she mirrors that which is within, using different techniques. The mime learns to be aware of the performer, and what is being projected, how the performance is seen, and what is seen. The mime learns how he writes on stage with his body on the canvas of that space. The human body is a brush, and the space in which we perform is the canvas, and what we perform is the spectrum of color, senses, sentiments, and feelings. The intensity of the color is what makes the artist last, rather than being just another passerby, who leaves no lasting impression.

We have to be both here and there at the same time. It's a paradox, but of course, we have to reconcile the fact that the paradox is something that doesn't exist. What we really want to do is to actualize the idea. The artist learns to train the body, in order to listen to the dictations of the soul, and to bring that out in performance. When you develop that balance and the ability to project it, you feel fulfilled.

There is time to give to the technology of the art, to learning the mechanics of it. And both alternately, and simultaneously, there is time to give to what is added from your soul. And that's what every artist – and actually every being – is contributing to the whole.

The art of mime in particular, demands a certain attitude, for the art of mime unifies all the arts. I call it the mother of all arts. In music, there is you and the instrument – the piano, the flute, or the violin. You are activating an instrument outside of you. In most arts, there is a separate instrument of the art – this is true for the painter, the actor, and so forth. And even if you master that instrument, you may become a fantastic violinist, but without soul. But in mime, you yourself are the instrument.

Dance today has reached a very high peak of technology, especially in America. Yet it is lacking the ancient tunes of the necessity of dancing. Today, dances and concerts are just for entertainment, with no other purpose or motive than self-gratification. It doesn't have the necessity it had in ancient times. Art was a necessity. When people made ceramic plates, for example, they did it to eat from them, not to put them in museums.

Now, when we come to the art of mime, it has what we call the triangle of theater: mime, acting, and dance. In other words, that's the Westernization of the word Ka-Bu-Ki. One uses the body. One uses the voice. And one, the unifier of both of them, which is the mime, doesn't use the words of the actor, but does use the body of the dancer *and* something else. That something else is the invisible, what is called the unknown. Because when you shut off the words, you let the body express. And when you let the body express, not by dancing a situation, but by being the situation, you come to what they call in Japanese culture, the Haiku. The Haiku poem, though it has few words, has everything in it.

The mime shuts off the mouth, the gate of speech, which intensifies the expression of the physical body, allowing that innate force to come out. In mime, we tend to condense communication. Condensing communication preserves and conserves energy, something which we are all concerned about these days.

Mime puts you in a situation in which you have to create yourself, you have to interpret your creation, and you have to perform it yourself. In other words, you are the painter, the painting, and the canvas, all at once.

It is demanding, to the degree that you have to be the Shakespeare, the great play-write of yourself. Not all mimes are Shakespeares of themselves. And not all dancers are Nijinskys or Nureyevs or Baryshnakovs. The more you demand from yourself through technical discipline, the better you are able to find the unlimited. You let that invisible soul soar and express and project in a harmonious way. That expression happens in a condensed way, without the brouhaha and hoorah-rah of the theatre-for-the-rich. You strip from the stage all the décor, music, the noise of the world, and you are by yourself, relying on yourself. You are the only source, and you are the expression of that source, right on stage.

Not all these ideals are actually being practiced today. The art of mime is in a very peculiar situation today, and these ideals could help bring this art to a turning point. I think it is the art of the future. We need to condense the blah blah blah talking of communication, and stop abusing energy and giving attention to that which is not important at this moment. Instead of the dragging, dragging, of a drunken turtle, we need alert eagles to fly and apply those ideals. Then we can succeed in the next 10 or 20 years in bringing this space-age art, finally, into its own rightful place of existence.

In the future, I see people communicating more as mimes do. Even today in some mime shows, you can see the magic of an almost telepathic communication on stage between mimes. We have neglected our fantastic ability of telepathy. The telephone would not have been invented if this telepathy didn't exist. The telephone is a manifestation of telepathy. Telepathy exists in each of us, and you can see that actually intensified between true lovers. Really, true lovers don't talk that much.

We learn certain techniques, certain tools, certain keys of how to use the body. This is in order to teach the body. The body is just a community of cells. We must train it to do what we dictate to it, and we must not take for granted that we know how to walk and talk. The art of mime is the silent outcry – to stop being hypnotized by unnecessities and illusions.

There are techniques of illusion in mime, in which you can express, in a very magical way, that which is not there. But when you take this technique and just perform it on stage without any artistic statement, that's not important, it's nothing. That statement could last one year and then die off. We are trying to project a long-run goal for the art itself. And that's how I see the marriage, finally, between matter and spirit, and not the fight between matter and spirit, between the body and the director of the body.

The instrument of the mime is the body, the spirit is the player, if you will. Or in another way of looking at it, the visible player is the body, but it is conscious of its spiritual guidance. The uniqueness is that you are the instrument, and you are the echo of that instrument. This is what it means to be the Shakespeare of yourself: to do it yourself, to create it yourself, to perform it yourself, and to be the resource and the source of everything.

Remember that matter is condensed spirit. It's a visible spirit, if you will. But if you function only from the matter, which is the body, it makes you a clone, an automaton. The art of mime tries to dehypnotize. By restoring yourself, you become able to restore others. You can finally get to the level of the artist as a transformer, a synthesizer. And that could affect the audience at a very high level. Do you ever go to see some dance or theater, or mime, and you go out unaffected? Why didn't you get into it? Because there was nothing there. The one who can put something into the performance is the artist. Artist and audience is one. It's the same spirit that moves them. But the activator of this motivating energy is the artist, who is projecting that which is in a dormant state in everyone in the audience.

Another important reason why we may be unaffected by a performance is that, when we go to the theater today, we don't go out of necessity. We go to entertain ourselves, so art becomes merely entertainment. But, if as a being who lives in the 20th century, I feel very entertained by the state of affairs of man, I could project that observation through the art of mime. The true artist of mime is a provocateur.

Another important aspect of mime is that it doesn't rob you of your imagination, like other arts. It leaves your imagination to its own fantastic spheres. It allows your own telepathic inner vision (that's like your own television: TIV). And so, if a painter paints his painting and gives it to you to see it, and you dare to ask him or her, "What is that?" The artist says, "It's there. *See*. Learn to *see*." Now, a dancer dances the situation they see, an actor acts out the comedy or the tragedy of the times, and the painter's painting reflects the reality of that time. But the mime **becomes it.**

The mime artist has to be evident, suggestive, and project a conscious innocence. The artist of mime is trying to reawaken, to kindle the flame of conscious innocence, functioning as a restorer in society. If you are an artist of mime, or an artist of music, or any kind of artist, you can apply these same ideals, to make that art better.

You are clear, you are balanced, and you can live calmly and in total peace in the midst of madness. After all, you know, the mime is a conscious fool. To be a conscious fool is not just to wear colored clothes in the streets and white makeup on your face. To be a conscious fool, there must be some investment. This is the kind of investment that we as artists have to make. To be totally, consciously, a fool, you have to achieve a high degree of wisdom. That's another paradox.

In the last years, mime has grown considerably, unbelievably, through the contribution of some mimes in the community. I think it is a statement of the times. If you study the history of theater, you will find that this art has flourished since the ancient times. It was in initiation rites in the Egyptian pyramids, among primitive peoples, in the Renaissance, in Greek times, and so on. This art flourished, whenever the times evolved into a dangerous period of decadence. Whenever there is a crisis in human affairs, these mimes appear with their white faces in town squares, as though to give a message to humanity.

At one time, Napoleon forbade speaking in the theaters of Paris, so everyone tried a little mime – pantomime. He was afraid that a revolution might be incited in the theater, and so he said "Stop! Don't talk!" They became mimes and their silent outcry, I think, somehow changed humanity. These mime beings, here and there, give some message to the world, by their way of living. However, it is most important that the mime artist knows consciously what he or she is doing, and is not just standing there, pulling invisible ropes, and walking in place, and things like that. A little more conscious effort would do good for the art of mime and for all the arts.

How is mime, which has the least technology of any art form, going to get across its message in the modern world? To answer this, we have to take a look at different ways of thinking.

Now, it is known that there is no such thing as a straight line in the universe, right? All art is circular. The art of mime has the ability, the uniqueness, to embrace both hemispheres of the brain, the linear, and the non-linear. I call it a spiral way of thinking. Technology itself is going toward the spiral way of thinking, and there are a few art forms which are going that way as well. People will get used to it, and in the future, it will be a usual thing, like walking is today. It will be easy.

But now, we are still slaves to only one linear way of thinking. Since the art of mime deals with the body, I move my right arm, I move my left arm. I move clockwise, I move counterclockwise, and so on. In doing this, I build my world, my universe. I create the illusion of that and make it visible for the audience. But in doing that, I have to use both the right and the left. I can't just turn right all the time. I have to turn left too. So, this spiral way of thinking is made visible in the art. The spiral way of thinking is what the art of mime is aiming for. The mime has to transcend both right and left, and find a way to govern the body, in balance and harmony.

The art of mime is both scientific and mystic in one. The mime has to use the scientific left-side of the brain to analyze and put things right. And they have to use the intuitive right side, to make the soul explode out from their movement. So, if you want, the artist of mime is a living computer, that computes both right and left, and brings a synthesis on the spot, without waiting 5,000 years for the revolution. That's why I think it's a futuristic art.

The mime is a being of paradox, who has reconciled themselves with the universe, and with themselves, and that's what the future is about. That is the balance that we are looking for.

Know Yourself

לְעוֹלָם מְדַבְּרִים בְּךָ שְׁנֵי קוֹלוֹת.
הַשֶּׁקֶט יוֹתֵר הוּא בְּדֶרֶךְ כְּלָל הַקּוֹל הֶחָפֵץ בְּתַכְלִית.
ליקוטי מוהר"ן כב. ז.

**"The world speaks within you with two voices.
The silence is generally the most essential, desired and most important."**
Likutei Moharan 22.7

The Harmonious Cell

"Be whole in the detail, and a detail in the whole."
—Samuel Avital

THE HUMAN BODY is a community of cells. It is a macrocosm made up of millions of little bits matter. Each little part has its own unique work to do. Each cell has its own consciousness. Ears, liver, uterus, blood, vertebrae, muscle, tongue, tooth, heart – every little part is vital to the totality.

In the same way, the cosmos is a community of cells, made up of many elements. Each person is a little dot in relation to the universe. Each dot has its unique place in the whole. A group of people is also a collection of cells. Every person has a ray, a color, a spark of light that he brings with him. And there is always a thought or common theme that brings any group or totality together.

Whether it is a single being, or many together, it must be harmonious. A unifying thought has to be there, or else it is not one being. When a being or group is harmonious, it has a certain balance that is clearly visible. In order for the balance to manifest, each cell must know its place and its work. Each little part must know how it is vital to the totality. If the being is fully awake and lucid, each cell will move and act very consciously.

We have to perceive totality before we can express it. The "Elephant in the Dark Mentality" occurs when a person sees only their own perception of the totality. Six blind men each got hold of a different part of one elephant, explored it thoroughly by touch, and then got together to discuss their six perceptions of "elephant." One described the trunk, another the ear, another the tail, and the other three described the leg, back, and tusk. Each was sure he knew what an elephant was, and each thought the other five were stupid. See how this works?

An ensemble must serve an idea of harmony. Each person must know his place within the ensemble. Everyone occupies territory. Do you always choose the place you sit, and then accept your position because you chose to sit there?

When there is harmony in a person or in a group, there is a transformation of thought into form. A "physical mandala" is an example of such a transformation. Three or four people move together and then freeze in a harmonious form, as if they were a mandala. Then, at the exact same moment, they all start moving very slowly, changing the structure. Suddenly the motion simply stops – and miraculously, a new mandala is revealed. Unless each member of the group sees the whole picture, the mandala will not happen.

Every group contains leaders and followers. Is the shepherd for the flock, or is the flock for the shepherd? The leader takes a certain initiative. An engine, for example, is the leader of the train. If the freight cars rebelled, trying to go in different directions, the freight would never be delivered.

If you start with one dot and add others to it, you have a line. It is the same in movement and this can be explored through physical exercises. The first dot, the initiating part, is the leader. All the rest of the body parts are pulled along behind it, like train cars following the engine. For example, if the nose is the leader, it goes as far as it can on its own, and then the head is pulled along after it. Next the neck follows, then the chest, waist, and pelvis.

Walking is perfectly blended. Neither foot is the leader. The leader was where the follower is, and the follower will be where the leader is. It is simple. Accept that that which leads, leads and that which follows, follows. This will lead to a continuation of no leader, no follower. Any part of the body can be a leader. Any person in a group can be a leader. Just be careful not to allow the leader to become a dictator, while the followers become sheep.

Necessity is the leader of walking. An itch is the leader of scratching. Are you leading the movement, or is the movement leading you? A true leader is not seen. It does not make itself known, instead it remains hidden. As the root is hidden, the tree grows. Just as the blood stays in the body and is never seen, so the leader should always remain hidden. An audience doesn't want to see where the impulse to move in a performing group originates. And yet, in order to be hidden, you have to be very visible. It is because we stay tuned to that hidden leader that we succeed.

Mime is the only art form in which you can make the picture come out of the frame or the sculpture breathe. The picture moves! The idea, the unifying thought, must project through the movements. Every movement done by every person, and every cell, is seen by the audience.

A movement is a transition. In everyday life, transitions happen too fast for us to see what takes place. And so, these transitions, such as taking the cap off the toothpaste, or going through a door, are things most people don't give attention to. In mime, movements are done slowly, one at a time, so they can be seen.

Every movement must be done consciously, in order for the idea to manifest. Every member of the group must know what part of his body, or which person, is the leader at any given moment. Each must give up some of his individuality to find the group balance. I can be her leg and she can be my arm! By moving consciously and by perceiving the totality, the invisible can be made visible.

If the ensemble is truly serving the idea in harmony, it should be as though one person were performing. Nothing happens until the right people, with right skills, come together at the right time, in the right place. Until all these things come together, we spend our time perfecting our skills and learning to listen. Then, when the right time comes, we'll be able to hear. We'll each be able to bring our own unique spark of light to full fruition, by unifying the macrocosm/microcosm, that is our being, with the expression of totality.

> **"Whether you think you can, or you think you can't... you're right."**

The Poetry of Activity

THE FOLLOWING VERSES may sound poetic, but in fact, they are also actual instructions to the Mime student. They contain specific experiential techniques and improvisations, which can be explored by the budding artist.

The summary expresses the urgent demands required for the one who is interested in becoming a genuine artist, who wishes to penetrate through to new frontiers of Being. It is for the person ready to abide by the ubiquitous law of the artist, "Thou Shalt Not Worship Mediocrity."

1. HOLY WORKSPACE

Jump Into your
Symphony of being;
You are the center of silence
You are the dot in space,
The drop in the sea,
Become
The essence of yourself

2. STILL AS A MOUNTAIN

The moving thoughts are
Slower than that
The body cannot lie;
The truth of the mountain is the ability
To space the time and
Time the space
As you know, all this might just be blah blah blah

3. THE ONE WHO

Suicide, but don't die;
Swim, but don't drown;
Burn, but not to ashes
Listen to your body,
The center of yourself
And, aha
Thank you for being here

4. FROM ECSTASY TO LUNCH

Alert like a cat, send a telegram to
Sharpen your sword
Brick by brick, word for word,
Build a mold
Measure your energy with a verbal fast,
One day of silence
Now – ecstasy – lunch – now

5. GENESIS OF THE SELF

With one great breath
Be a whole in the detail and a
Detail in the whole
Always come back to zero;
No leader follower, no philosophy,
But follow the path faithfully on your
Journey from thought to action

6. TO BE AND NOT TO BE

A pinpoint of light (POL)
Makes the body like a brush;
With yourself here, as tubes of vision,
tubes of communication.
You dance as a beggar in a circle inside itself
Then with the echo of a whisper, in
crystallized thought,
You be AND not be
And that, my friend, is the quest

7. SERVE THE IDEA

Penetrate inner space,
Be true to yourself,
Explore without fear,
Cut through the space/time continuum,
Don't rape the sound,
It is known, indeed,
You are unique

8. ORGANIZED PANIC

Think with your body,
Confront the situation;
Move gently into space,
Challenge yourself;
Try not to try,
And no acting, please
What is, is stand still and Be

9. LABORATORY OF THE SELF

We are after the essence
And the essence is after us
We jump in and swim into it,
We write the text of our history with the
human body.
Keen awareness, my friend, prevents accidents
So – not revolution,
But evolution, please

52 Weeks: From Thought to Action

Fifty-Two Weeks of Practice:
The Journey from Thought to Action — 145

First Thought, Last Thought — 159

The Day Map — 160

The Eye Compass — 163

אַל־תְּבַהֵל עַל־פִּיךָ וְלִבְּךָ אַל־יְמַהֵר לְהוֹצִיא דָבָר לִפְנֵי הָאֱלֹהִים
כִּי הָאֱלֹהִים בַּשָּׁמַיִם וְאַתָּה עַל־הָאָרֶץ עַל־כֵּן יִהְיוּ דְבָרֶיךָ מְעַטִּים:

Keep your mouth from being rash,
and let not your throat be quick to bring forth speech before God.
For God is in heaven and you are on earth;
Therefore, let your words be few.
Kohelet (Ecclesiastes) 5:1

שַׁמַּאי אוֹמֵר, עֲשֵׂה תוֹרָתְךָ קֶבַע.
אֱמֹר מְעַט וַעֲשֵׂה הַרְבֵּה,
וֶהֱוֵי מְקַבֵּל אֶת כָּל הָאָדָם בְּסֵבֶר פָּנִים יָפוֹת

Shammai used to say:
Make your study a fixed practice;
Speak little, but do much;
And receive all men with a pleasant countenance.
Pirkei Avot 1:15

Fifty-Two Weeks of Practice

The Journey from Thought to Action

"I swear to do the possible and only the possible."
—Samuel Avital, the Teacher of the Obvious, 1971

ENJOY THIS 52-WEEK journey from thought to action, in which you can explore many creative and practical principles. These practical suggestions were not written with the intention to put a spoon in your mouth, but rather to allow you to use your creative imagination to apply them. These practices can be explored during one year (52 weeks), according to your needs, and your time and environment.

Consider well the inner thoughts that come to your mind as you read these practices. Observe if anything seems to you as easy, simple, strange, superfluous, "a waste of my time," or "I already know it." Is there anything you find mysterious, controversial, or nonsense, "not logical", "out of your mind," "it's crazy," stupid, etc.?

Your immediate reactions such as those above are actually a good sign, and mean that you are on the right track. Therefore, when a door appears before you and written on it are the words "**UNKNOWN**," thus provoking the reactions above, you will know that it is ok to **DARE TO GO IN.**

The **THOUGHTS** suggested here will provoke wonder and even AWE. The series may appear alternately intense or very simple, and none of it should be taken for granted. Many of these suggestions are so obvious and even hilarious – don't let this cause you to overlook them. They are reminders that we often forget to examine everything that is happening to us in this "passing moment," while we exist on this planet. So simply enjoy your practice, without expecting any results, and you will be amazed what you discover.

> "Shakespeare said: **To be OR not to be**, that is the question."
> We say: "**TO BE AND NOT TO BE**." And that is the life puzzle."
> —Samuel Avital, Boulder, CO 1972.

Instructions: The Model for the 52 Weeks practice:

THOUGHT: This is the abstract. Actively cultivate this thought during the week in all your daily occupations.

SPEECH: When you speak, express the above thought in the different situations that occur during that week.

ACTION: Act on the abstract thought. Do it. Move it. Make it concrete and real, so that the triple learning is complete. The repetition of it every day during the week will seal it within you, and you will absorb its knowledge, naturally becoming it, without any effort.

> *"In the beginning was the word, BEFORE the word there was motion, vibration, movement, the source of all life."*
> —Samuel Avital

Week 1
THOUGHT: **SPEAK LESS AND DO MORE.**
SPEECH: Speak less.
ACTION: Do only what is necessary.

Week 2
THOUGHT: **SILENCE IS BETTER THAN GOLD.**
SPEECH: Choose one day a week to be silent.
ACTION: Let your action be silent.

Week 3
THOUGHT: **I AM SANE IN THE MIDST OF MADNESS.**
SPEECH: Let all your words be true.
ACTION: Do a few sane actions toward another this week. For example, write a letter to your friend telling them, "I am happy you exist."

Week 4
THOUGHT: **FUNCTION FROM RELAXATION.**
SPEECH: Use words that don't harm anyone.
ACTION: Observe and do all movements in a relaxed and calm way.

Week 5
THOUGHT: **OBSERVE WHAT PEOPLE DON'T SAY.**
SPEECH: Listen to nonverbal human expression.
ACTION: Count how many unnecessary words you use every day.

Week 6
THOUGHT: **HOW MANY "EYES" DO YOU THINK YOU HAVE?**
SPEECH: What can "eye" see?
ACTION: Practice the "eye compass" exercise. See chart following this article.

Week 7
THOUGHT: **RESPOND INSTEAD OF REACTING.**
SPEECH: Use words of response rather than reaction.
ACTION: Let all your actions be relaxed, ready to respond calmly, and not to react. Do this in every situation. We call this the **RESPONSE ABILITY.**

Week 8
THOUGHT: **HOW MANY EXCUSES DO YOU HAVE EVERY DAY THAT MAKE YOU FAR FROM YOURSELF?**
SPEECH: Do not say words such as: "**I can't**," "**I'm not able to**," "**It's impossible**," or any words that block you from being. (See the Excuses Article in this book)
ACTION: Write down all your supposed excuses from doing or manifesting what you love, so that you can **BE THE ONE YOU WERE MEANT TO BE.**

Week 9
THOUGHT: **"ARE YOU WRITING YOUR OWN LIFE SCRIPT?"**
SPEECH: Don't utter any word that is not True, Necessary and Kind.
ACTION: Observe your movements that are not harmonious with yourself. Consider the following ancient counsel:

The Three Gates of Speech – A practical suggestion

There is a proverb that every word should pass through three gates before being uttered. At the first gate, the gatekeeper asks "**Is it true?**" At the second, he asks, "**Is it necessary?**" At the third, he asks "**Is it kind?**" If your immediate response to all three questions is positive, you may speak without harming anyone.

Week 10
THOUGHT: **CONSCIOUS INNOCENCE: IMPOSSIBLE OR INEVITABLE?**
SPEECH: Speak only conscious words.
ACTION: Act and be totally conscious and totally innocent.

Week 11
THOUGHT: **DO YOU EAT TO LIVE OR LIVE TO EAT?**
SPEECH: Whatever you eat, eat consciously, and chew a lot.
ACTION: Don't walk and eat, sleep and eat, text and eat, e-mail and eat, etc. **JUST EAT.**

Week 12
THOUGHT: **CAN YOU EAT THE WHOLE ELEPHANT IN ONE BITE? CAN YOU DRINK THE WHOLE OCEAN IN ONE GULP?**
SPEECH: Dare **to Speak** the obvious.
ACTION: Dare **to Be** the obvious.

Week 13
THOUGHT: **THE CURSE OF MORE (ALSO KNOWN AS, THE "MORE SYNDROME") AND THE "BLESSING" (SANITY) OF ENOUGHNESS.**
SPEECH: **"Do not say 'I will study when I have time.' You may never have it."**
—*Pirke Avoth 2:5*
ACTION: Eat and stay hungry. Don't eat to your fullness. Apply this to everything. Done?

Week 14
THOUGHT: **DO EVERYTHING WTH POISE AND CALM.**
SPEECH: Speak from a state of calm.
ACTION: Align your posture to be straight and relaxed, aligned with your breath.

Week 15
THOUGHT: **"REST" IS ESSENTIAL FOR "REST"ORATION.**
SPEECH: Pause and breath between speaking: Allow moments of silent communication.
ACTION: Take Conscious, Creative Naps.

Week 16
THOUGHT: **THE SECRET OF LIFE IS: BE AWARE OF YOUR BREATHING.**
SPEECH: When asked a question, take a full breath in and out before you answer.
ACTION: Breathe like a baby, that is **"THE SECRET."**

Week 17
THOUGHT: **WHY RUSH TOWARD YOUR END? THE POINT IS THE JOURNEY, NOT THE DESTINATION.**
SPEECH: Pronounce your words. Enunciate and speak every word clearly (Cut the letters with your lips).
ACTION: Always focus your attention 100% to be with what you are doing now. No exceptions or excuses.
Read the Fish Story at GoKabbalahNow.com under Writings/Stories

Week 18
THOUGHT: **LET YOUR BODY SPEAK.**
SPEECH: Listen to how the movement speaks. Find the natural harmony between the movement and the breath.
ACTION: Pay attention to every part of your body. Take time to move and stretch every day. Don't miss it. (Consult **the BodySpeak Manual** for specific exercises.)

Week 19
THOUGHT: **DO YOU THINK YOU ARE AWAKE OR ASLEEP?**
SPEECH: Observe if you speak your dream or you speak your sleep.
ACTION: Write down your dreams in a book and don't look at them again. Practice the First Thought/Last Thought exercise, following this article, to reorganize your dreaming and sleeping.

Week 20
THOUGHT: **WHATEVER YOU WANT: <u>GIVE IT FIRST</u>.**
SPEECH: Give your friend 100% attention when they speak, instead of thinking of what you will say next. Listen carefully.
ACTION: Identify what the other is lacking and fulfill it, discreetly.

Week 21
THOUGHT: **COULD YOU DARE NOT TO NEED ANYONE ELSE'S APPROVAL? IS THIS POSSIBLE?**
SPEECH: Do not speak something unless you feel it **100,000%**.
ACTION: If you see everyone headed in one direction, go the opposite way. Do not encourage "**<u>the mass hypnosis consciousness of the followers.</u>**"

Week 22
THOUGHT: WHO IS GUIDING YOUR DIRECTION? DO YOU HAVE AN INNER COMPASS TO ORIENT YOURSELF?
SPEECH: Count every word you speak in a day. Seems impossible? TRY IT!
ACTION: Count every step you make during the day. Make a map of your day.
(See The Day Map Illustrated Exercise later in this section)

Patterns of Movement: Making a Map of Your Day*

Definition: Observe the patterns of movement you make from place-to-place, for one day. Notice how your day takes shape.

Exercise: Draw a map of your daily activities from the moment you wake up until you go to sleep. Write down every activity in detail. Draw every movement of the day right after you do it. (For example, if you go to the store, draw lines representing the road from your house to the store, through the store, and back home again, etc.)

Benefits: Keep awake, alert and ready, and stay open to the present moment. Become consciously aware of unnecessary movements, and observe how you could eliminate them and conserve energy.

* *Exercise is taken from the Bodyspeak Manual by Samuel Avital*

Week 23
THOUGHT: WHAT IS LOVE? AN ILLUSION, A DREAM, SUFFERING, A "CRUSH," OR JUST NONSENSE?
SPEECH: Observe whether your words and actions match. Also observe this in those around you.
ACTION: Write down everything you want the other to give you. Resolve to create it yourself instead. By doing this, actually, you are recognizing yourself.

Week 24
THOUGHT: DEPENDENCE AND INDEPENDENCE, SIMILAR OR DIFFERENT?
SPEECH: Write your own **personal declaration of independence**. Read it aloud every night before you sleep.
ACTION: Visualize what you want to create. Then DARE TO BE IT, and DO IT.

Week 25

THOUGHT: "NO PAIN, NO GAIN": DANGEROUS OR BENEFICIAL TO YOUR HEALTH? (Don't overlook this question)

SPEECH: Examine the "<u>common wisdom</u>" nonsense of this thought, and write down what you REALLY think.

ACTION: Don't overdo it. Don't invest excessive effort in anything. Avoid excessive and extreme exercise, etc. The password for this is: **"EVERYTHING IN MODERATION, NOTHING IN EXCESS."**

Week 26

THOUGHT: **IS THE "OTHER" A FRIEND OR AN ENEMY?**
Ask yourself, "AM I THE "OTHER" FOR THE "OTHER?""

SPEECH: Spend 80% of conversation listening to the other and asking about their interests. Spend only 20% talking about the topic or yourself (i.e. only when you are asked to do so).

ACTION: Observe the good in the other, and apply it in your own way. "**Don't judge your friend until you have been in his place.**" —*Pirke Avoth 2:5*

Week 27

THOUGHT: **HEAL YOURSELF BEFORE YOU ARE SICK. PREVENT PROBLEMS BEFORE THEY HAPPEN.**

SPEECH: Devote 95% of words to Learning and Inspiration and only 5% to myself and my small concerns.

ACTION: Use your power of awareness to prevent accidents. Think good thoughts. Eat healthy food. If you see a nail in the road, remove it, so that the "other" person will not get hurt, and so that their tire will not explode.

Week 28

THOUGHT: **DO YOU LIVE THIS MOMENT IN YOUR LIFE FULLY? 50%, OR 100%? OR DO YOU JUST SURVIVE?**

SPEECH: When you speak, speak with 100% of your being, passionately and calmly. If you have nothing to say, be silent, will you, please?

ACTION: When you walk, feel every texture and fiber of the carpet as you walk over it. Apply this level of awareness to everything.

> Now ponder on this nugget of practical wisdom. There is a French proverb that says:
> "SI CE QUE TU VAS DIRE N'EST PAS
> PLUS BEAU QUE LE SILENCE NE LE DIT PAS."
>
> "IF WHAT YOU ARE GOING TO SAY IS NOT
> MORE BEAUTIFUL THAN SILENCE, DO NOT SAY IT."

Week 29
THOUGHT: **WALKING ON A TIGHT-ROPE, DANGEROUS OR NATURAL? Could you walk on the knife edge?**
SPEECH: If what you are going to say is balanced, say it.
ACTION: Anything you do this moment, this week, this year, this life, DO IT as if for the first and last time. Comprende?

Week 30
THOUGHT: **"NOWNESS" IS VERY DANGEROUS. ARE YOU A CONSCIOUS PROCRASTINATOR? OR?....**
SPEECH: If you observe yourself postponing, remember, "**This moment will never come again.**" Once it passes, it is gone forever.
ACTION: "If I am not for myself, who will be for me? But if I am only for myself, what am I? And if not now, then when?" —*Hillel*.
In plain English, **anything that you need to do. Do it now.**

Week 31
THOUGHT: **EXPECT THE UNEXPECTED. BE THE UNEXPECTED.**
SPEECH: If someone insults you, say "Thank you." Don't sue them.
ACTION: Most people are afraid to make mistakes. Instead, make mistakes on purpose. Let the mistake show you how to correct it, and please **Consciously Make New Mistakes**... and you will be surprised what you discover, now that you know the "**Great Secret of Authentic Learning.**"

Week 32
THOUGHT: **DO YOU FOLLOW THE MAILMAN UNTIL HE DELIVERS YOUR MAIL? OR DO YOU TRUST THAT YOUR MAIL WILL BE DELIVERED?**
SPEECH: **DARE** to speak with certainty. **DARE** to envision good outcomes.
ACTION: Observe and release any unnecessary tension in your movements. It sounds easy, but a kinder effort on your part will do.

Week 33

THOUGHT: **COULD YOU MAINTAIN CALM WITHIN THE CHAOS, BALANCE AND STILLNESS WITHIN THE STORM, EQUANIMITY IN ALL LIFE'S EVENTS?**

SPEECH: In any circumstance, whether you categorize it to be good or bad, practice this Kabbalistic way of being. Say to yourself, "**This Too Shall Pass**," and also "**This Too is for the Good.**"

ACTION: Enjoy your happiness and enjoy your sadness with the same breath. It is a unique moment of being.

Week 34

THOUGHT: **SELF-SUFFICIENCY: IMPOSSIBLE OR ESSENTIAL?**

SPEECH: Choose consciously and use only the words you **need** to use.

ACTION: And please, **PRODUCE MORE AND CONSUME LESS.** This is so rare in this perplexed time of existence now!

Week 35

THOUGHT: **SHOULD LEARNING BE PAINFUL, OR PLAYFUL? DO YOU HAVE TO SUFFER TO LEARN, OR DO YOU LEARN WHEN YOU ENJOY IT?**

SPEECH: Laugh at your mistakes, always.

ACTION: **DARE TO BE SILLY.**

Week 36

THOUGHT: **EXPERIENCE LIFE WITH A CLEAN SLATE.**

SPEECH: Clean your slate every night before bed. Write down and consider all your actions for the day and forgive everyone who has wronged you. (See the First Thought Last Thought Exercise following this section)

ACTION: Wake in the morning with the awareness that you are a brand new person. Actually, Science has yet to discover this **Obvious Secret**. Or maybe they know, it and they do not want you to know it.

Week 37

THOUGHT: **UNITING THE OPPOSITES: UNHEARD OF? EASY? OR IMPOSSIBLE?**

SPEECH: Speak from a place we call the **Center of Silence.**

ACTION: **Rest** while in movement. **Be Inwardly Still, While Every Part of You Is In Motion.**

> **INHALE IMPORTANCE AND EXHALE INSIGNIFICANCE.**
> This is the way to embrace **the** "**paradox**".
> From the Bodyspeak Manual: "**Paradox**" is a deeply imposed conflict of intelligence that is directed only to one small aspect of being. In reality, this is a tool in the hands of people who manipulate others for their own benefit.
> —*BodySpeak Manual, Defintuitions*

Week 38
THOUGHT: **CAN I EAT 80 HOTDOGS IN 5 SECONDS?**
SPEECH: Count how many unnecessary words you use in a day.
ACTION: Use only what you **NEED**, **NOT** what you **WANT**.

Week 39
THOUGHT: **STOP AND CONSIDER**.
SPEECH: Consider what you are about to say, before you speak.
ACTION: "Take" time to stop and consider, in order to **Respond**, rather than **React** to all life events.

Week 40
THOUGHT: **ARE YOU THE CAPTAIN OF YOUR OWN SHIP? ARE YOU STEERING INTO STORMS OR INTO CLEAR CALM WATERS?**
SPEECH: **Speak words that Build the other.**
ACTION: Take one day in which you only think of harmonious outcomes, good for yourself and for all concerned.

Week 41
THOUGHT: **DO YOU "HAVE A LIFE"? OR ARE YOU LIFE ITSELF?**
SPEECH: Notice how often you use the words "**I Have**" and "**I Am.**" When you say "**I have time**," you are lying, because actually **Time** has you.
ACTION: Consider the difference between **HAVING** and **BEING**. What things in life <u>**do you think You Have**</u> and what things <u>**do you think You Are?**</u>

Week 42
THOUGHT: **LIFE IS 99% PREPARATION AND 1% INSPIRATION.**
SPEECH: Think before you speak. Roll your tongue seven times inside your mouth before uttering a "word."
ACTION: Show up fifteen minutes early **for all appointments this week**. Pack your lunch the night before.

> **Spy On Yourself.**
> All these 52 practices have a purpose, which is to spy on yourself. And when you observe yourself making a mistake, **CORRECT IT IMMEDIATELY**, until this becomes second nature for you. And now my friend, you are becoming a **SPIRITUAL SPY**, and a very conscious and effective ONE.

Week 43
THOUGHT: **BECOME A SECRET AGENT, A "007"**
SPEECH: Do an act of goodness and don't tell anyone.
ACTION: Give without being known to the recipient, and without expecting a reward or tax deduction.

Week 44
THOUGHT: **BE THE ACTOR AND DIRECTOR IN YOUR OWN LIFE.**
SPEECH: On a daily basis, create an accounting list of your thoughts, speech, and actions, to see if they are taking you to the direction and state of being that you **Really** want in life. Are they helping you be **The Being You Were Meant to Be?**
ACTION: Practice **75/25: 75%** of your attention is completely engaged with what you are doing. Use the other **25%** to observe yourself, in order to function from objectivity, and consciously direct your actions.
75% DOER, 25% OBSERVER.

Week 45
THOUGHT: **YOU WOULDN'T LET UNINVITED GUESTS IN YOUR HOUSE. WHY LET IN UNIVITED THOUGHTS?**
SPEECH: Write down every important thought you have over the course of a half hour.
ACTION: Learn to develop the thoughts that you **NEED** and to turn away the ones that you don't **NEED**.

Week 46
THOUGHT: **WHAT IS MORE IMPORTANT: QUALITY OR QUANTITY?**
SPEECH: **Speak as though every word is a treasure**.
ACTION: Move more slowly and appreciate the movement. Chew your food thoroughly and savor every taste. And please make sure you do this practice in every action this week.

Week 47

THOUGHT: WHAT WOULD HAPPEN IF YOU BELIEVED EVERYTHING YOU HEARD? WHAT WOULD HAPPEN IF THE CAR DROVE YOU? You would probably say to the Judge, "the car caused the accident."

SPEECH: Consider whether you have really verified, examined and experienced what you speak about, or whether you are just repeating what others have told you. Are you a parrot? Come on! Wake up?

ACTION: "Truth is what stands the test of experience" —*Einstein*
Always Verify Everything. The Kabbalistic Tradition emphasizes:
"<u>**HONOR THEM and SUSPECT THEM.**</u>" In English, you would say "<u>**Trust but verify.**</u>" Is that clear?

Week 48

THOUGHT: BE A MASTER OF "YOUR" TIME

SPEECH: Practice speaking concisely. Use less time to communicate the same idea. This is what I call "**WORD ECONOMY**". (See personal story below.)

ACTION: Observe and organize how you use your time. Create set times in your schedule for things that you want to do and achieve.

WORD ECONOMY

"My grandfather once told me that we are born with a certain number of words in our "**word bank**." If one uses too many words (just like if one overspends their money), it empties our word bank account. We become overdrawn, and become mute. When we use words only when necessary, we practice word economy.

"Words are only one of the ways to communicate. **99%** of our real communication occurs in silence, through body language.

"I highly recommend to practice one day of silence a week, to achieve the ability to <u>**speak less and do more**</u>, and <u>**produce more and consume less**</u> – practicing consistently the practical wisdom of the "**Word Economy**."

This is what is called in Kabbalah the TIKKUN = RESTORATION.

Week 49

THOUGHT: LIFE IS TELLING YOU WHAT YOU NEED TO LEARN. ARE YOU LISTENING?

SPEECH: Ask yourself in all life circumstances, "What am I learning in this situation now?"

ACTION: Catch yourself in the act, surprise yourself. See how many mistakes you can catch yourself making in a day. Then, **correct them immediately.** When you master this, you are now ready to **MAKE YOUR OWN NEW MISTAKES and CONSCIOUSLY KNOW WHAT AUTHENTIC AND LASTING LEARNING IS ABOUT. That is what I call practicing your "enlightenment."**

The 4 C's

היה זה הפסיכולוג הצרפתי גוסטב לה-בון שטען לפני מאה שנה שכל רעיון חדש מיושן כבר ברגע שהוא מתקבל על-ידי ההמונים. התהליך פועל כך: מישהו הוגה את הרעיון. עובר דור עד שהרעיון מתקבל על-ידי האינטליגנציה. עובר עוד דור עד שזו מנחילה אותו להמונים. כאשר הרעיון מגיע לשלטון, הנסיבות שהולידו אותו כבר השתנו ודרוש רעיון חדש המציאות משתנה הרבה יותר מהר. מאשר התפיסה האנושית.

The first is to make a <u>Commitment</u>. This commitment gives you the willpower and energy you need for the second C: <u>Courage</u>. With commitment and courage, you have the power to create <u>Capability</u>. And finally, armed with commitment, courage and capability, you then have <u>Confidence</u> to execute your vision.
—*Dan Sullivan*

Week 50

THOUGHT: **DARE TO BE YOURSELF ! COULD YOU?**
SURE YOU CAN.

SPEECH: **"Do not say one thing with the mouth and another with the heart"**
—*Baba Metsiah 49a.*

ACTION: Practice 5 minutes a day of conscious laughter. After you finish your morning rituals, stop for a moment, and **look at the mirror.** Observe yourself looking at you, and have hearty laugh at yourself **for no reason whatsoever.** See how funny you are. And, mon ami, **Welcome to "SILLY LAND,"** Le monde de l'absurde.

Week 51

THOUGHT: "WHEN LOVE depends on something, if the thing ceases to exist, love ceases to exist. But if it does not depend on something, then it never ceases to exist."
—*Pirke Avoth 5:16.*

SPEECH: In every situation, recognize and pursue the values of integrity and totally practiced honesty, even when it doesn't seem to benefit you. In simple words, be honest with both yourself and others – without needing a reason or any approval.

ACTION: Create something not for any reason, except that your inner being and sense of love inspires you to do it, and <u>**experience a new sense of PLEASURE.**</u>

Week 52
THOUGHT: DO EVERYTHING AS IF FOR THE FIRST AND LAST TIME
SPEECH: **Speak** every word as if for the first and last time.
ACTION: **Do** every movement as if for the first and last time.

**LIFE IS NOW IN SESSION.
ARE YOU PRESENT ?**

**Write this saying and place it before you
so you will see it all times.
Put it on your refrigerator as a constant reminder.**

• • •

REMEMBER AND REALIZE FOR SELF-GUIDANCE

A suggested philosophy for a balanced, happy and productive life:
"Identify and eliminate laziness and dishonesty in yourself and around you.

Live passionately without guilt. Be always ready, alert, creative
and responsive to the beautiful and vibrant life within you.

Happiness is your natural state of being and does not depend on anyone else
but your own self. Enjoy 100% every present moment of your life.

Remember! Your life is your only moment in eternity, precious and full
with joie-de-vivre. Focus your energy with vitality to produce values
and earn your super happiness – your natural state of being.

Give more than you take. Produce more than you consume.

"Vive La Vie, Vive L'Amour, Vive La Liberté, Vive La Difference."
—Samuel Avital

First Thought and Last Thought – Consciously

Practice and Master
First Thought and Last Thought Exercise (FTLT) – Consciously

PRACTICE FIRST THOUGHT/LAST Thought every day, becoming aware of the FIRST THOUGHT that comes to you in the morning, and the LAST THOUGHT that you think before going to sleep.

When you master this technique, you can consciously use the following statements, making a clear decision to live and be grateful for the gift of life.

MORNING FIRST THOUGHT

When you awake from sleep in the morning, repeat this thought loudly
to yourself 3 times before getting out of bed, giving meaning to each word, and
setting out to carry this attitude all day long.

I am grateful for the gift of life.
I consciously decide to live today fully awake and ready.

EVENING LAST THOUGHT

At night, before you go to sleep, as you place your head on your pillow,
read and repeat this last thought consciously,
carrying it with you into sleep.

I am fully grateful that I have lived today to
the best of my ability and potential. I love life
and I will wake up tomorrow to greater possibilities.

"Souls that recognize one another...Congregate. Those who don't...argue"

The Day Map

THE DAY MAP is an exercise I gave to students to pay attention to details and develop awareness and consciousness.

A Student Experience by Steve Rusan

In this workspace, we began to learn to expect the unexpected, for Samuel truly lives in the moment. We tried to be "awake and ready," open to the present. Samuel is a mirror, reflecting yourself, if your eyes and heart are open enough to see. He uses many means to do this – one of these is homework. One assignment we were given was to make a map of our day. Following this, the assignment was to make a pattern map of consciousness. The instructions were to use a structure to depict our states of consciousness during one day, working intuitively rather than intellectually.

My map is a series of twelve drawings:

1. *Awakening* – greeting the day, accepting the gift of another day of life
2. *Preparation* – preparing the body and mind to meet this day
3. *Oneness with Nature* – walking outside, paying attention to my place in the world order
4. *Focused Awareness* – attention on intricacies and details
5. *Harmony* – a drive through the mountains, feeling the order of all things
6. *Reconciling* – meeting others, finding sameness and difference at the same time
7. *As Above, So Below* – sitting on top of a mountain, seeing the reflection of the higher in the lower
8. *Habits* – keeping the home space in order and balance
9. *Nurturing* – provision of food
10. *Sharing* – a meeting to share energy, ideas, and experiences on the path
11. *Unification* – the union of male and female
12. *Completion* – the day ends, the circle is complete
    (See illustrations on following pages.)

Steve Rusan, Boulder, Colorado 1981.

The Eye Compass™

**A special exercise of the BodySpeak™ method
benefiting one's orientation, direction, and decisions.**

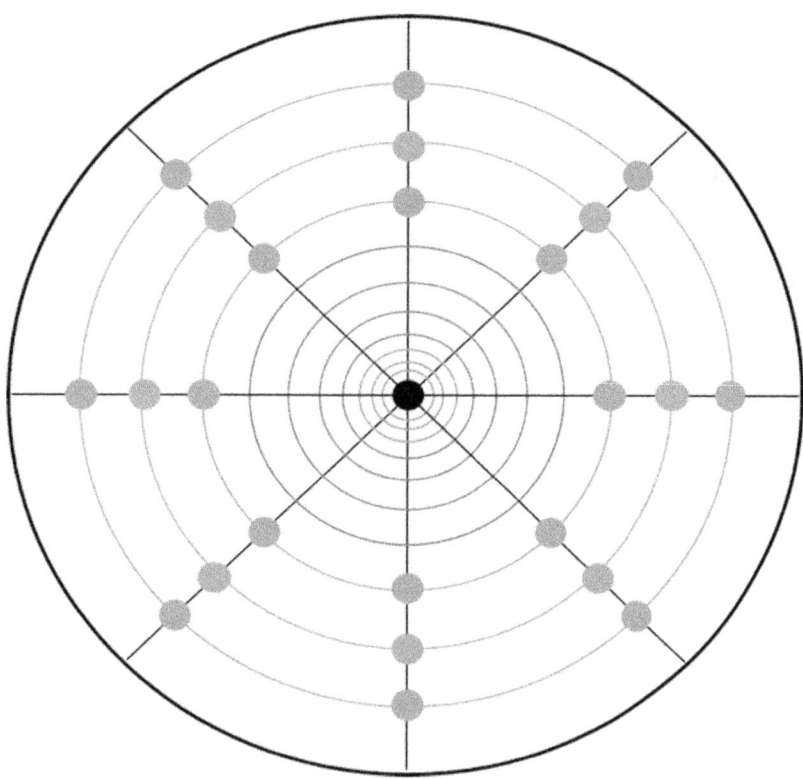

Directions:

1. Focus on the center black dot.
2. Follow the smallest violet circle with your eyes 6 times clockwise and then 6 times counter clockwise. Repeat with each violet circle from the smallest to the largest.
3. Follow the blue circle stopping and focusing the eye movement at each dot. Follow the circle 6 times clockwise and then 6 times counter clockwise. Repeat with the green circle and then the pink circle.
4. Finally, follow the outermost black circle with your eyes 3 times clockwise and then 6 times counter clockwise.

Articles

What is a Sane and Balanced Life?	**167**
A Look at Myself	**171**
Memes: Dangerous Minefields	**175**
Fear Does Not Exist	**178**
What If?	**183**
11 Commandments for Students	**185**
Meditation Anesthesia	**187**

What is a Sane and Balanced Life?

A BALANCED AND healthy life depends on control of one's thoughts. This control of thoughts allows us to experience our physical and mental life, in a way that is harmonious, and integrated as one with all creation.

Many random thoughts tend to dominate our being during this life. So, we must learn to channel our thoughts with focused direction, in every action we do during the day.

Happiness cannot inhabit or occupy the space where despair and sadness exist. The joy of being fully in this very miraculous moment is actually the key to being happy in "these times."

It is becoming very obvious in this world now, that everything is upside down. This is exactly as the Prophets of Israel repeated and shouted in their eternal messages. This "screenology generation" is addicted to what is fed to them through their telephone screens. As a result, they call darkness light. They call the sweet bitter and the bitter, sweet. They call the day, night and the night, day. That which is light is accepted as dark, and that which is right is considered wrong.

For a spiritually balanced and enlightened being, it is possible to govern oneself and be balanced, where imbalance is the norm. This calls for a clear and sane way of thinking, which requires guided and focused thoughts, sane and sharp.

We have been given the power to be self-leaders and to use our self-governing ability. When we use these given abilities within ourselves, we can see clearly, and make the sane decision NOT to accept or allow strange and unbalanced thoughts to inhabit us within.

There is a constant disturbance, and a daily assault on our senses, caused by the many disbalanced human thoughts that we encounter every day, in every place. Every day, everywhere, the insanity and imbalance we meet is only increasing. In the face of this, we tend to follow like sheep, rather than being the shepherd, the self-leader. I call that "sheep consciousness." Every day, we see so many unhealthy thoughts appearing around us, seemingly from nowhere. And we witness the increasing discomfort within each human mind that allows and accepts this chaotic behavior.

We came to this world to LIVE in it, and to overcome that which is not balanced for us. Our innate intelligence, if used fully and completely, can assist us to choose how to be, and where to go, and what to think. And as we follow this way, it leads over time to balance and harmony with the world. We have to realize the complexity of the paradoxes, unconditionally accept both sides, right and left, up and down, etc. Then naturally we can function harmoniously in this world, with ourselves and each other.

Yes, many beings now deeply sense that "something is wrong." Yet we seem to be so blind, that we do not see its source. It is all around us, like the very air we breathe. The greed of a few has come to a dangerous edge. And now it is sweeping away with it, all those who have forgotten how to self-lead. It is sweeping away all those who have gotten caught in sheep consciousness.

The root of this whole state of madness is in the thoughts we think every day. So, we must begin to learn how to choose and control our thoughts. Then, we become strong and powerful. We do this by making the healthy decision NOT TO SUPPORT THAT WHICH IS HARMFUL to myself or others, or to my inner environment.

When you do not support that which is harmful to yourself, you have begun to taste what self-governance is. By that sheer ability, you experience true balance and harmony within your being. That will guide you to perpetuate a sane way of thinking. And from there, you can overcome all the toxic thoughts, that are harming you and me, and the many others who are not even aware of this.

This is a new way of being, in which we are in control of our thoughts, and we discover the power of choosing sanity. Cultivating this, each of us can actually make a big difference. We can become a healthy and balancing factor that could really cause the true change. This is not the fake change that is imposed on us from all directions at this time, but a true change.

This new power can be used by withdrawing all support from those who perpetuate the lies and imbalance. This means, NOT to support those "leaders," or career politicians, or those who call themselves your "friends," yet who show no self-responsibility, no respect, and no concern, let alone active compassion, toward themselves and others.

There are those who pretend to be warriors, while in real life, they are cowards. This is deceptive. However, through this newly learned and acquired power, we can recognize that which is really right instead of wrong, sane instead of insane, good instead of evil. And through healthy choice, we become balanced and healthy – This is the key to being and becoming "sane in the midst of madness."

So, here is a small piece of healthy counsel. When you meet people who create problems where they do not exist, that is your "red-light." It is a signal, from your own healthy being, to "stay away" and remove yourself from that negative association. In my culture, it is called "honor your legs."

Ponder and study this ancient nugget of wisdom: "Those who are merciful to the cruel will end up becoming cruel to the merciful." You can observe with your inner compassion, how this learning can lead you to your birthright – which is to experience true sanity and balance in life.

When you sense that "something is wrong," that something is rotten in the human mind today, your sane being is sending you a message, and you <u>MUST NOT SWEEP IT UNDER THE CARPET</u>. You must explore it with an open heart and open eyes. Ask questions. And when you find your sane truth, dare to stand for it. You earned it. Experience this and become a self-leader. Use the ability to govern yourself like a sovereign and independent being. Then you can be the being you were meant to be in the first place. For that is actually the purpose for which you came to this world.

There is a time when you make that healthy decision to make all the right and directed efforts. This is when you decide to live in a balanced way on this earth, with your thoughts, actions and movements in sync with your desires, aims and dreams. Then you have the clear possibility "to be that dream" and "be the balance" you were meant to be.

So, with this earned sanity, you actually develop the ability to balance yourself in every situation, in every moment or event you encounter. Function with calm in the midst of confusion, while deafening noise is around you. Be serene within the chaos everywhere. Be enthusiastic among the bored, and real among the fakes. Be convinced with your inner meditations, passionate and compassionate with the same breath. Know then to savor deliciously and appreciate the serenity of this very sacred moment.

Therefore, this is the sane path to the balanced and harmonious way that I call, "**Being Sane in the Midst of Madness.**" By being spiritually strong and self-governing, through the mastery of your thoughts, I am very confident that you can overcome all the "difficulties" that are now being constructed before our very eyes.

There is a dialogue between the body and the animator of the body. When this dialogue is listened to closely, and activated in our lives, we can be in the state of love. This is passionately living and being that connection. It is called in Kabbalah "The sacred connection of the Neshamah and the body." The Neshamah is the divine spark that animates and activates life within the body.

So, your attitude between you and your body has a great importance. It has a great power, when we use it consciously, with focused intention, in order to better our lives and the lives of others.

This dialogue between your body, and your thoughts and feelings, is a power that is disregarded by a great many people, who are just living casually, with no purpose of their being. This dialogue is not with words. It communicates mainly in silence and stillness, a definite "inner voice." When one listens naturally, one can detect and use this silent language effectively.

The life that is balanced and harmonious is within all creation, and its great beauty is whispering to us with each breath, each moment. It is an unspoken eternal language, that only the sane being can experience and know with certainty. This is what I call "The Center of Silence," the stillness and creative solitude with all that is, and all that is not.

Life on this earth is very healthy, rich, good and balanced. Strive to savor it, knowing the wisdom of that ancient saying: "This Too Shall Pass."

כִּי כְּמוֹ שָׁעַר בְּנַפְשׁוֹ כֶּן הוּא
אֱכֹל וּשְׁתֵה יֹאמַר לָךְ וְלִבּוֹ בַּל עִמָּךְ.
משלי כ״ג, י״ג

**As you imagine, think, arrange and organize within your soul,
so it will become. Eat and drink he says to you,
but his heart is not with you.**
Proverbs 23. 13

In other words, this verse clearly affirms and teaches that what you think, conceive and believe, you have the ability to achieve and manifest in your life right now.

**What you think consciously, you can become.
What you feel 100%, you will attract.
What you can imagine vividly, you create.
Observe these powerful words and know their great value to serve you.**

אִמְסַר עָלְמָא בִּידָא דְטִפְשָׁאֵי סנהדרין מו
"The world was given to the stupid to govern."
Talmud Sanhedrin 46

A Look at Myself

THIS MORNING I woke up with a new discovery. This was a self-discovery, the kind that doesn't come from analysis – but rather, by observing my life in a certain way, I had a clear view of myself in this world.

To understand what I observed, first of all, we have to look at how education generally works in this world. In this culture, you go to kindergarten, and elementary school, and then junior high, and high school, and college, and so on. All of it is oriented and guided for a purpose. You do it, so you can be educated. You do it, so you can be good at it. You do it, so you can make money at it, etcetera.

For example, you may study therapy, or to be a doctor, or to be a lawyer, or some other career, in order to make money, to "make a living." You have a goal. And you strive for that goal. These are the normal aspects of education today.

In other words, you have been educated in a university, in an institution, which gives you its stamp of approval, by giving you a certificate or a degree. And everyone is seeking that approval. And if, for example, you publish a book, you do it in order to be known, to be famous, to "be somebody," right?

This is the normal way of being educated in this world. You have goals. You strive. You stay up late at night for that. There are exams and grades: A,B,C,D,F. You work hard to get that PhD.

Now, if you will observe it, you will see that before you complete all this education, that's not considered life. Instead, you're *preparing* for life. You're trying to finish that, to complete it. So, all that education actually sways you from living.

You're busy worrying. You're busy preparing to live. You have to write that paper to go to the director of the school, you have to please the parents, etc. And when you finally think you are ready, you get married, have children, and so on, and you are not satisfied with your life. You are anxious, and you still want to achieve that and that, and are not at peace with yourself, and then you get sick and need medications. And you still owe your student loan by the time you are 50, if you are lucky. You are talking about life, you are preparing for life, rather than living, and studying with no condition.

Now, one thing that I remember is that before going to teach at Southern Methodist University, they asked me to send a bio or credentials. In the bio, I wrote, jokingly, "Graduate of the University of the Streets in Paris." And they thought there actually was such a place. So that inspired my thinking. I asked myself "What was my university?"

This led me to have a look at myself. All the things I listed above were non-existent for me. At the school I went to, in the place of my birth, I simply wanted to learn. There were no grades there. There were no degrees. None of that. I went to study, that's all. It was not even to study in order to become a Rabbi. Normally you see that a person does this for the sake of something else. In other words, you have a goal. I don't remember in my life that I had a goal to anything.

So, the discovery is, **I was living it**.

Because, I didn't worry about degrees. In the city I grew up in, there was another school, the Alliance Israelite Universelle, that was designed to teach universal education on the French model. They taught in French, and they had grades there. But the school I went to, which was called Em Habanim, was not like that. They did not have grades.

We grew up studying Hebrew and the Jewish tradition, Torah and grammar and more. You grew up respecting your teachers. And I was just busy studying, with no goal in mind. They did guide some students to become Rabbis, but even that was not the point of it. I was just busy learning and living. And in my life, when I look at it, that is the way I have been teaching, until today. There is no future goal in mind. You don't do it for a because.

But in this world, in kindergarten, your parents already want you to be a certain way. In college, they want you to get a certain degree. In work, they want you to work a certain job. The way I grew up was a different world. My parents didn't want me to be anything. They just let me live.

And as a result, I didn't have a stressful childhood at all. Later, as an adult, there was a time I was interviewed to give a set of workshops for executives and CEOs at large companies. I told the CEO of that company that I'm glad I do not have a degree from any University. As we talked, I told her the truth, that as a child, I was not abused, I didn't have any trauma. I don't even know what trauma is. I don't know what depression is at all. I don't know what all of those things are. I did not get that job. There was a doctor she worked with, who had recommended me to the company. He was a very nice man. When he heard what I told her, he told me that is why I didn't get the job. But he said to me, "That's actually why you are the exact right person to give these retreats." That job would have paid a lot of money. But it did not work, because I told the truth.

But as my students observed, I am actually very glad that I don't have a degree from any university. In my work, I didn't look for outside approval from anyone. And in running my school, I never took a grant from any institution. I don't have a title to give myself authority over others, or make myself different from them. The same thing projected in how I worked with my students. Because I see my students as teachers. I learned from them in every possible way, not through words, but through living.

In my work in mime and theater, I explored how you can get messages through movement. You can know so much about a person through the words that they use, through posture, through their movements, etc. And so, the BodySpeak™ Method was born.

And it is true to this day, when I study something, I don't have any goal whatsoever. If I'm guided to that book, I just open and study. That's it. And I don't have books of western philosophy. Even my knowledge of theater was never from books, but from live theater and acting. My teachers did not use many words, and it was not the words I learned from. For me, the teaching words were pointing out a direction, to give me exercises and indicators for actual practice.

It is the same thing with all of my behavior – my behavior was not the norm. And it isn't now either. And so, this morning I was just observing that. It was a clear look at myself. And until now, because of that, some people like me, and some cannot stand me. And because of that, many students told me until now that I am an enigma.

So, you see, it is a different approach towards life. When you study the BodySpeak™ method, you can detect that. When you read one of my books, you can detect that. The way I used to refer to this was as a constant living presence. Constant. And when you live like this, it affects others around you too.

Now, do you know how I maintained that state? One key word: Playfulness.

In the classes I teach, everything is a playground. And so, all through the years, I can say that nobody in my classes felt stressful or pressed to do anything. Because they enter an atmosphere of playfulness. And like that, the child within comes and lives it. And as I mentioned in my classes many times, I'm not interested in displays of technique. Just experience the learning, and trust the confidence of the body. It is a constant, continuous presence.

So, you can see the difference. If you go the one way, you're not living – Instead you're preparing to live, you're planning to live, you're talking about living, you're thinking about living. You're busy running to get that. But we are talking about something else completely, which is to live now.

And so, I told my students, don't wait for approval from anybody. Just get busy living what you are doing. Even when you are writing, just write. Enjoy it. Don't do it to get it done. Don't do it for a reward. Enjoy, and be that moment of writing. You will be amazed at what you discover. That attitude helped me to stay sane in the midst of madness all through my life.

My suggestion: Please use the example here of how I looked at myself, to look at yourself. Just look at yourself, in your own way, in order to make the greatest discovery of being and becoming. Being what? Being yourself. Becoming what? Becoming the one that you are meant to be yourself. And as for me, I consider myself as a temporary resident on this planet.

Samuel Avital as seen by Nada, 1976.

Memes: Dangerous Minefields

MANY PEOPLE ARE not even aware of the word "Meme", unless they are scholars or academics. A "meme" was originally defined as a "mind virus". They are words or suggestions of behavior, that influence a person to accept an idea as truth, without investigation or examination – without one even being aware of it.

Human languages are full with many, many thousands of memes, both positive and negative. But many people will find this unacceptable to consider. For example, "common sense" is a meme. "Common sense" is something that attempts to contain half-truths, which we accept, mostly when we are unaware. Most of this is instilled in us in our youth, during our years of formation.

Many systems of education are full with these kinds of memes, which have been implanted in our consciousness. It is like a virus that has been inserted in our systems. People believe that meme is true and that it is healing, but actually, it may be the opposite. It is a thought virus.

The obvious example in American culture is commercials, which introduce you to need that which you don't need. That is where they insert those memes, those programmed ways of thinking. The commercials have become one of the most effective assaults on human consciousness, and now they are even becoming verbally violent, instead of using persuasion as they did in the past.

There are many of these memes in the languages of the world. You will find them in academia, in legal studies, in university curriculums, in high school textbooks, and so on. All of these are full of memes. And they are accepted as is. These memes have even succeeded in entering the greatest dictionaries of the world.

Since most human education systems depend on these thought viruses, introducing them to young minds in their early formation, I suggest examining and re-examining the words we use every day, in our relationships with everyone. In doing this, identify the virus-meme. Examine it, and decide if you truly want to use it or not; This is the most sane way to be harmonious and serene in a perplexed life.

An example that I observed when I came to this country, was that in stores, the saleswoman would ask me "May I help you?" And so, I would ask "Do you mean it? Can you really help me?" And they told me, "Samuel, we have to say that. It's a script they give us." That is a meme. When I ask if they really mean it, I am bringing attention to whether you are saying the truth, or just asking because you want to please your boss. Is there a because, or are you kind to the other person for no reason? Marketing is the art of using memes to make the sell.

Now a few memes are positive, but unfortunately, those are generally not taught, only through certain families who keep their old traditions. And memes are very subtle and easy to accept, because not everyone examines the words that they speak. Because most human nature is gullible, and easy to hypnotize.

Non sequiturs are one common way of shifting from positive memes to negative memes. When someone uses a non sequitur, they shift the conversation to something that has nothing to do with the subject you are talking about. For example, a man and woman are having a picnic and he tells her that he loves her, and she says "Would you like a sandwich?" You shift from a value to non-value. Politicians do this constantly. They cover up the truth, and dodge the question.

The great majority of these memes, in almost all the languages of the world, are mostly negative. And unfortunately, the schools and universities that are supposed to teach students to distinguish the difference, are not doing so. They do not teach students **how to think**, but **what they are supposed to think**. Therefore, students are not even taught the tools to examine what they say, how they say it, and why they say it. If you teach them how to think, they will be aware of every word they say.

And so, the words we use are important. This is why in the Defintuitions section, we point out certain corrections of terms that we normally use, in order to become aware if the definitions or ideas we have of things are of benefit, or actually not of benefit. Actually, the whole idea of "I" is the most dangerous meme in most languages. For instance, when one says "I am hungry," they are lying. The stomach, the system of hunger, is what is hungry, not the "I". The real spiritual "I" is never hungry.

And so, everybody expresses different emotions to each other without even knowing the truth of it. The expression "I love you" is actually the greatest abuse of language, because it separates the "I" from the "you". And if you ask anyone in the street to give you a simple definition of love, they will always refer to a physical action.

Hence, the most abused words in the English language, as I know it, are "God", "love", "freedom", "knowing", "life", "happiness", etc. These are all memes, that are influenced by people's emotional states. But the teachers do not teach the children how to examine them.

People think that they are not going to live longer than 60 or 70 – that's a meme. And by 50, you are supposed to retire and apply for social security – that's a meme. So, longevity becomes a disease.

And so, it is important to know the words you are using. Don't say a word until you know what it means. Begin from there. Because the memes become a societal permission to lie and to cheat. You can use the Three Gates of Words from the Sages:

The Three Gates of Speech – A practical suggestion

There is a proverb that every word should pass through three gates, before being uttered.
At the first gate, the gatekeeper asks "**Is it true?**"
At the second, he asks, "**Is it necessary**?"
At the third, he asks "**Is it kind**?"

If your immediate response to all three questions is positive,
you may speak without harming anyone.

Here is a French proverb to always remember before uttering a word:
"Si ce que tu vas dire n'est pas plus beau que le silence ne le dis pas"
"If what you are going to say is not more beautiful than silence, do not say it."

**"Make no mistake about it—enlightenment is a destructive process.
It has nothing to do with becoming better or being happier.
Enlightenment is the crumbling away of untruth.
It's seeing through the façade of pretense.
It's the complete eradication of everything we imagined to be true."
—Adyashanti**

Fear Does Not Exist

The Edge Between Sanity and Imagination

**"The one who fears the ONE,
fears no one."**

DOES FEAR EXIST? What do you think?

Warning. Fear is a myth that has conditioned humanity until now, causing war and bloodshed. The cause of it is the many memes, the thought-viruses and programmed ways of thinking, that have been instilled in us over the generations, and across all nations and cultures. Those thoughts were repeated, until now, at this time, they appear to be true and seem real for us. And I call that true madness.

Semantics is how we form meaning of the world, based on our language. And according to this, semantics has begun to affect human life everywhere. I am not a scholar, but a good scholar could elaborate on how those false thoughts were built into the language over history, and how it is impacting the current human situation.

One realization we can come to is that we create our fear with our IMAGINATION. One phrase I liked to use over the years was F.E.A.R – false evidence appears real. An unrealistic perception of life is the BASIS of FEAR.

People are not willing to live, people are not willing to die, that is the predicament right now. The fear simply means that you are not living with life, you are living in your mind. Your fear is of what is going to happen next, which does not yet exist. If your fear is about the non-existent, then your fear is 100% IMAGINATION. If your suffering is about what does not exist, we call that insanity. So, people just accept different levels of insanity.

People are always suffering, either about what happened yesterday, or what will happen tomorrow. So your suffering is always about that which does not exist – simply because you are not rooted in REALITY, you are always rooted in your mind. But if the memes around you influence you to a high degree, you will start to believe it, and then the problems begin. By thinking it, you invoke it, and therefore, it is established, and that's how we create problems where they don't exist.

One part of the Mind is MEMORY, another part is IMAGINATION. In one way, both of them are IMAGINATION. They DO NOT EXIST right now. You are lost in your IMAGINATION, and that is the BASIS of FEAR. If you are not rooted in IMAGINATION, there will be no fear.

Fear does not exist. It does not exist. But it exists for those who accepted those ancient memes, those false thoughts. And there are so many, many of those memes, that have been inserted in our subconscious over the years. They have been taught to us from academia, from law, from philosophy, from so many fields of knowledge today. Therefore, those programmed thoughts are accepted, without us examining it.

If we do examine it, however, and come to that sane way of thinking, many obstacles and confusions will be solved naturally. But this will take time. Because most humans now don't "have the time" to study this to a certain degree. And some attention is needed in order to clean our consciousness and thought processes from this plague of ancient memes, which was inserted while we were totally unconscious, no matter which culture we are from, whether eastern or western.

However, from the other side, fear actually has a benefit: to trigger creativity and a strong tendency to accept change. And in the future consciousness, this will be understood by itself.

The power of fear is something to explore. Fear is the effective cause of true and valuable individual and collective change. There is both the good and the bad in fear. It depends on how one defines the word fear, positively or negatively. Generally, in this society that creates problems where they don't exist, the memes (or programmed ways of thinking) about fear, are all harmful. But many times, a person does not change until they are scared to hell. And fear could also be a deterrence, not to harm others. It depends on how one uses it, positively or negatively.

I found a verse in Mishlei/Proverbs 28:14, which may appear as a paradox, but it is not. The verse says "אַשְׁרֵי אָדָם מְפַחֵד תָּמִיד וּמַקְשֶׁה לִבּוֹ יִפּוֹל בְּרָעָה" "Fortunate is the man who always fears (or is always anxious). And the one who hardens his heart, will fall into the trap of evil."

Now why would someone who is anxious be fortunate? On the surface, it doesn't appear to make sense. I would translate that anxiousness or fear, as stress, which is something that 99% of humans feel – but they don't use it as a trigger to live a creative life. I can say that stress is a very positive experience for any artist.

A large percentage of humans today interpret stress in a negative way, but as an artist, I know that if I don't feel that nervousness, if I don't have stage-fright, my performance will not express as I intended it. My heart will become hard and I will fail in my performance. But if I have respect, and feel that awe of my audience, using that "stress" in a positive way, that is what focuses me to communicate my creative expression.

So, stress is a driving force, a trigger to creativity. Instead of using it as a negative, I use it as a positive. All of these are ways to behave in order not to create problems. Because the whole idea of stress was actually recently invented, it is just an idea that is imposed on people and it conditions our behavior unintentionally.

Here, however, I can indicate one essential thought about the source of suffering and lack of happiness in humanity today. Authentic wisdom suggests that the addiction to intellectuality, to overthinking, in many fields of human knowledge, has almost destroyed the natural state of happiness of humans.

Now, we have the key to restore human happiness, with no war, and no conflicts — if we use the intellect carefully, without abusing it in every field. This can be done individually, in the renewal of a new consciousness (see the article The Great Shift), that humanity is in the process of completing now.

And so conflict instead becomes a challenge, and I welcome it. But generally, people resist conflict, they flee from it, because of the fear of what is going to happen.

Now, this is a revolutionary thought, that in spite of all the evil permeating everywhere now, happiness is our natural state of being. Health is the natural state of being. We were born to be healthy, period. All this is true, considering the human goodness that exists within every human being.

Metaphorically, we can relate to the interpretation of the story of Adam and Eve in the Kabbalah and the Zohar. The story of the sin of Adam and Eve, for those who know, is the story of the loss of their innocence.

They were ordered not to eat from the Tree of Knowledge of Good and Evil, because on the day they ate from it, they would discover death. After that, they would die, and all the easy eternal life of the Edenic state of the Garden of Eden would be removed from them. This was the expulsion from Gan Eden (the Garden of Eden).

Now, the snake intellect interfered, camouflaging his intent with the idea that when they ate from the tree, they would become like God. Here the snake symbolizes the overuse of the intellect in order to abuse humanity, something which has caused suffering and increased violence and wars across human history.

As the Zohar speaks about, we are still suffering from the introduction of death, which happened through that event called the sin of Adam, which is the loss of Edenic innocence. And our main, essential role now, is to restore that Edenic state anew, by the great change of consciousness that humanity has been going through the process of, throughout all the thousands of years.

Now, millions of philosophers and intellectuals have tried to figure out the "mystery of being" on this planet. And they are still continuing to guess and hypothesize, without going anywhere. They are still busy intellectualizing the "mysteries", while neglecting to be the mystery itself, free of all suffering.

Everyone wants to be happy, free of suffering. But the memes (thought-viruses) of war and suffering have been implanted deep in the consciousness of humanity, and so we have to introduce new constructive and positive ways of thinking (see the article, "The Great Shift.") And I found the best way to do this is through the BodySpeak™ exercises I developed over the years. In this way, our consciousness can contain a greater ability to understand ourselves and our environment.

But for now, over the thousands of years, we have abused the ability to think in a balanced way, without hurting the other.

I say this because we have only words, and humans have created a violent reality, full of wars and hatred, because of over-intellectualization of everything – which is also the abuse of language. We are obsessed with creating fear day and night, and it is fiction.

Once we realize the goodness that exists within every living being, wars will stop, violence will cease, and life will become much easier – until we reach the conclusion of actually living in Gan Eden (the Garden of Eden), in this world, free of suffering, free of conflict. But if you, reader, think that this is a utopian impossibility, sorry, you are still in the dark age of abuse of the intellect.

We can contemplate this possible reality, in a focused way. But the over-intellectualism has destroyed all the good in humans, by thinking that humans are violent and animalistic. Actually, the Tikkun HaOlam, "the restoration of the world" is in the hand of every individual on this planet. But most are ignorant of this possibility. We build hills and mountains of doubts, and have forgotten the essential and balanced way of human thinking.

So, for a person who still has some iota of intelligence, one must uproot this unconscious meme of fear, that was planted and installed in the human psyche over thousands of years. The person who examines this can come to the way to delete it or uproot it from his or her consciousness, which is the most difficult thing to do.

And my friend, if you are an authentic human being, please observe and figure this out yourself. And I will close with a hint from Einstein:

> **"I think 99 times and find nothing.
> I stop thinking, swim in silence, and the truth comes to me"**
> *Albert Einstein*

What If?

Various Ways of Using this Ancient Meme

HUMANS HAVE A tendency to ask questions that begin with "What if…?" "What if" is actually another subtle meme (programmed way of thinking) that can go in both directions, both positive and negative. But we mostly use it on the negative side. This is because our tendency to try to understand the dual reality around us causes us to suppose that things are like this or that. So we develop guesses, based on suppositions, that have no basis.

Let's find a positive example of "what if." A novelist who is writing his first novel explores characteristics of his characters. He creates a story through exploring this question – "What if the grandpa suggests going to the beach at 12 midnight?"

The challenge of our novelist is to develop his characters, according to his knowledge and intention, and he does this with words and dialogues and guesses. And so, he uses 'What if?' as a trigger to create that novel. This is a positive what if. And sometimes, if the writer or artist is aligned and allowing themselves to listen carefully, the characters may practically write themselves, suggesting their own line of development to the writer. That can happen in many fields: music, painting, writing, mime, etc.

The negative what if could be thinking, "What if tomorrow there is a big snowstorm and I cannot go sign that contract? That may cost me a lot of money. Plus, I am sensitive to the cold. And even if I call to postpone it, what if they cancel, and take on another client instead?" So this is a guess, not knowing the weather, not knowing many things. It is guessing what will happen – which has not yet happened. And as a result, that creates fear, doubt, and lack of confidence.

Part of this tendency to ask "what if?" is done through unconscious fear. "What if the "monster" will snatch me while I am drinking my Starbucks coffee?" There are no monsters in Starbucks. And you are not in Starbucks now in any case. In other words, you are creating a false imagination. So, you are using the gift of imagination in a negative way.

You can go on and find out for yourself how you use these types of suppositions and guesses. That is also an escape from this moment. In this moment, you are not at Starbucks, there are no strangers, you are just supposing. We just create that idea in our imagination.

If one thinks that way, it means only one thing: The level of consciousness of that person is undeveloped. Therefore, it depends on the angle of your consciousness. So, try to look from different angles and you will find your understanding. It all depends on the individual human evolution. (*See the preceding article – Fear Does Not Exist*)

Eleven Commandments for Students

THESE ARE ELEVEN (11) suggestions for students who are more than curious. This is for those ready to study in depth that which is taken for granted and obvious, those willing to dedicate valued time to learn. It is for those daring enough to examine "reality" through experience, manifestation and a joyous heart, and not just through words and theories.

1. **You shall integrate education and learning as a first priority.**

2. **You shall not glorify mediocrity. Always honor excellence.**

3. **You shall apply the learnings in order to experience them, and verify their truth yourself.**

4. **You shall not pretend that you understand.**

5. **You shall not be shy, and know how to ask the "right" questions, from context.**

6. **You shall not cultivate curiosity. Go beyond being curious only.**

7. **You shall not confuse innovation with progress. Adopt the motto "<u>KEEP ME SANE IN THE MIDST OF MADNESS</u>" in all situations.**

8. **You shall honor your Teacher (your fountain of knowledge and wisdom), and listen carefully to the teachings with all your heart and mind (with the profound intention to apply them).**

9. **You shall not court popularity, self-approval, and self-aggrandizement. Always aim to the "Ocean", not only the "streams, the "Central-Core," not only the periphery. (Streams = information. Ocean = knowledge)**

10. **You shall strive for excellence in conscious thought, speech and action. And welcome all mistakes with a gentle heart, so you can correct them immediately. This way you may shape your own "key," and, enter that <u>Mysterious Place</u> called the <u>Hidden Obvious</u>.**

11. **In any situation in life, adopt this attitude that will simplify life complexities: "<u>THIS TOO SHALL PASS</u>" and "<u>THIS ALSO IS FOR THE GOOD</u>".**

"המנהיג הטוב ביותר הוא זה שהעם אינו מרגיש צורך להודות לו.
כשמלאכתו נעשית ויעדו מושג, העם יאמר: 'עשינו זאת בעצמנו.'"

**The great conscious leader is the one that the people don't feel any need to thank.
His work is done, and its purpose is for the good of the people,
and the people would say, we did it ourselves.**
Anonymous Quote

Meditation Anesthesia

"Meditation is Hazardous for Your Health"

WHAT IS ANESTHESIA? It is a loss of consciousness induced by an anesthetic used in surgery. It can put people to sleep altogether, or cause numbness in parts of the body. But there is also, "spiritual anesthesia." In Hebrew, it is called תרדמה Tardema. What is this spiritual anesthesia?

Spiritual anesthesia is a technique that is done consciously to people. It happens in various methods of meditation. If done correctly, meditation can be a very sacred practice. If not, it can affect a person negatively. Starting in the 60s and 70s, I witnessed the so-called "spiritual awakening" that was happening, which continues until now. In it, I saw a really consciously evil way to put people to sleep.

At the time that I witnessed this, the town of Boulder, where my theater school is located, was swamped with gurus. There were boys that came from India, and the people spoiled them, and gave them cars and riches, and would do anything they said. Seeing this, I tried to warn my students about it. So, at the time, I started telling them that meditation is hazardous for your health. I was attacked for saying that, since it was à la mode at the time, but I wanted to warn them.

They thought that these "spiritual" learnings were supposedly developing then. But actually, they were not developing at all, it was just a repetition of what happened before, in the last century in Europe, with figures like Blavatsky and others. There is a whole history to this that few are aware of. And at the time, there were westerners who were supposedly students of Tibetans, but they converted that knowledge into their own frames of thinking.

To understand this, first we must understand that there is such a thing as an original idea. But when you transport meditation practices from the east to here, they get distorted along the way. That is what I witnessed. In yoga, for example, people thought that Asanas were just physical movements. And so today, there are thousands of videos everywhere with people teaching yoga movements, but the meaning of the movements, the Asanas, is more than just physical. Understood physically only, it gets distorted. The same thing happened with the Torah, the bible. It comes from a very deep spiritual context, but when people read translations of it, they read it on the surface level only, and it gets distorted. I emphasized this throughout my teachings.

That distortion develops over the years, and they spread it, using certain terms, that the people who spread them have no clue what they actually mean. In many of these places, India, China, Tibet, there are traditions that do meditation in a certain way, but when they try to transport that to the west, they destroy it. Why? Because of the western abuse of left-brain thinking only. The deep context that tradition came from gets lost.

I experienced this in teaching about the kabbalistic system, teaching the tree of life and the maps of consciousness of Kabbalah. People wanted to compare it to chakras, and different systems, which is wrong. The system of the chakras is very beautiful, and I have respect for that system. It is from a certain area, and a certain ancient and meaningful culture, and it works for them. But when you try to export that, it gets distorted.

And so, there is what I call anesthesia meditation. "Relax, sit, everything is done for you. Relax." This is a deep programming that is done in the west. And even if people go to India and study for a few years, when they come back, the language they transmit this knowledge in, be it English, French, etc, is already crooked.

I can say this. If you are reading this and you are sane, go to the TV or YouTube and look at how this distortion is done so cleverly that nobody notices it. It's very subtle. Anesthesia meditation. It's a deep sleep, designed to distort your consciousness. Yet the language is to be awake, to be conscious, right?

In the Zohar they speak about awakening also, but the Kabbalists come and say, it is not the awakening that we know in this world, because actually they call that deep sleep. This life is a deep, deep slumber. That state of sleep was instilled on purpose, and even though humanity has been shaken by various historical events, they still didn't wake up.

I can say this even more crudely; Anesthesia meditation is there to keep you in a deep sleep. And the amnesia gurus are doing it to this very day. Go and look at the gurus of today. I even studied with some of them to observe it directly. They dare and have the brazenness to tell you, "Sleep, it's good for you. Just relax."

So that is a deep amnesia and anesthesia that they will never wake from. And that is why a lot of people quit, because it doesn't work. There are some people who study for years in India, and learn about chakras etc, but all of this is still done only on the level of information; Nobody wants to dive deep and really explore and know that tradition from experience.

Because they are programmed to sleep, to relax. It is total inactivity, and when it is done by millions of people, they live in a fake reality. And that is what is going on now – virtual reality. The technology is good, but it destroys people little by little. I suggest watching the film Kumare, which reveals how easily this type of hypnosis is done.

This spiritual anesthesia, spiritual amnesia has been going on for a very long time, and it continues until this very day. And if you read this and you are shocked, it means that you are one of the people who enforces and assists this anesthesia.

So I warned my students that meditation is hazardous for your health. Why is it hazardous? Because it is deep anesthesia. They make you sleep. And they can shout about awakening and consciousness and all that, but they are doing the opposite. Why do I say that? Because over the years, I found out this very sophisticated art of lying that they do, full of harmful and destructive memes, ways of thinking that are totally fake.

I said it many times, if you want to learn the language of lying, study English. And this is why some people didn't like me. Take all the fields of knowledge in the western world. The academicians are lying, the lawyers are liars, the politicians use these same lying techniques in their ideologies. And they know it. They know what they are doing. But they want people to stay asleep. They say "You've got to vote, you can change the world." They give you that supposed amnesia power.

In Kabbalah, they explore this principle that only the human being can talk, and that speech is the greatest gift. But we abuse it. In the story of Noah, the flood came because of the abuse of words, which was taken to the edge. So, the edges of the edges, that's a restart.

In the Zohar they speak about this state of sleep, and that state of sleep is actually the state we call awakening now. So in the 70's, I reversed the word sleep, and the opposite is please. When you say please, it is a code word to tell you to sleep. When we look at it on the surface, I'm either physically asleep, or I'm physically awake. That is one way of understanding awake and asleep. But I told my students many times to be aware that they sleep. That's a different way of operating, which really is possible.

This anesthesia meditation is happening now, and I can show it to you. For example, I have observed one of the most popular 'spiritual teachers' of today, who has built a big following. This is actually a man who has psychological problems, but he speaks very beautiful English and people are drawn in by it. But if you go and listen to anything he says, if you are really lucid enough, you can see in between the words to know what is really going on. But unfortunately, there are so many examples of so many people doing the exact same thing

They do this through the half-truths. And if you try to point out any of the flaws in their thinking, you are wrong, according to them. They tell their followers it is for them, but actually it's not. They say things about changing consciousness, but actually all their language is a clever and dangerous meme (a thought virus), and when it is established, you take it for granted, and you don't even use your own healthy faculty of thinking anymore. Once those false memes, programmed ways of thinking, are established, your original way of thinking isn't even there anymore.

So, you become a parrot. You repeat the words and ideas they created, and it sounds good, but it isn't true. Actually, you have your own unique way of thinking. But because of these words and movements that they pretend are for your own good, people get hypnotized. That is why this is a red light for me. They pretend to be for your good. You can observe this everywhere.

I said it many times, that they keep you busy, so you will never look into yourself or examine your life. But when you begin to look into yourself, you can begin to correct yourself, and you discover your own unique way, which is different from what they tell you to think, and how they tell you to think. This is why what we call waking now, the kabbalists referred to as a state of sleep.

This is what I call the greatest evil in the world today – fake meditation. It is fake meditation, because when this art form was transported from the east to here, they changed it. But when they present it, they have all the answers, supposedly.

I can demonstrate how their tactics are hidden, in such an artistic way that nobody notices it. After I observed this, there was an example I gave to my students to help them detect it. I demonstrated how people can do the same movement, but one movement is totally absent. It truly shows in the movement, it doesn't look the same.

So, you can do that physical movement, you just do it like nothing, and it is meaningless. But if you do that same physical movement, and you pause in it – if the movement breathes and has awareness – it is both physical and nonphysical. This is to turn people's awareness toward something, to simplify very complicated ideas into simplicity. So, I called it the art of simplifying the complex. This way it becomes very easy and very accessible to everyone.

Observe it, nowadays in this culture, on the high-tech campuses, they have a room for meditation, alongside with the cafeteria and restaurant. And they even claim it is spiritual. But why is it there? It is so the workers can recharge their energy, so they can work harder for them and never leave that campus and keep working constantly. And they say it is so they can be 'creative.' So that is fake creativity again. And they try to cover what they are doing with the idea of "upgrading yourself," but upgrades are for machines, not human beings.

They keep the people working constantly, not leaving that campus, so the campus becomes a prison without them knowing it. That is imposing a personal prison on people, assisting them to create their own self-prison – and they are highly paid for it, for staying in that high-tech, robotic state of slavery. The words around it sound good – enlightenment, relaxation – but it is all on the surface. And when it accumulates, the person can get very confused, and even become mentally ill, because what they have learned conflicts with reality and with their personal history. It can really cause harm.

And once that harm is caused, then the psychiatrist or the scientist comes and gives you a shot or a pill and that's how they supposedly solve it. But hopefully in the future, once humanity has experienced a spiritual reset, these fake tactics will be obvious to everyone. They will say, how stupid that generation was, that they accepted being hypnotized for hundreds and hundreds of years. So that is anesthesia hypnosis.

But they "have the answers" for everything. As long as you ask a question on how to be present, they "have the answer." I saw an interview with the popular "spiritual" teacher I mentioned, and a very widely known teacher from the 70's, and in it I could see that they both deepen this state of anesthesia. I knew this teacher from the 70's, when I did big workshops in the Lama Foundation, and I encountered him there. But what I see is that they know the language well, and they can twist it in any way they want. If I was a scholar, I would identify how all this came about, through the history of it, but I am not a scholar. Meditation was supposed to bring you harmony and creative being, that is why it was originally created, not to deepen your sleep. But they distort it and misuse it.

These anesthesia gurus use affirmations, and subliminals, and many sayings like "go with the flow." All of those are valid in one context, but when they are used with a spiritual agenda the problems begin. They could leave you relaxed, happy and breathing with every breath and could make you aware. But on the negative side, they can be used to program people and they could put you to sleep. It depends on what you think yourself is. Therefore, it could be anesthesia – instead of becoming aware, you become unaware. So, there is some truth about it, but it is presented in a negative agenda by some of those "spiritual teachers."

This is why in the 90's, I read about Café-Salon Philosophique, the philosophical meeting that was done in Paris, and I started one here. That way people could experience abusing words for two hours, and we recorded every session.

So, what do we see? Abuse of words. But it sounds very logical, and it contradicts everything – If you say that, he says that. In the Jewish tradition, we had this kind of logical discussion in the Talmud, but there is a big difference. In the Talmud, it was to understand something, whereas here, the purpose is to prove that I am right and you are wrong. And so, you create a theory one week, and the next week, another scientist comes and refutes it. But there are great scientists like Einstein who refuted their own theories, right there on the spot.

For instance, can you prove what happens after your death? In the cafe, that was a topic we explored – "Death: Is It Inevitable or Unacceptable?" We explored it. And I said, "Anyway, we are going to die someday, so what's the discussion? Get busy living."

I detected these tactics over the years. It even exists in the arts, in theater school teachings. It appears in many different ways, in many different places. And its purpose is to cloud your clarity through logic, to cloud your clarity. Because actually the human being was awake before birth. When a person comes to this world, they come to the school of distortions – and part of that is the 'spiritual' paths that are using these same distorted techniques. This even exists in certain branches of Judaism. This is just the tip of the iceburg, and I really wonder why it is done.

This is why the Talmud and the Kabbalah consider this world, in which you and I live now, to be "the World of Lies," an illusion. And now, since all the libraries of the world contain books filled with lies, it is a message for the really awakened and learned human being, to be aware that one is born with the natural intelligence to think for oneself. That is called having your head on your shoulders. It means you can develop your own way of thinking and being, your own original way.

But as I said, this world of lies is structured to keep you constantly busy for nothing, and mainly to keep you away from your real self. That real self is your true and right way of being, but to take you away from that, they distract you constantly. And especially in our confused times, the over-technology of the AI that is being developed leads people to a state of robotic thinking and being. People look to the machine for answers, instead of relying on their own intelligence. But on the positive side, the AI technology and what comes after it, will free up people's time to really study themselves. And that happens by being comfortable with silence and stillness.

But everybody can find that true sense of balance, because it is innate in us. If you notice that you have a pain somewhere in your body, that pain signals to you, so you can heal it. The problem is laziness, it's taking everything for granted, it's thinking the pills will save us, which is another meme that has been planted, that is difficult to remove. So when we say the world of lies, that is really what it is.

This is why ultimately, we come to those three powerful things that guide the behavior of humans, and also cause them to distort things: power, money, and sex. Those are the three pillars of this culture. And if you want to have power, you control millions of people by telling them what they want to hear. Do you understand this? It's very subtle.

But I was aware of this subtlety since I was little. I could detect if someone was speaking from the knowledge of the sources, or just guessing. You can interpret, but you have to stay in the perimeter of that knowledge. That is why I say, respectfully, wherever you are, whatever tradition you are in, follow the river, you will get to the ocean. It's King Solomon who said that "All the rivers run to the sea, and the ocean is never full." But that also introduces the idea that humans never have enough. I call it the more disease. They are never satisfied.

People are sincere in wanting to learn, but in the anesthesia cultures they abuse that sincerity, that is where they insert subtle doubt. I don't have anything against doubt, because doubt and curiosity go together, and you can discover things with that. But since I came to America, I saw that tendency in people. They study yoga or they study the BodySpeak™ method with me, and they go back to the University and make a thesis about it. It is like they study the finger and they want to teach the whole body, as if they know the whole thing. And that's why academia is the center of programming people to insanity. This is from my experience, which I observed, because I was in those academic institutions.

So, there is a phrase I used to write on some of my teaching materials: "Those who recognize one another congregate, those who don't argue." I'm not against argumentation, if both people are versed in that field, they can learn a lot from one another. Unfortunately, the art of conversation has disappeared in our times. Now they want you to agree with their view exactly, and if you don't, they will force you to agree with it. But in the Kabbalah, they went beyond the questions and interpretations, and found a new state and developed a new language. They explore what is a dot, what is a line, what is space. If you are a mathematician, it will occur to you as if they are speaking mathematics, and if you are a mystic, you find it amazing.

Now, one of the technologies of anesthesia meditation is they insert it when people are not aware. And they make them unaware so they can program that in. It is so subtle, I'm telling you. So, I tried to express these ideas in my teachings over the years, to share conscious tools to deal with this and understand why it happens.

They don't want you to think for yourself, and so they fill in false memes, confused ways of thinking, through abuse of cliches – and they do it brazenly. But if you have a solid base, you say, it doesn't make sense to me. Does one need to develop a strong sense of depression and misbalance to be a spiritual being? Of course not. You can even look and pinpoint how they sway you from your own natural understanding.

But this anti-civilization does everything to use anesthesia on the population, using the big mask of caring for you. For example, in healthcare, I'm not normal if I'm healthy. This anesthesia is done through the pills and the pharmaceuticals. If anything happens, you resort to their pill or their shot, or their supposed supplement, not to yourself. They keep you stuck on that and they make a lot of money. But now they are discovering that many of these supplements are not what you think they are.

And really, the simple way of healing is to think that you are healthy, and it is. But that's too simple, and for them it takes too much effort to install that themselves, to be themselves. So here you see that these words are masks to hide the truth from you, supposedly healing you. And many of those drugs have terrible side effects, some of them can even kill you. So, it is like honey on the outside, masking a poisonous inside.

That is why I said many times, they keep you busy, so busy that you never have time to be yourself. And there is no book that can tell you how to go to yourself. So, in the Torah and the Kabbalah, the stories teach us how to learn from every situation in life, so you can begin to understand for yourself. As I said, once you begin to detect and remember that you are a spiritual agent, you have to have a strong sense of observation and distinction, to dare to be yourself. Dare to be a human, dare to be yourself. That's the program we have here, to dare to be.

They don't teach you to the tools to reimagine yourself in this culture. If you are a young kid and you have an invisible friend, you are condemned. The kids have access to those dimensions, but then they open the big psychiatry book and identify them as ADHD, and all those things. They do that to erase your intelligence from your consciousness, so you can be obedient and believe whatever they say. I saw that in a treatment center where I did volunteer workshops for kids in Dallas. The kids were very gifted, but their parents didn't know what to do with them, because they had so much energy, so they sent them away.

So, we are looking at anesthesia meditation, which is amnesia meditation too. Anesthesia is what makes you numb, so that you don't sense and feel. But amnesia is erasing the memory that you are that. So both words apply. Many things that claim to awaken you, or to make you feel good, many things that they say are spiritual, are actually designed to make you completely unconscious, completely asleep. And they call that awakening.

And so they become the very masters of keeping people asleep. They always escape from the now, while they keep saying now.

People ask what is Jewish meditation, but in Hebrew it is Hitbonenut, contemplation, a deep exploration of something. But for that, you have to purify yourself.

The power to control is good, if I'm controlling myself. People are against the ego, they want to kill the ego, to kill the Buddha. But Judaism doesn't do that, if it is authentic Judaism. But even in Judaism, there is fake Judaism, fake Kabbalah.

How is it fake? Because here, you think if you read a book about yoga, you can open a yoga teacher studio. It has been done, and it's being done, I'm telling you. You learn the movements, and you have a good voice, and you make videos and have 10,000 people look at it and give you likes. And if you have 500,000 likes, then you are a big ego. But the edge of that is that it detaches you from life, or from relating to other human beings. Because even if you have 500,000 followers, it doesn't mean that you are right. We have to wake up to these subtleties, but the average human being is not aware of these things.

This is because we live in an age of abused information, and thinking that information is knowledge. Doing so exposes us to accept negative memes without protest, and deepens our sleep state.

Spiritual anesthesia, it exists. And the people who will be against what I say are those who are part of the spiritual ratatouille, where they took this and that from different spiritual traditions without knowing what it is (see the article **Spiritual Ratatouille** in the book, *From Ecstasy to Lunch*). But this anesthesia is even worse than the ratatouille that was done with spirituality.

So, there is anesthesia, where they put you to sleep, and there is amnesia. But from that anesthesia, crossing the line to amnesia, to a state of total forgetfulness, is very easy.

This is what I call the greatest evil in the world today: fake meditation. It's fake meditation, because when an art form was transported from the east to here, they made it into something else completely. They use it to tell you to close your eyes and be totally passive. So, I call it meditation anesthesia. And it continues until this very day.

Therefore, this article is a call to sanity, if it didn't leave the planet yet.

Postscript:
I recommend reading the article "Madness and Sanity on Broadway" in the Last Word section, and the article "Keep Me Sane in the Midst of Madness" in the book *From Ecstasy to Lunch*, for some background on what this article is based on.

And if you succeeded to read all the ideas here, it means that there is still hope in the human condition. And I thank you for that.

Stories and Poems

Sefrou, the City of Roses   199

Time and Space, TI-PACE   203

Waiting for the Messiah   204

The Mother Who Loved Her Son   206

Sefrou, the City of Roses

THE PLACE OF my birth, Sefrou, was the physical cradle of my early formation. It was the scene of many events and strange happenings, mixed with comic and tragic flavors, where I grew until I left my home for Israel.

In Morocco, not far from the famous city of Fez, lie many small villages with names like Bhalil, Imouzzar, Ifran, and my own village of Sefrou. The large lakes nearby make this area an oasis of natural beauty. Many rivers stream through the valley, cascading from the nearby mountains, running eventually between the huge trees along the central river, the "Ouad Aggai," or "Ouad Al-Yehudi" – the river of the Jews. The color green dominates the whole lush valley.

Olive trees grow in abundance in Sefrou, supplying a large area with tons of olive oil. Many fruits are grown there, all reaching exceedingly large sizes. In addition to the peaches, apples, and many kinds of nuts, Sefrou is known for cherries, which are shipped to all the other Moroccan cities. Some days are even set aside during the year to celebrate this fruit with special ceremonies. Among the many flowers cultivated there, roses in particular, are grown in great quantities. Both rose oil and rosewater fill every house with their fragrance.

On Thursdays, merchants come from all the surrounding villages to the "Souk," the marketplace, to sell their products – milk, chickens, fruits, herbs, perfumes, and every imaginable thing you can sell. Going to the Souk is like going to a festival. Business is in full swing everywhere. It is like entering into a bath of perfume and spices. Merchants debate and bargain about prices, while acrobatic dervishes whirl in full performance. Exotic belly dancers gyrate in dark tents, and snake charmers chant and play their flutes all over the market. Beautiful Berber women come from the surrounding mountains to sell jewelry.

Profane and sacred are so mixed that one needs a quick sense of discernment and a strong intuition to distinguish the true from the false. One can get absorbed in so many things as to forget the world. For children, it is a weekly garden of marvels.

In my childhood, about 25,000 people lived in and around Sefrou. Of those, 2,500 were Jewish. Six hundred families occupied about 65 houses all concentrated in the "Mellah" – The Jewish quarter.

There were a few synagogues beyond the borders of the Mellah, in addition to the five within its walls.

The Jews mostly traded with the nearby mountain people, whose clothing was very similar. They also wore ornaments, handicrafts, and jewelry, mostly expertly made by the Jews. On holidays, people clothed themselves exquisitely to show off their riches. Many Jewish merchants spent the week outside the city in the mountains, selling their wares, and returned Friday afternoon for the celebration of the Shabbat.

Many factors kept the Jewish community close. The unity and intimacy of the family, the respect for elders, familiarity with history and ancestry, the continuing study of scriptures, the nurturing and careful education of the children, the observance of the Shabbat and holy days, and the integration of the spiritual into daily life, all created strong links between the Jewish youth and their elders. Respect and assistance to the poor were an obvious manifestation of the Jewish people of Sefrou.

Thus, in spite of the continuing Arabic persecution, the Jewish community was close-knit and loving. The factors mentioned above, combined with the simple, natural surroundings of Sefrou, created an atmosphere of health and vigor. People lived long, fruitful years, and Sefrou became known for the great longevity of its inhabitants. There was a great respect for the elders and teachers.

The Jewish people worked silver, lead, leather, and gold, producing beautiful shoes called, "Baboushas," candelabras, and ritualistic religious objects like Hanukkah candles. Works in wool were another specialty. Tapestries and carpets were made with great care and concentration. Other professions included woodworking, carving, and the making of excellent wines.

The history of Sefrou is marked with several great floods. In 1890, the rising river, abetted by the strong rains, flooded the Jewish quarter, resulting in much loss of life and damage to houses. Another flood in 1950 brought even greater damage. I witnessed a flood in Sefrou during the Second World War, and it was a fearsome time for me. I imagined that flood, which also destroyed many lives and houses, to be like the flood of Noah. It changed the whole demography of this beautiful place, for many Jewish families had to move outside the Mellah (The Jewish quarter) to live in newly built houses after the flood subsided.

Many learned men and women lived in Sefrou, poets, writers, Kabbalists, Talmudists, judges, teachers of all kinds, and skilled leather bookbinders. Historically, this little place gave much to other Jewish communities in Morocco. Many young Rabbis were sent from Sefrou, with great success, to be the spiritual leaders of other communities. And there was always a movement of students, coming and going, studying in the Yeshiva in Sefrou.

In school, children learned in a very simple way, sitting on the floor waiting their turn for the teacher to teach them personally. When they grew up, students were encouraged to pursue their higher education. The study of the Talmud and the Zohar was especially stressed. The literature of the great poets of the golden age of Spain, like Yehuda HaLevi, Solomon Ibn Gabirol, and Avraham Ibn Ezra was also studied in class. Wealthy people supported the students with food, clothing and living quarters.

Thus, the community was knit by the intimacy of sharing. People lived with the consciousness that they had been in exile for thousands of years and that they were waiting for the "Geoula" (the redemption) of the Jewish people. This manifested in their pious daily practices, in prayers to become worthy so that they might return to Israel, the land of their fathers, in their own lifetimes. They carried on these age-old practices while adapting to their living situations with their Muslim neighbors.

One thing that I observed growing up was the notion of enoughness in the behavior of the Jewish people in Sefrou. Actually, even the rich were not spoiled. Most of the rich Jewish people in Sefrou contributed constantly to the support of the Jewish community. This giving was without any obligation or solicitation, it was a natural tendency. It was a relatively small community, of around 2,500 people, so the community was able to manage and provide for one another's needs.

I grew up with that sense of what I call "enoughness," and so it was obvious to me. It was only in the western world, in America and Paris, where I noticed immediately that the attitude of most humans is spoiled. An egg is an egg, whether it is from a fine restaurant for the rich, or prepared simply in the restaurants of the poor. So therefore, I always sought simplicity in the food I ate, in the relations I had with students, friends, and family. And I had enough. Enough means to live simply, and continue my life. That is the environment I grew up in, and so I call it enoughness. That means, in another way, to live life rather than talking about it.

This principle of enoughness helped me to deal with the challenges of this world, wherever I went – that and the two famous sayings of "This too shall pass" and "This also is for the good." These assisted my spiritual upbringing, to this day, as I live my life on this earth.

There were a few central, lived characteristics of behavior of the people of Sefrou, like moderation, modesty, tolerance, patience, and enoughness. These are traits that I maintained all my life, living them naturally, without even needing a word for them. Now I know to name those characteristics that assisted my spiritual balance and sane attitude. They also created a way of tolerance toward everyone I meet. And I am constantly grateful for that. Throughout the years, living in different countries, people I met noticed those traits, like patience. Some of them told me they were surprised in situations when I did not become angry with them. But the practice of these qualities assisted me to be sane in this mad world.

• • •

שָׁנוּ חֲכָמִים: הָרוֹאֶה אֲכְלוּסֵי יִשְׂרָאֵל אוֹמֵר:
בָּרוּךְ חֲכַם הָרָזִים, שֶׁאֵין דַּעְתָּם דּוֹמָה זֶה לָזֶה, וְאֵין פַּרְצוּפֵיהֶן דּוֹמִים זֶה לָזֶה.
בֶּן זוֹמָא רָאָה אֲכְלוּסָא עַל גַּב מַעֲלָה בְּהַר הַבַּיִת, אָמַר: בָּרוּךְ חֲכַם הָרָזִים וּבָרוּךְ שֶׁבָּרָא כָּל אֵלּוּ לְשַׁמְּשֵׁנִי.

הוּא הָיָה אוֹמֵר: כַּמָּה יְגִיעוֹת יָגַע אָדָם הָרִאשׁוֹן עַד שֶׁמָּצָא פַּת לֶחֶם לֶאֱכֹל: חָרַשׁ זָרַע וְקָצַר, וְעָמַר וְדָשׁ וְזָרָה, וּבֵרַר וְטָחַן וְהִרְקִיד, וְלָשׁ וְאָפָה וְאַחַר כָּךְ אָכַל, וַאֲנִי מַשְׁכִּים וּמוֹצֵא כָּל אֵלּוּ מְתֻקָּנִין לְפָנַי.

וְכַמָּה יְגִיעוֹת יָגַע אָדָם הָרִאשׁוֹן עַד שֶׁמָּצָא בֶּגֶד לִלְבֹּשׁ, גָּזַז וְלִבֵּן וְנִפֵּץ, וְטָוָה וְאָרַג, וְאַחַר כָּךְ מָצָא בֶּגֶד לִלְבֹּשׁ, וַאֲנִי מַשְׁכִּים וּמוֹצֵא כָּל אֵלּוּ מְתֻקָּנִין לְפָנַי. כַּמָּה אֻמָּנִיּוֹת שׁוֹקְדוֹת וּבָאוֹת לְפֶתַח בֵּיתִי, וַאֲנִי מַשְׁכִּים וּמוֹצֵא כָּל אֵלּוּ לְפָנַי.
ברכות נח. א.

**Ben Zoma once found himself among a crowd of people
in the Holy Temple Mount in Jerusalem, and he said:
"Blessed be The One who is wise of the secrets, Blessed be The Creator that has created
all these people to serve me." Continuing, he mused aloud:**

**"Think how much Adam had to endure to eat bread?
He plowed, planted, reaped, bound the sheaves, threshed and winnowed, he ground the
ears, he sifted the flour, and then kneaded and baked, and then at last he ate.
Whereas I get up each morning and find all these things done for me.**

**"How much did Adam have to do to obtain clothi collective consciousness ng?
He had to shear sheep, wash the wool, comb it, spin it and weave it. I get up each
morning and find all these things done for me. And all kinds of craftsmen come to the
very door of my house and supply me with whatever I need."**
Babylonian Talmud. Tractate Berachot 58a

**Therefore, the idea is suggested from sources in Judaism that the world was created for me.
And so, every human being should adopt the idea that the world was created for him or her.**

Time and Space – TI-PACE

Once upon a time, there was a girl named "time" and a boy named "space." Time was short and little, and Space was big and tall. One day, Time went for a walk in the forest, and she found a scorpion trail, which she followed until she came to a great tree. She climbed up the tree to its uppermost leaf and came face to face with Mr. Space.

"Hello, Miss Time," he said. And she said, "Hello, Mr. Space." Space then asked Time if she had a little time to talk. And she answered, "I am time – I have all the time in the world!" "Do you have space?" she asked. "I have all the space we could possibly need," he answered.

And they talked and they talked and they talked. First, they spoke with words, about everything imaginable. Then, a very strong wind came up and muffled their speech, and in that moment Time and Space discovered a new language – without words.

They wondered what they should call this new language. They searched and searched for a name, but no name came to them, so they decided to call the new language, "name." The three friends, Time, Space and Name, laughed together at the top of the tree.

An invisible wedding ceremony was now taking place, joining Time and Space together for all eternity. There was a love so great in this marriage between Time and Space that flashes of lightning streaked across the sky. Bright sparks of light and color descended around the lovers.

One little spark spiraled down and landed on the very top of the tree, where it began to build a nest. Time and space could not take their eyes from the little spark, that soon realized that she was being watched, and began to speak a secret language. She spoke, and her words were like the song of a bird to Space and Time.

As she sang and built her nest. Time, Space and Name – the three together – stood witnessing the creation of the world. Thus, the pyramid of being was and is formed.

Waiting for the Messiah

Torn between the real and the imaginary,
      between being and becoming,
      between lucidity and madness,
TALIEL wants to catch a cloud to reach
      the state of the Messiah.

TALIEL is a living symbol – the image of Israel –
      waiting over all the centuries;
Waiting, waiting, waiting for the deliverer,
      the restorer,
Waiting for the Messiah.

TALIEL personifies the collective consciousness
      of the Hebrew people, and by the same token
      he is the interrelation of all the Hebrew letters
      in their eternal effort to return to the dot,
      the source,
To return to the Messiah.

TALIEL demonstrates the passage through
      waiting, hope, youth, old age,
      jumping from cloud to cloud,
But each time he awakens with a shock —
History has taken another turn;
      the Temple destroyed, the destruction of Masada,
      the expulsion from Spain, the Holocaust,
Exile after exile.
And yet – TALIEL waits, ever reaching for
      the ephemeral cloud.
He knows that the restoration of a being
      can happen in the wink of an eye.

And then – suddenly, finally,
Is it true? Can it be
TALIEL has captured that cloud and rides atop it
    like the true King of Israel.
He rides high above the earthly growth pains
    of a struggling planet in its effort to become.

He looks down.
Behold!
TALIEL rides the holy cloud over
    the celestial City of Peace.

Originally Published in Agada – אגדה – Vol 1 #3 5472 (1989)

The Mother Who Loved Her Son

Everyone must read this. Otherwise....

THE SKY IS clear and cloudless blue. Amidst rows of cream-colored suburban houses with white trim, Mercyna, a nurse, pulls her silver Lumina into her driveway after a day of work at the local Mercy hospital.

She wipes her feet on the welcome mat. It depicts a simple country scene: a red barn and cows grazing in a green field. As the clock in the hallways chimes the hour, she puts her groceries on the kitchen counter. She drinks a cup of coffee. She scans over the recent newspaper headlines on her Macbook. She puts potatoes in a pot to boil. She sets a timer. She chops up chicken for dinner.

She hears the front door swing open and thud closed.
 "Hi Shanyon," she calls to her seventeen-year-old son.
 "Did you have a good day at school?"
 "Eh" he responds. The potatoes boil. A quiet, rapid clicking in the background. Shanyon must be texting friends on his cell phone again, as he always seems to be. Clicking stops. Footsteps up the creaky stairs. Mercyna hears his door click shut. She sighs.

The kitchen becomes aromatic with the smell of cooking food.
 "Dinner time," Mercyna calls out to her son.
 "Coming" he calls back. "Just let me finish chatting with Sandi on Facebook."
 A minute later, his lanky form appears in the dining room. Mercyna is already setting the table. The Macbook perches on a nearby counter, beside the usual motley assortment of pens, notepads, and a pile of junk mail she hasn't yet sorted through.

Shanyon sits and looks up at her, his dark blue eyes peering out beneath unkempt, chin-length brown hair. He is tall, but always slouched and his growing body still doesn't seem to have caught up with his large feet. He leans back in his chair.
 Shanyon uncaps a pen and starts sketching lines on his paper napkin. Mercyna smiles. Shanyon loves art. Usually, he draws her cartoons at dinner and his blue eyes sparkle with laughter. Then suddenly, over the last few weeks, she never sees him drawing, and his blue eyes seem out of

focus, like a foggy sky, like he is looking at a faraway sea no one else can see. He rarely looks at her directly.

She passes him the plate of chicken. "Have you heard anything back from Cal Arts?"

He looks down at the napkin. "Dad says that artists all end up as broke losers and that I should go pre-med instead."

"Your father is.." the words sound strained and bitter. Mercyna stops, softens her tone. "Hey, Shan, you can be anything you want. You're a very good artist."

"His new girlfriend said I'm smart and I should become a businessman like dad."

"There are many things your father has gained from being in business, but I think there's more to success than money. Will a Mercedes make you happy, or going to college where you want?"

"It doesn't matter anyway…"

Shanyon looks down at his plate. "Mom, I'm not going to college anyway. I don't want to live anymore. I'm going to kill myself."

Mercyna's hand freezes in mid-air, still holding a spoon-full of mashed potatoes. She drops the spoon.

She takes a breath and looks her son dead on. "Well, if that's what you want to do, that's okay with me. After all, that's reality. That's how it is."

Mercyna stands up matter-of-factly, clicks a button on the Macbook and picks up a sheet of paper and a pen from the counter. "Would you please take that piece of paper there?" she says, handing it to him. "If you are going to kill yourself, you need to plan it out, step by step." She sits back down next to him.

"Okay, step one. How are you going to kill yourself? With a gun? By hanging yourself? Driving the car off a cliff?"

Shanyon gulps perceptibly. "Um, with a gun."

"You're sure? Okay, write it down."

"And what is your motive?" Mercyna asks. "You need to write that down too. Why have you decided to kill yourself?"

"Cause I'm a loser. The new art teacher doesn't think I'm any good. She said that at my skill level, I better apply to the community college, so I won't be disappointed if I don't make it into schools like Pratt or Cal Arts. And I don't know if my SAT scores are even good enough go to business school or pre-med. And the girls think I'm stupid. I probably need a Mercedes for them to even look at me. I asked Kelly to the prom and she laughed in my face. She wrote on her Facebook page that she thinks I'm a creep, and so now everyone at school knows. I asked Shana out and now I think she doesn't even want to be friends with me anymore. And I'm not good at sports like Brad. My teachers think I'm stupid. Everyone thinks I'm stupid. Maybe I am. Maybe I'm not going anywhere anyways. So what's the point? I'll just end up as a loser. I could probably fall into the ocean and no one would even notice anyway."

"Okay. Write that down."

Silence. The sound of pen scratching pure white paper.

"Now, how exactly are you going to shoot yourself?"

"What?"

"This is important. If you shoot yourself in the stomach for example, you could bleed for quite a while before you die and it would be very painful. In the head maybe?"

"Um, yes. In the head."

"Okay, you are planning to shoot yourself in the head. Write it down."

"So, where are you going to kill yourself?" Mercyna asks. "In your room?"

"Yes, I suppose so."

"Good, write it down."

"And after you die?" she asks.

"Huh?"

"A funeral, I suppose. We will need to have a funeral for you. We can't just leave your dead body lying around upstairs."

"Yeah, I guess."

"Write it down then."

"Anything else to add?"

"I don't think so."

As soon, as the pen stops moving, Mercyna leans in close to look at the paper. "Okay, let's look at it, point by point."

"First, the gun. Where are you going to get it? You're too young to buy firearms and I'm not going to buy it for you. That's illegal. Are you going to break into a store and steal it?"

"Um, I guess so."

"Okay, write that down too."

"Now, your plan is to shoot yourself in the head. Let's consider. When you shoot yourself in the head, the blood will spatter all over the wall, and probably little pieces of your brains as well. I'll have to come find you and your face will be all blown off and I'll have to clean off the wall. Plus, your blood will soak the carpet. I'll have to get a new carpet, because every time I see it, I will think of the sight of your face blown off and your eyeballs sticking out from where your face used to be, and I'll have nightmares. Replacing the carpet will probably cost me around eight hundred dollars. I don't imagine that you have eight hundred dollars, do you?"

Shanyon shakes his head, no.

"Probably I will end up paying for it then. You can write that down."

"After that, the police will arrive. They will want to know if I killed you. An ambulance will come. They will bring your dead body outside of the house on a stretcher. All the neighbors will be watching and wonder what happened to you. They'll mark the upstairs as a crime scene."

"Jeff will probably want to come by and want to play basketball, but he can't because you're gone. Tim and Mark and your other friends won't be able to hang out with you on the weekends. They will come by and ask me what happened and I'll have to tell them. All your friends from art class will miss you, but you won't be there to make art with them anymore. Your grandmother will call and she will cry. Your dad will probably never talk to me again, because he thinks I caused you to suicide. All of this will show up in the papers."

Silence.

"Okay, next item on the list: the funeral? Do you know how much a funeral costs?"

"No."

"About $13,000. You don't even have $800 for the carpet, so you won't be paying for it. I don't have that much money saved up, so I'll have to sell the car and borrow the rest and I'll have to take the bus to work from then on. You don't have any other ways of getting $13,000 do you?"

"Dad has money."

"Good idea. If he pays half I will still have to sell the car, but I won't have to take out a loan. Okay, write that down."

"My real concern though," Mercyna continues, "is that the police will think I killed you. They'll arrest me while they try to figure out whether I killed you or not. I'll go to jail and I'll have to get a lawyer. Except that I don't have money for a lawyer, so I'll have to mortgage the house. Hopefully they'll let me come to the funeral. All your friends and family will be there and they will cry because you're dead. After that, I will have to go on trial to prove that I didn't kill you."

"I will write a suicide note so that they know it wasn't you," says Shanyon.

"They won't know if I forged the note. I'll have to prove it in court."

The phone rings, it's mad ringing reverberating through the tension of the room.

Mercyna stands up calmly and answers it "Hello, Preston residence."

She hands Shanyon the phone. "It's for you dear."

"Um… okay." Shanyon picks up the phone hesitantly and walks into the other room. In the distance she can hear the muffled sound of his speaking.

"Hello." *Pause.* "Oh, hi Shana." *Pause.* "Uh, not much. What are you up to?" *Pause.* "Oh, the prom? Yeah, I still want to go with you." *Pause.* "Well, okay, great." *Pause.* "How about 7:00?" *Pause.* "Great. I'll see you then." Click. He hangs up the phone.

Footsteps.

Shanyon reenters the room. He looks around as if unsure what to do next.

"Here, sit back down," his mom says, pushing the pen and paper in front of him again. "Let's continue. Now where were we? Oh, yes, I'm on trial. Hopefully I won't be fired while I'm in court, because I'm not making it into work while I'm in jail and besides everyone will be so horrified that I might have killed my son. They won't want a mother like that working in a hospital."

I'll probably panic because you're dead and I'm in jail and I've been fired and I'm losing my house to pay for legal fees, and all the time I won't be able to get it out of my head, the idea of your face all blown to pieces, looking up at me."

"The other thing you should write down," Mercyna added "is all the things you won't be able to do if you kill yourself. You won't be able to play basketball with your friends, and you'll miss the prom, and you won't be able to go to art school. You will never draw a comic book again or have an art show in New York. You won't ever see your friends again." Mercyna glances up at the clock. It's 6:30.

"You won't get to go on dates or get married. You'll never be able to go surfing in Hawaii or learn how to rock climb, or go on road trips with your friends. You won't get to go to college, and you won't get to go to parties anymore. You'll never learn to fly an airplane or go skydiving, or any of the other things you wanted to do. Write those down too."

"The other thing that we haven't said yet" Mercyna continues "is that if you kill yourself, I will miss you and I will cry myself to sleep every night until the day I die."

Shanyon looks down at the sheet of paper as if he is afraid to look her in the eye. Mercyna's chair-legs squeak alarmingly against the linoleum floor. She stands up and picks up the sheet of paper.

Mercyna crosses her arms and leans back against the counter. Shanyon's eyes scan the paper. The room is so silent that even the sound of their breathing seems loud. He reaches the end of the first page. The paper rustles as he turns it over. "Hey mom."

"Yes."

Shanyon looks up at her, with tears in those beautiful blue eyes that she loves so much. He looks down at the paper then back up at her "Mom, I've decided I don't want to kill myself."

"Oh? How come?" she asks.

"It's just not worth it."

"Well, if you think so."

Shanyon suddenly rushes over to her and hugs his mom tightly. She hugs him and tousles his hair.

"Hey, it's time to go do your homework before it gets late."

"No, mom. I'm going to the prom."

She looks down at him "Oh you are?"

"Shana said she wanted to go with me."

"What time does it start?"

"7:00"

"Well, you better get going then."

"Okay. Can I take the car?"

"Yes."

He hugs her tighter. He stays for a minute, then dashes away on his too-big feet. His footsteps seem lighter.

The second he is out of sight, Mercyna crumples against the counter with her head in her hands. She breathes a huge, frightened sigh. She looks in the mirror. One tear pours down her cheek, and then another. She cleans her face, and returns to the kitchen.

Visions from Nowhere

One Night I Could Not Sleep	**215**
A Dream: The Missing Piece of the Puzzle	**219**
The Vision of the Serpent and the Unicorn	**221**
Admission to the Sacred Chamber	**224**
The Listening Ears	**226**
The Vagabond I	**227**
The Vagabond II	**232**

One Night I Could Not Sleep

ONE NIGHT, I could not sleep. My spirit was awake this night. Various images of the universe flooded my mind, as if they were a performance set up for me. I was totally still, as if my body was caught unprepared, and the objects on my desk were still arranged neatly in their silent order. My hand tried to grasp and write down the flood of images from that two-thousand-year-old village of my childhood.

Images and events of my life passed before the screen of my eyes, like moving pictures, as if they were entertaining me, or reminding me of something ancient I may have forgotten. I saw a past that seems like now, like it is very much here in this place where I dwell. I saw where I am now, and where I will be in some future. I saw events that made me what I am today, in many subtle details. It was as if a timeline was spread before me.

Somewhere within me, I knew it was late at night. Part of me was physically here, and another part was showing me film-like images, which seized and captivated my being. I know I had a red pen. With it, I was writing symbols, letters, and other signs, that were both familiar and new to me, at the same time.

My hand hesitated at times, but it was as if the images were being transmitted to me via some subtle element that moved my hand to write, just write. My hand obeyed the images and wrote and wrote. A million thoughts raced within me. I saw events I was familiar with, and ones that were totally new, ones that it seemed were not yet manifested in this life.

And now I was turning and turning over in my bed, sideways, holding my head with my hands, with my eyes closed, contemplating. And at the same time, I was writing all that I viewed in this seemingly strange dimension of being, using this red pen.

It was as if I was both awake and asleep, both here and there, dancing between the worlds of thought and action. I could feel and sense with all my organism. It was a vivid sense of touching and sensing everything at once, as if I was trying to drink the whole ocean with one gulp. Yet I was also very aware of being in this finite body.

I knew I was in a room, a box with separate walls, protected from the natural elements. I saw through these dense walls all that was happening, beyond all walls. I saw humans caught up in the walls of limitation and paralysis in the face of the events around them, causing self-suffering. I saw them cursing the others for their problems, which they had created themselves. They were trapped inside their own personal prisons, as if slaves to their own thoughts.

My hand was sketching those events in detail, as if my fingers were obliged to write about them. It was as if the events were trying to imprint their essence into my fingers. What am I, a puppet or a puppeteer? What am I doing here? Did I forget my identity? Why all these walls and screeching cries, filling the air, and deafening all my being? Why am I feeling all this, at this late-night hour?

Suddenly there was a noisy silence that faded into a totality of silence. Quiet and calm fell all over me and around me. My hand was still writing, almost in spite of myself. Write, sleep, contemplate, and think. How did I come here to this "new-old" place, at this time in my life?

Suddenly, I saw a beautiful house of light, that seemed elevated in space, suspended on "nothing". Well yes, to be suspended on nothing, that is possible here. Beautiful, old, white trees surrounded the house, and there was a golden fence around it. There were seven stairs leading to the entrance, which was a majestic gate. I stopped there for a moment to contemplate this beauty, that seemed beyond human.

The gate of the house was made of ornate carved wood, designed with gold and purple colors, and there was an aroma coming through it that was very inviting and attractive. For whom was this gate made? And why? I circulated the possibilities in my mind: To open it, or not to open it? Is it the gate of all gates, for all to enter and learn? Is this "**The gate of learning**"? Is it here performing its destiny, to be open and available for those who are hungry to know? And what is there to know?

All my body was like a question mark, being invited to open and discover. Discover what? This was a sacred moment of great wonder for me. I stood before this wondrous gate for an infinite time. As I stood there, I saw the letters I was writing, flying from the paper and becoming alive before me, as if many beings I had created in my thoughts were now manifested and assisting in my great decision; To open the gate, or not to open it?

I saw the dots which formed the letters, and they transformed into lines. And the lines transformed into a million forms, so alive and full, each with a colorful way of moving and being. I thought to myself, if this beauty is outside the gate, what kind of greater beauty awaits me inside the gate? I realized these signs were actually communicating with me HOW to open the gate. I was hypnotized by the beauty of their appearance. And then I received the magic word to write and utter in order to open the gate.

What? How can one open a gate with a word? Just utter a word and the gate opens? While I was contemplating this possibility, suddenly I was inside the gate already, and I bathed in a greater and stronger beauty than I had ever known. What? The gate is the inside, and the inside is the gate? Now that I was here, I walked inside the gates. Stairways and illuminated windows appeared as I went. Then I thought that actually, I myself was the gate, and I was the stairs and the splendid windows. I thought that, actually, I was the gate of the gates.

And who lives in this house? Now that I was here inside, the dots and lines became very clear. They began to form letters, in a language I knew well, and that was easy for me to understand. Are there many rooms in this Mansion? Is it actually a Palace?

Every room had a function, a role to play in the existence of the house. Each time I opened a room, I immediately perceived its purpose in the house. Passing from room to room, I absorbed that knowledge, as if my whole organism recognized it and was familiar with it. It was as if it was made for me. So, I just drank in that knowing, without thinking. It was like a "feast of knowledge and wisdom." I knew I might need it someday, when I woke up again to the everyday world.

All my being was experiencing the eternity of a moment, in "that world" of unity. And with that experience, something was transmitted to me. What I understood then was the way to share with others, so they would see how to open the gates of knowing, and not be afraid of the limitations of "this world," the limited world.

The way is open to dare and be oneself. The way is open to allow the infinite possibilities to manifest with one's thoughts, creating beauty, and new ways of communicating in "this world." In that way, we can bring that inspiration, from "that world" to "this world," from "nowhere" to "somewhere," from invisible inspiration, to a form that is visible to our senses.

So many hands and hearts are reaching to this gate. They are pleading to enter and learn, entering and leaving again. It is like the ladder of Jacob, with beings ascending and descending. Everyone has a role to play in a new dimension of being that is our destiny – a new play of light, of words, letters, and colorful ways of being.

At that very moment, I became aware of my red pen, which was writing all my visions on white paper – and it made me aware once more of where I was. The time was late at night, the place was my body, dwelling here in "this world." I was back to "this self," which has a name and an "identity." But now that I am here behind the gate, I see we are all included in this new and possible reality. Yet many are unaware of it, and are swimming in the "great illusion" of a reality that consists only of matter and the material world.

Well, here I am now. The day comes after the night, and the night comes after the day. What simplicity! And then, there is another day and another night. And we pass here, blind, unaware. We are like sleepwalkers, imagining, giving attention to that which is insignificant. We pass our time attached only to what appears to be, without exploring the interior of the appearance.

Realizing and experiencing all of this, I sensed that had I encountered a great obvious truth, that if were to I utter it, I would put myself in danger. Therefore, I decided to break that indescribable experience down into many small doses, which I spread throughout my teachings.

A Dream: The Missing Piece of the Puzzle

I experienced this dream on Sat, Nov 15, 2003 towards the dawn.
Hebrew date: 20 Heshvan 5764.

I DREAMT THAT a great Painter created an enormous painting made up of many pieces. He was going to open a big exhibit to present all the pieces together. He planned the exhibit as a performance. In it, people would be able to view his way of putting them all together as ONE image.

The Painter dedicated one piece of the painting to me. I received it, and I was invited to be present at the exhibit at a certain day, time and place.

I did not know this Painter. Nor did I know WHY he had given me a piece of it and dedicated his work to me. I saw that on that piece, he had written my name and his dedication.

On the day of the exhibit, many people came to the opening, from all over the world. I was also among those present. The Painter began assembling the pieces in a big wall space. A very peaceful, and suiting music played. He began to assemble all the pieces, one by one, showing how to put them together. But… one was missing.

He turned to the audience and declared that one among the people present was holding the missing piece to complete the whole image – and he asked that they please deliver that piece now. Discreetly, I gave that piece to the person sitting next to me, and I asked her to please pass it on to the painter, so he could complete his work.

She did so. After the exhibit finished, and the whole image was completed, I noticed a certain smile from the Painter, looking at me from his place. And I smiled back. The Painter approached me gently. He said that I had done good to pass on the missing piece via my neighbor. He expressed that it was good I had remained "hidden" from the audience, so that they did not know who was the person holding the missing piece.

The lesson I understood from the dream was to give without being noticed or recognized. In some of his writings, Maimonides identified 8 ways of giving charity. The last and best one, he suggests, is when the giver and receiver are not known to each other. That is probably the hidden meaning of this "dream."

The "dream" reflected the desire to deepen learning of how to put "separated" things together in one place. It showed that one must know how to conceal the obvious, in order to impart knowledge effectively. As a whole, it showed me to recognize the UNITY in everything and in everyone – and to better see the common connector within **all Creation**.

Design by Kohirama

The Vision of the Serpent and the Unicorn

This vision was so vivid and lucid, I was aware of every detail. I was in the mountains, in one of my regular spots of reflective wondering. I sat down on a rock to view the beauty of nature, and as my eyes gazed deeply into "space," I saw the following scene very clearly:

I was standing in a green field, in an ordered and beautiful landscape, near a big lake. On the horizon was a mountain. It was a beautiful place, serene and calm, like a sanctuary. I breathed in the fresh air, and just enjoyed it immensely. I felt free of all the worries of everyday, noisy life.

I approached a huge rock in the midst of this field, and sat there for a moment. Suddenly, from my left side, there came a giant serpent with two heads, appearing as if out of nowhere. And from my right side, there came a beautiful mythical animal, a Unicorn, in all its splendor. They approached one another, as though they had a sacred rendezvous, an appointment in this "**time**" and "**space**" before me.

It was like a dance. The Unicorn came very close to the Serpent with two heads, and gently placed its horn between the two heads. At that very moment, there was a luminous light of all colors, and a sound such as I have never heard before – a thunder with a powerful stillness. A radical and meaningful transformation seemed to be occurring before my very eyes. After some time, when the Unicorn gently removed its head from the Serpent, there stood a beautiful woman, bright and shining with a golden light. She was wearing a purple and golden garment, and holding in her hand an object with light at the end of it. I called it then "**The Golden Edge**."

This graceful, beautiful being, emanating a special quality of light, started walking toward the lake. I felt that she was aware of my presence, but she continued walking. Meanwhile, in the middle of the lake, a spiral staircase appeared from the waters. The golden and silver colors of the stairs were surrounded by a magnificent light. The woman walked on the water, and when she reached the staircase, she began to climb upward, like an angel.

When she arrived at the top of the stairway, she stepped off and landed on the top of the mountain. What I saw was the tip of her stick, which she held in her hands. Then she disappeared at once beyond my vision.

After a "time of waiting," she appeared again with all her majesty. She said to me, "**Walk to the top of the stairway.**" Without any hesitation, I walked, and stood there at the top. Now, I had a beautiful view of the whole area. I sat there, not knowing what would come next.

Suddenly, from the surface of the waters, her face appeared, and I saw her brightness, and then it immediately disappeared again. This happened three times. The third time, she showed her hand above the waters and said: "**Be patient in this life, and know that I am always with you, even when you are not consciously aware of me.**" Then, she disappeared from view.

After another "time of waiting" here at the top of the stairway, I looked to the awesome horizon, and there was the image of my mother, Hannah. I recognized her immediately, with her gentle and benevolent smile. She said to me, "**Be gentle with yourself and all beings**, while you are passing through this life, which is like the "eye of the needle."" And as she said this to me, she raised her hand in a sign I know from my childhood as a blessing. I cried, and as I wiped the salty tears from my face, I held their solidity. I cherished these tears as "**the jewels of realization.**"

The teardrops in my hands turned into three crystals. They were like bright, "solid waters." They were my mother's precious gift from "there." Then, I thought to ask her to appear to me again, and tell me more of what my soul yearns to know. As if she had read my thoughts, she said: "**Read the signs and the symbols of the sacred letters. Increase implementing the law of love toward yourself and all beings who come into orbit around you during this life. And know that I am always with you, My beloved Shemouel.**"

Then a scroll flew from her hand into the air. The holy letters flew forth from the scroll, forming various words and sentences. I read them very clearly, as if I was reading them from a book. I was full of such a curiosity beyond this world.

Then, I looked upon the waters, trying to see the image of my "mother" in its reflections. I blinked my eyes and she reappeared again. She smiled and leaped again from the waters, and I threw a golden cord to her. She held it in her hand, and leapt quickly to where I was standing, at the top of the stairway.

Then she came closer and said to me "I shall always return to BE with You. Call me as you did before." And then she disappeared.

At that very moment, I sensed a deep and profound peace within every cell and bone of my entire being. And I sensed, heard, and saw a great light, circulating and spiraling above the waters. Finally, after some time, the waters stilled, and they appeared again as we see them in this world.

At that moment, I found myself in the same quiet place on the mountain, where I had come to rest and reflect. Returning to my actual time and space, I played the vision back in my memory, and I recorded it right there.

After I finished writing down this meaningful and moving event, the First Thought that came to me was to share with some friends what I had sensed and felt there. I would develop my own special ways to decipher and transmit this with spiritual abundance, I wanted to give back the beauty, serenity and creative power that I received. My direction would be to teach it in a way that is easy and accessible, to those who come to me with an honest heart and a ready soul to receive.

When I walked back to my regular life, it was as if I was floating, and leaping with a special joy that I cannot express with any human word. I was grateful and with a greatly increased appreciation for being alive and healthy to walk in life, holding my constant motto, *"**Keep me sane in the midst of madness.**"* And within me, I added the words, *"**Keep me serene and calm in the midst of the turbulence of this "perplexed world."**"*

I thought that someday when I collected reflections, I would be happy to add this vision among the other writings, to share with my friends, students and other readers, for their inspiration and well-being.

Admission to the Sacred Chamber

BEFORE ADMISSION, I am told first to listen to the voice within, giving exact instructions on how the marriage of Self occurs.

PREPARATION occurs through spiritual attunement with the Higher Self, the knower of all things. This is done with constant observation of one's conduct, without conditions.

NOURISHING the positive aspect of the self, while acknowledging the negative, by fasting properly and opening the **VESSEL** for the influx of the Light, the Peace nothingness, the Palace of splendor, the apex of the triangle, where the opposites are reconciled.

TWO "Masters" guide me to an outer chamber of admission. I sense the invisible presence of Light with my being, through this vehicle, this body, where I reside now.

WALKING in this world, silent worker, to radiate peace and harmony. In my heart, I feel this mighty presence guide me to the ONE.

WITH me in the middle, the two guiding Masters hold my elbows as we leave the chamber. On the horizon, a palace appears. My heart beats faster. "Calm, my son," says the Master on my right. "Peace, my son," says the Master on my left.

BRIGHT light surrounds this place of splendor. The Golden gate is open. Walking between rows of columns, I inhale the scent of roses from both sides. I stand now near a door, carved with symbols familiar to me.

THREE words are said by the Masters, which I repeat. A sign is made by the three of us, and the door opens wide. A draft of fresh air welcomes us.

BEING in the midst of this light, the words flow through my mouth saying, "I am overwhelmed, Beings of Light. My heart is full of gratitude for this gift to be among you. You know my inner thoughts and ideals. I humbly ask to serve the cause of all causes. So shall it be. Let me be the instrument of truth, knowledge, wisdom and peace."

SILENT images now are shown to me. The Presence is awesome. I see the creation and its marvels, and I hear bells – I see in front of me the sound of a scent unknown to me before now.

ONE of the Masters approaches me, and I feel an intensity of light as He comes to me. All the Masters stand in silence.

HE puts his hand on my head and I soar. Rivers of water flow from my eyes, as though the center of my head is compacted with the intensity of his hand's vibration. I close my eyes to savor this experience.

WHEN I open my eyes, I am in the center of a purple triangle of marble. The Masters are standing, four on each side of the triangle, wearing white robes, and this sight is illumined with the beauty and crystalline clarity of the inner being. During this awesome silence, the voice says:

"**THROUGH this silent communication, you learn now the "ANSWER."** Keep it in your heart. You are now admitted to this chamber of the purple triangle of marble. This is your place, and your "work" is empowered now to serve the cause of all causes. Now you will be led to the material plane again, and you must remember the sign of how to recognize us in that world. Peace be with you. The **Shalom of EL** guides you in **THIS WORK**."

NOW I am led by the two Masters, holding me gently, taking me back to the place where we met. "Go with Peace now, silent worker, and Invisible One." As they walk to the horizon, I pray fervently, and come back to this Vessel-body. I feel as though washed with a mighty shower of Light.

IN my chamber, looking at the flame of the candle facing me, I am comforted. I feel Peace in all my organs and limbs, as though all my cells are new, as if I have just been born. It is a feeling I will nourish all the days of my life. I am new, yet as ancient as the One residing in my heart, the "Master of my heart."

A PRAYER of gratitude comes from my mouth. This body is a physical envelope of matter, in which I live. Every cell of it sings a great song of love of life, for all that is. When I walk it is important. Every movement I make is done with full awareness and conscious intent. I am not this body. In essence, I am spirit residing in this vessel now, renewed and re-generated with light and power. All thoughts become clearer, and I see through the density of matter, and keep silent. My reverence for life in this world increases, and the King of my heart sings with infinite joy. I go now in peace, confident, without fear. I am here to work silently and invisibly, for the benefit of all humankind, knowing that I am guided and protected in all my thoughts and actions.

The Listening Ears

I SEE MANY ears sitting in a great valley, listening. So many ears – that have legs and hands and heels. They can hear from every pore of their skin.

The Voice coming from behind the mountains says to the ears sitting in the valley, "HEAR!" They don't ask what, they just want to hear. They are present, ready to hear every single word.

The Voice is vibrant, from the rocks of the mountains, to the hollow space of the valley and the inner eardrums. The sound cannot be heard by the human ears, only by the inner ear. And the Voice speaks again, saying "The days are counted. The earth supports its children in silence and gives abundantly. It gives plenty of food, to feed the physical bodies of humans, the plants on the earth, and all living beings." And so, the earth listens and thanks all who feed her and assist her, even while she is being purified through earthquakes and other upheavals.

And the ears that sit in the valley listen and begin the dance of listening – thousands of ears dancing the dance of silence – hearing the Voice that calls humans to return to their essential being. And the Voice fades and fades beyond the rocks, until it evaporates like a flaming cloud.

The ears walk from the valley to every corner of the earth, to give what they received to all who want to hear. And it will take time until what they heard is digested and understood. In that time, they will learn to act when the time is right, to do things now.

As it is said, "If not now, when?" And I say, "If not now, there is no when!"

This is the time to hear.

Listen........

The Vagabond – I

(Deposé a L'Association Des Auteurs De Film 5, Rue Ballu – Paris, December, 1961)

Note: The Vagabond I and II, were originally written as scripts for a Swedish television program, but could not be produced at the time, because they lacked the technology to express certain elements of the script, such as walking horizontally. Elements that would have been possible with today's technology, were simply not possible at the time.

MOST OF US dream of a form of happiness, a state of true peace and moral serenity. Our age is the era of supreme science, which dominates our existence. Yet still, all forms of happiness are accessible to us – This is in spite of all obstacles, and in spite of the constant psychosis of war, which directs the deeds and acts of humanity.

Somewhere, in spite of everything, I know that there must be a place on this little earth where happiness and serenity rule. Like a wandering gypsy, I set out at random to search for the splendor of that place, conscious of the innumerable difficulties which would spring up in my way. And here is what I found:

A glacial cold hovers over nature. It is winter. I am light-hearted, my soul on holiday. I travel across mountains and valleys. Under my arm, a "red attaché case" contains a razor, a notepad, and a plain black pencil. I follow a serpentine path through the deserted countryside. Night falls, and the freshness of the evening makes me shiver lightly. To warm myself, I give free rein to my fantasy, and I walk, changing my rhythm at each step. I move in a cadence that is joyful, then jerking, etc. My normal vertical movement suddenly changes and I am able to walk horizontally, and then I return to the vertical, and so on, all along my route.

Suddenly, far off, an abandoned village appears, asleep amidst its scattered, shining lights. I find myself in a strange courtyard. A tower, with monumental walls, rises at my right. A stairway with high steps, leads up to the tower. In the courtyard, at the base of the stairway, groups of people are tossing a ball back and forth. On every other step of the stairway, stand impeccably uniformed men.

In contemplating this scene, all sense of time and place is lost. An impressive silence hangs over all, and suddenly, an immense curiosity seizes me. All life seems unreal in this setting.

I am invisible, since I do not belong to this place, but I want to go up to visit this tower as a tourist. Everything is strange. I notice all at once that the ball has reached the guards, and that they are passing it back and forth among themselves, with rigid motions.

Still there is silence, and there is a new surprise: The group of people has disappeared. I approach the stairway with the intention of climbing it, but a triangle of well-built, bare-chested men bar my path.

For an instant, I reassure myself that my "red briefcase" is still under my arm. Face-to-face with this barrier, I do the impossible, I leap into the air. I orient myself in space, and I make a mocking gesture at the guards. I continue to go up, creeping up through the air itself, and finally, I arrive at the last steps.

My curiosity is satisfied. Suddenly, I notice a heavy door of iron, and, as if by magic, it opens before me. A tiny man shows me the way. He is charming, but with a diabolical smile on his lips.

First, I go by a dressing room that is very clean; one would think that no one ever used it. Leaving there, miraculously, I find myself in a marvelous drawing room, where everything is of an extraordinary and unimaginable richness. The walls are of varicolored marble. Gigantic statues adorn the corners of the room. Oriental tapestries, in rich shades of warm red, introduce a divine harmony.

Amazed by such unheard-of splendor, I stay frozen in place. I forget the presence of the little man, and not a word is exchanged between us. All at once, I realize that I am outside, and in spite of myself, I continue on my way. A simple rustic countryside, reflecting poverty, appears before me. Some wooden huts sit in a triangle, with expressionless faces at their windows. I examine these distant faces, and I see a glimmer of expectation in their eyes. I try to get into the hovels, but there is no door, no stairway, no ladder, and no elevator. There is no way to enter.

I signal to the people, but it appears that I am invisible, since I obtain no response. All the same, I again try to enter. I am tenacious, trying to get in at any cost. Finally, my strong effort leads me to find a hole, but only a four-footed creature could crawl through it.

What can I do? I stoop to enter it. Aware that I may never be able to leave, I feel as if I'm buried alive. I crawl along, and suddenly a glimmer of light appears, and I feel the hope of standing on my two legs again. Finding myself on the inside of a hut, I put down my "red briefcase" without realizing it. I want to be able to freely admire the beauty which is revealed before my eyes.

Evidently, I am still invisible. Around me, I notice some couples of a rare beauty, whose expressions reflect happiness itself. The extreme poverty of this place, alongside the gleam of the spirits of these unimaginable creatures, appears a paradox.

I approach one of the windows. There too, everything is transformed. The countryside is of a beauty I have never seen before, and all at once, I feel as if I have been carried to paradise itself.

These people exchange not a word. Their gestures and their expressions say enough about them. In their faces one reads the moral serenity of people who are fulfilled. This atmosphere of calm and of silence, makes me tremble. Unconsciously, my enthusiasm makes me feel a pang of jealousy toward these totally fearless beings.

This mystery penetrates me, and I let myself go. In spite of myself, I am carried away with wonder and admiration. As if in a dream, I suddenly find myself once again in the marvelous drawing room. I do not know how I left those mysterious and fantastic huts.

I cross the drawing room to leave it, and I pass by the dressing room. After I have passed through the great iron door, it closes magically behind me. On the steps of the stairway, the guards are still there, impassible.

I try to pass, but the first guard stops me. I do not insist, but fantasy awakens in me once again. I leap into the air and from empty space, I grab something that resembles an umbrella. I descend to the earth, calmly, like a parachutist. This seems normal to me, for I have lost my sense of reality. I land calmly, naturally, as if nothing out of the ordinary has happened to me.

Within me, something new has been born, created by the unforgettable sensation aroused by the place I have just visited. Joy rules in me, and a sweet feeling of inner peace guides my joyful steps. All at once, from empty space, an immense silhouette springs forth, three times as large as I am. Its face seems familiar to me. I shiver, for I fear this apparition which stares at me. Suddenly, there is nothing more. Everything has disappeared.

I continue along a few steps, and I realize that I have forgotten "my red briefcase." I retrace my steps, and a frenzied hurry takes hold of me. I walk vertically, horizontally, vertically. I think I am lost, when in the middle of my path, I see a gigantic door, huge and monumental, encrusted with leather and precious gems in a thousand colors. It is a splendid spectacle which appears before my eyes. I approach the door, which seems impossible to open.

I face the door. I lift my right foot, and I push lightly. Miraculously, the door swings open gently, slowly. A grandiose spectacle welcomes me. On a highway, an immense crowd lines up on either side of the road, roaring and chanting. This seems like a ceremony for someone of great importance.

Stately music bursts forth and floods out from everywhere. I become aware of myself, and I feel ridiculous in my much-patched coat, and yet, this welcome seems intended for me. I advance timidly in my ridiculous coat, thinking, "What is this for? Me? Was this reception prepared for me? Who am I? What have I done? Who is this celebration for, this tumult?"

I come forward, slowly, timidly. I take a few more steps, and I begin to be convinced that all this has been prepared for me, for there is no one else near me. A divine voice rises out of space and says to me: "Lift up your head! Throw your chest out proudly! It is true, all this has been prepared for you. Courage… courage…courage…" (The voice fades away slowly).

This voice encourages me, it gives me back my confidence. I throw my chest forward, and assume at last the gait of someone of importance. I pretend to be walking with a cane, although I have none. I lift my hand into space, and grasp a real cane. I salute the crowd, always continuing to walk along. I pretend to doff my hat. My hand touches my head, and I realize that there is a real hat on it.

As if by enchantment, my rags are transformed into an elegant suit. I look at myself and I am amazed. Suddenly, a deathly silence falls. No more noise, no more music, no more crowd. All the lights have vanished.

I find myself again in my rags, my shoes ripped. A very loud, mocking voice, hurls forth a strident laugh. Along the road, two rows of trees thrust toward the sky, their clipped black branches stripped bare, pointed and sinister.

I am stupefied before this landscape. All the sadness of the world engulfs me. "My red briefcase?" I must get it back. I continue on my way. All at once, I hear the noise of a bomb exploding. It seems like the end of the world.

I look around me, and I see machines of war, weapons of all sorts. Fuses ready to blow appear on all sides. I ready myself for death, as I dodge these agents of death. I wait. I have no idea how much time goes by, but what I am waiting for happens. A bomb explodes close to me. Shaken by the explosion, I think I am dead.

But now, I keep on breathing, and looking into the darkness. I see some matches arranged in pyramids, which are dancing the glory of the devil. I no longer know what to expect, but I continue on my way. Finally, I see the tower and I approach it. On the stairs, the guards are still frozen. This time, without consulting them, I jump vertically to the height of the first guard. I land on the step behind him, and then I do the same with each guard, until I get all the way to the top of the stairs. I pass the dressing room, the drawing room, and the huts. I take my red briefcase.

Obsessed, I come out again, and at last I want to go home. Alas, I must pass through a narrow, winding pathway. I whistle to drive away my fears. Suddenly, on the trunk of a tree, there appears a rooster with an enormous red comb, proud and strong. He is splendid, but I am consumed with fear.

Immobile, I seem transformed into a statue.

He beats his wings with a majestic grandeur, in a nervous rhythm. The noise of the beating of his wings spreads through the silence and seems to threaten my life. My face freezes. My hands search along my body for a hiding place. (Here the camera will cut from the expression of the face, to the head of the cock, to his wings, to the hands of the man, and to the cock's feet with their long, menacing talons).

At a certain point, I feel brave, and I make a more menacing expression, and stare fixedly at the cock. Then, from one side I hear the happy, romantic clucking of the hen, who is sitting on another little tree trunk. She seems happy about the exhibition of the strength and ferocity of the rooster.

The cock jumps into the air and lands again on his tree trunk, more threatening than ever. Remaining still, I look at the cock's smallest movements fixedly. I move, as if in order to hypnotize him, by raising my hands and lowering them with great calm.

The cock becomes smaller and smaller, until he disappears altogether. I breathe freely at last. I hear the tearful clucking of the disappointed hen. After the cruel tension of this encounter, I continue my journey toward the staircase.

The guard keeps me from going down. I lift my hand and put it on his shoulder. He disappears, and so in the same fashion do all the guards. When I get to the bottom, I contemplate the sky, spangled with shimmering stars.

I continue on my way with light and joyful steps, walking over mountains and through valleys. A sweet, rhythmic, cadenced music guides my horizontal and vertical wanderings.

I mingle with the light of the stars. My face appears in the distance, with dazed eyes which seem to demand something. A voice says, "Once upon a time."

The Vagabond – II

(Deposé a L'Association Des Auteurs De Film 5, Rue Ballu – Paris, December, 1961)

Note: The Vagabond I and II, were originally written as scripts for a Swedish television program, but could not be produced at the time, because they lacked the technology to express certain elements of the script, such as walking horizontally. Elements that would have been possible with today's technology, were simply not possible at the time.

HE HAS COME to rest awhile on a bench in the garden, to read his paper. (You first see his feet, his shoes, and the paper that hides him). After a moment of relaxation, he feels himself pulled by some cords, now invisible, now visible. There are four little birds playing with a thread which is caught on the man. He is pulled into the air, startled, right up to the treetops, and then he is dropped. The birds fly off, and he falls into a deep lake. He doesn't know how to swim. He discovers the beauty of this universe of little fish, which play about him, and he discovers also that there are men in the water, who are not at all different from those on the earth. He does not know that he has drowned, and that actually he is dead. He begins to adjust to his surroundings, and he falls into a light sleep.

There is a draft at his back. He gets up to move, and he finds himself in a palace of white marble, glistening like water. He doesn't know where he is. Pillars surround him on all sides, like a great forest, and it seems to him that these are the pillars which support the palace.

He tries to climb up on one pillar, but he cannot. He looks up. The sky seems adorned with little black dots. He flies up, gently, until he gets to the top of a pillar. He stands up to put his foot on another pillar, and he starts to walk along on the pillars. They begin to move in all directions, making a sound like the music of shattered violins.

He jumps from one pillar to another. A human voice cries out. The pillars stop. He stops, his feet spread between two pillars that seem to be moving apart from each other.

His face convulses, and his head begins to unscrew itself from his neck. He leaps to a nearby pillar. He lifts his hands, preparing for another leap, but this time he lands with his hands on two other pillars. His body and legs remain on two other pillars. The cry grows louder.

"Where are you? Come back to earth, and describe your vision to men." He reunites his body, as the pillars start to dance. He wants to return to the other side, and he feels something, like a sweet and firm caress, which moves over his body. It is a little insect, which is strolling gently over him.

Unmoving, he looks at the strolling insect, as if paralyzed. He cannot move any part of his body. The little creature dominates him. Now a little ballet of insects begins on his body. Drums and bells accompany the whispering of their wings, which kiss one another.

He wants very much to wake up, but knowing the wickedness of men on the earth, he prefers to let these darling little animals dance and jump on him. They do not harm him; they only feel like strange pricks on his body.

He wants to fly away on the pillars and dance, but he stays immobile, without strength, without will. Suddenly a huge hand appears in space, moves toward him, and becomes smaller. The little insects fly off toward the powerful hand, as if toward a magnet.

Now, he finds himself standing on the solid branch of a tree. He cries, and the teardrops dampen him. Some white pigeons fly by. He calms himself and contemplates them. He notices that the teardrops have different colors, and the pigeons play with them, and take on their colors.

Some men and women pass, taking on the colors of the drops which touch them. The women's gowns are of livelier colors than the clothes of the men. Then, little by little, they all transform into colored pigeons. He wonders why he too has not been changed into a pigeon.

At this moment, a blue eagle flies over him. He lifts his head to look at it. Suddenly, the bird seizes him with its talons. His jacket begins to split, but he is lifted up, dragged off, and dropped over a turbulent sea. He does not know how to swim, and fights with all his might to resist. Far off, he sees a large boat, which is coming toward him. He cries out. A rope is thrown out to him, and he is helped into the boat. He is made to understand through gestures, that they wish to see his papers, for he does not understand the language of the men. He is given something to eat, and shown to a cabin furnished with a bed.

On his awakening, he is shown around the boat. He laughs before each new discovery, and thinks himself invisible. Suddenly, he leaves these places and moves toward the unknown. He finds himself in a desert, going toward a black tree planted on the horizon. A terrible wind whistles. From this wind rises a silhouette, half-man, half-camel. The wind stops. Across from him, he sees this strange majestic being pinned down in the sand.

A moment of silence . . . He can think of nothing to say to it. He makes some gestures and some grimaces, trying to find some means of communication with the creature. Receiving no response, he steps back, watching the monster disappear. He rubs his eyes at this disappearance.

Now, he sees machines and planes that are made to conquer space. The monster reappears beside him, and every time it stretches its hand toward one of these planes, the plane flies off. The monster moves its hand toward the man, who then falls asleep.

He awakens, stretched out in a very green meadow. The voices of children cry out, running after each other. The children line up in two groups, face to face, with a great deal of noise. One young child, a redhead with blue eyes, lifts his hands for silence. He begins his speech.

"Do you know who we are? We are the children of the earth, burned by the ambitions of an adult war; we have been victimized by human lack of understanding. Now we are thousands of miles from the earth. By the sacred order of our power, we are going to come back to earth today, and be born in different countries, with the knowledge that in thirty years, we will try to take power in each of these countries, and stop the menace of war which haunts the adults."

The redhead holds up a little silver baton. An invisible drum taps out a sharp and jolting rhythm, and at every beat, a child flies off into space, until the redhead alone remains.

The man approaches the redhead to speak to him, and the child jumps into his arms, pointing with his baton in the direction of departure. The two want to come back to earth to see what the children have accomplished ahead of them.

They march invisibly, holding each other by the hand, and they visit the places where the children have been born. Then, they come to a school.

The man finds himself facing a class of noisy children and tries to calm them. When the bell for recess rings, the man swoons. Opening his eyes, he sees some people dressed in white, and he falls back to sleep.

At the moment of the visit to the children's birthplaces, the screen flashes shots of births in different places in the world, like stars shining, to be born for a new world.

Quotes

Sparks from a Dancing Dot   237

Teaching Nuggets   243

Words from Samuel   247

Sparks from a Dancing Dot

SPARKS FROM A Dancing Dot represents memorable sayings from Samuel over the years, collected from classes, lectures, discussions, and interviews.

THE IMPORTANCE OF BEING THERE

We are living in a time of very rapid change, when evolution of thought and consciousness is proceeding by leaps and bounds. There are so many avenues open to us, so many voices competing for our attention, that we are sometimes overcome by confusion.

To meet and to transcend this confusion, we must increase our awareness. The artist considers this his or her chief work – not only for his or her own benefit, but also for the benefit of others – to eliminate confusion and to transmit the simple messages of the heart.

We respond with laughter and sometimes tears – the higher emotions lift us beyond the cares of daily life, to an experience of oneness with ourselves and with life.

If the artist has tapped the source of imagination, he or she gives us a glimpse of something very essential. When we have a look at the essence of another, we experience our own essence. There is no separation, there is only constant reflection in the mirror of the Self. In this spirit of community, we invite you to participate in the journey from matter to spirit – if it does matter to you.

ATTRACTIVE POWER OF THOUGHT

Once you begin to nourish a thought about something, you'll be amazed how everything happens for you. You attract what you are and what you look for. If you are in a negative state of mind, you attract negative conditions. If you choose to be in a place, you submit yourself to that atmosphere.

There are people who ask, "What's happening?" There are those who wonder how it is happening. And there are those who make things happen.

BALANCE

Finding one's inner balance is a process analogous to the movement of a pendulum. One's point of view swings from that of ego to the larger reality, from the realm of space to the realm of time, and then back again. Gradually, as we develop and mature, the swings become less extreme, the reactions and counter-reactions less violent, and one is able to look out from one's center.

COMPLAINING

If we understand ourselves as finite beings, we suffer and complain. But if we understand ourselves as infinite beings, we can overcome suffering and be happy.

DEATH/LIFE
If we could all arrange to be told by some medical specialist that we were to die in six months, we might finally begin to live.

DISCRETION
Roots grow when they are hidden beneath the earth and watered in the dark. Do not speak of your inner work, but let it be known by its fruits – your actions.

ENEMIES
Be grateful to your enemies for they can help you in a way your friends cannot. You cannot make peace with a friend, but only with an enemy. The enemy, not the friend, provides the battleground for transformation.

FLEETING MOMENTS
Moments are like birds; they pass quickly and soundlessly and are gone. If you do not attend to what is happening, when it is happening, you will have missed it forever. There are no second chances.

FOLLOWING THE PATH
There is a Sufi saying that the dogs can bark, but the caravan moves on. Once you know something, you shouldn't care what others think or say about you. Once you know you have a mission or a path, you have a star, and you soar to eternity.

GENIUS
Genius is to know what you do best and to use it.

GIVING
Anything given from a sense of obligation is not a true gift. To give from a sense of obligation is nothing more than the repayment of a debt. True gifts are given with conviction, from the heart, and without thought of recompense or gratitude. The highest form of charity is giving anonymously to an unknown recipient.

GOOD THOUGHTS
One good thought, well-formed and heartfelt, can clear a space clogged with negative and undisciplined mental creations. One must make a constant effort to choose the positive thoughts from the motley collection that rises to the surface of the mind.

HINDSIGHT
Life must be lived by looking forward, even though it often can be understood only by looking backward.

INITIATION
When a man can swallow his inner nothingness – a feat as difficult as a snake swallowing his own tail and turning himself inside out – then he can see the light of the infinite.

INNER TRANSFORMATION
To transform oneself, one must work alone and invisibly. One can be given tools from an outside source, but one must take them inside and work on the mechanism of the machine singlehandedly, and without an instruction manual.

INTELLECT
Intellect is one of the guardians that keeps us sane. If we abuse it, we'll become insane, if we use it properly, it is a great ally.

INVISIBILITY
Great alchemists have erased their personalities. This is very rare in a world where everyone wants

credit for what is done. To see and not to be seen, to work in humility, this is the invisibility. Instinct is your guide in the invisible realm.

KNOWLEDGE

Spiritual knowledge is always available. It is not locked away in mountain strongholds, or preserved on crumbling scrolls, in buried urns. It exists in our midst... but in disguise. Only those who are ready to receive the teachings can see through the innocent words and everyday events that clothe them. Those who are not ready, who might put their knowledge to ill use, pass by real teachings in search of illusive secrets, never recognizing the mystery in the ordinary.

KNOWLEDGE REALIZED

Knowledge, no matter how esoteric or precious, is of only theoretical interest until it is manifest in action.

LONELINESS

When you are lonely, remember the ocean. Imagine yourself a drop in that vast expanse of seawater. The drop, from its limited point of view, seems an entity quite unto itself, but from a higher vantage point, it is seen to be part of an invisible whole. How can you presume to think that you are separate and alone, when you are made of the same substance that makes up the entire universe? Someday, when you are older and wiser, you will realize that your sense of separation is only an illusion.

LOVE

If humanity needs to be told, "love thy neighbor as thyself," then it is a very low level of civilization. This shouldn't have to be said; it should be lived naturally. Around ones who are living it, you feel good.

MASK

A mask can mean many things. It may be thought of as a vessel that holds light, or the vibration of dots captured in matter, or the appearance connected with the essence, or as a tool for the creation of specific dramatic effects, or as an automatic depository for aspects of ourselves we don't understand, or as an edge, or as a layer of an onion. Every time you take off one mask, there is another.

A mask is a tool for communicating. It veils or unveils. A mask is a channel for allowing expression to come out from within.

MEDITATION

Meditation is both active and passive. For mime, you have to be in a state of active meditation. Relaxation, clear thoughts, stillness, breathing – you have to will all these. Meditation is the state of being the dot in the center of the circle.

MISTAKES

Mistakes are useful, for one can learn from them. Just be sure you make new mistakes.

MONEY

Money really belongs to no one. It is a means of action that passes from person to person. We should use it in accordance with our vision of universal progress. Until we conquer our desires for money, power, and sex, there is little chance for improvement in humanity's lot.

NATURE

If you study nature well, you will have no need for books. You will learn at least one important lesson: nature moves in circles. As the stream becomes the ocean, so does the ocean become the stream. Rain falls, the rivers gather their waters, and flow to the sea. The sun draws the seawater up to the sky, clouds form, and the rain falls once more. Every point in the circle is both an end and a beginning.

If you can allow everything to flow through you in a circular motion, you will come to no harm in this world.

NOTHINGNESS

Children are nothing. When they fall, they are nothing. If you are nothing, you don't have the consciousness of tension, and you don't resist gravity. Only when you realize this nothingness, can you do something.

PARADOX (ONE OF MANY)

That which appears foolish may be a reflection of wisdom, and that which appears wise may well be foolish.

PEACE

Peace is not the absence of chaos. It is a state of being, active, not passive, a space which, once visited, calls you forever to return. Sometimes you can find peace in an encounter with a friend, for peace is another face of love.

RELIGION OF TIME

Man can learn to live in time, rather than in space. He can learn to revere time and to see each moment as a gift, rich with treasures, like a cache of multi-colored jewels. A true religion can teach man how to leap from space into time, where God is found. True religions recognize that our contacts with divinity take place not in space, in cathedrals and sanctuaries, but in moments of transcendent experience, that carry us beyond space and time as well. To live in time is to live in infinity.

Rx FOR CONSTIPATION

When you know something, you have to give it away. If you keep it, you become constipated.

SACRIFICES

Giving up something to which one is attached is useless, unless the desire for it is drained from one's heart. Only the inner sacrifice, the voluntary relinquishing of one's dearest hopes and dreams, can bring about transformation. Transformation involves the in-corp-oration of knowledge. Bring knowledge into the body. To make room for it, one must clear out the old ideas and habits that clutter up the inner self. One must have a kind of garage sale of the psyche.

SEEING GHOSTS

If you know and accept yourself, including those parts you would prefer to be rid of, you will no longer project negative qualities onto others. Then you will not see the ghosts of your past in the faces of your friends and family.

SEEING THE POSITIVE

Say something positive to everyone in every situation. See something positive in every situation. After all, the half-empty glass is also half full.

Habitually think, 'It might work." Appoint yourself president of the "Why Not?" Club.

Practice positive expectations. Think, "I expect something new and beneficial will happen today."

All these efforts will build enthusiasm, and enthusiasm can put your life in orbit. Webster's dictionary describes the word enthusiasm as follows: En—inspired, Theos—God, Divine, En-theos—Inspired by the Divine.

SELFISHNESS

If you live only for yourself, you will never grow beyond your individual limits. But if you live for those around you, you will attain the full stature of a man.

SHABBAT

Six days a week, we try to dominate the world. On the seventh day we should try to dominate ourselves. Our bodies belong to the world, but our souls belong to someone else. The seventh day is for the soul, and it must not be viewed as an interruption in our worldly work, but as a climax of the week. We should not work, nor think nor talk of work, on Shabbat, but take a blessed rest. And unlike labor which is a craft, that is an art, requiring the accord of body, mind, and spirit.

SILENCE

The first law is to respect silence. You respect silence if you value your words. It has nothing to do with repressing your feelings. Words that come before realization are not important. But words that come after realization are very profound.

Silence, the "Golden Bit," is the fence of wisdom. When you know, you bite the Golden Bit.

SPARKS

When we are born, the angels take from us the light of knowledge, leaving only a spark. But that tiny spark is enough to kindle a fire, if, in our wanderings through the earth, we meet a person, or hear a tune, or read some words, in which we recognize something faintly familiar, a memory from another time and place. We are always longing for something, but what we really long for is no thing, it is that lost light. We are born into the world of matter so that we can find the knowledge that was once ours.

SPIRIT AND MATTER

You will have achieved a true union of spirit and matter, when your head is in the heavens and your two feet are planted firmly on the ground.

SPONTANEITY AND WISDOM

It is possible to have a marriage, a unity, between the wisdom that comes from the experience of many difficult and painful lessons, and the spontaneity and passion of youth – but it is very rare. Youth is busy with passion. The excitement of the wise man is enlarged from the excitement of youth.

Enlarge your idea of spontaneity. Spontaneity can be directed. So can passion, especially by the artist.

STRESS

The essence of an olive is contained in its oil. Press the olive, and the oil emerges. Subject a man to stress and his essence will emerge.

STUDENT-TEACHER RELATIONSHIP

Both teacher and student know; one remembers, and one has forgotten. When they get together, they remind one another. If the student puts the teacher on a pedestal, the flow of teaching stops. However eager the student is to learn, just as eager is the teacher to teach.

The teacher is a reflection of you, that expresses the things you do not dare express. If that reflection makes you angry, you are only angry at yourself. When you accept the reflection of yourself totally, then you have a teacher. Your heart opens, and everything is yours to be learned. The ideal student is the total reflection of the teacher.

When you evolve with a teacher who doesn't tell you what to do, you have to ask yourself the questions. This is how the genuine artist learns to think, live and work.

SUFFERING
Awareness is like soap – it always seems to slip from your hands. Suffering brings more feeling and more awareness. Pain is the signal of life. To escape suffering is to not want to be aware. Personal suffering is always ego. With empathy, you go beyond your personal suffering. If you are not ready to do this, you are not yet ready to be a student.

TALENT
Everyone is talented. Talent is the ability to create and live harmoniously, in your environment, with your friends. Talent is like a pearl; you have to clean up all the green seaweed before it shines, before you know you are a pearl.

If an art you are pursuing bores you, it is likely you do not have a talent for it. But, if you can transcend boredom, you discover talent.

THEORY INTO PRACTICE
The visible and invisible parts of you need to be fed in a balanced way. We can all be "with the flow," but it has to manifest, to be brought from the world of theory to the world of practice. When it comes to doing, we stumble. But it's not the work of one day, it's the work of an eternity. If something is perishable, don't gaze at it. All that is eternal, swim into it.

THINKING BEFORE SPEAKING
Before one word passes our lips, we should ask ourselves three questions about that which we intend to say:

> Is it true?
> Is it necessary?
> Is it kind?

If we answer "no" to any of these questions, we should remain silent, for we have nothing of value to say.

USES OF ADVERSITY
Without difficulty there is no joy. Difficulties should be seen as opportunities for growth, not as limitations that prevent growth.

WISDOM
Wisdom is knowledge properly applied to the affairs of the world. It is spiritual passion. King Solomon knew this, but few rulers of men have followed his example.

Teaching Nuggets

Quotes by Samuel Avital

THESE NUGGETS COME from various teachings of Samuel throughout the BodySpeak™ Mime workshops and the Gathering of the Sparks Kabbalah seminars. They came about as answers to questions, or were inspired by students' practice. These come from various knowledgeable sources, but are mostly based on immediate human situations and behaviors.

And if you want more nuggets, there are two beautiful books in the bible that do just that: Mishlei/Proverbs and Kohelet/Ecclesiastes. When one studies these two books, one acquires certain wisdom and the way to apply it. There are many gems of wisdom in those sources for you to explore.

"You can't eat the whole elephant
with one bite,
You can't drink the whole ocean
with one gulp."

"Whatever you want in life,
Give it first."

<u>Remember, 99.9% preparation
and only 1% realization.</u>
But you have to be constantly present,
in order to realize it.
Otherwise, it will pass you by,
because you were not there;
You were absent to feel it
notice it and appreciate it.

"Be Still Like a Mountain
and Alert Like a Cat."

"The Principle we seek is:
Minimum Movement,
Maximum Expression."

"If we don't know separation,
we can't know unity."

"Live so that no one can define you."

"There is no escape from yourself."

"Serve the idea."

"Within the limit,
you find the unlimited."

"Boredom is an ally of
concentration and clarity."

"When you say it's impossible,
that's a disease."

"You begin to live
when you come to your center."

"In such a mad world,
we have to be conscious fools."

"Decompose in order to recompose. Give place and time to every movement. Every action has intrinsic importance."

"Live your imagination = IN sanity."

"Consciously go beyond your limit. Build bridges to the limitless."

"Pain is the process of becoming aware."

"Inhale importance,
exhale insignificance."

"Shakespeare said
'To be or not to be, that is the question.'
I say "To be AND not to be,
and that is the quest."

"When you say "I have time,"
you are lying,
because actually Time has you."

"Most people create problems
where they don't exist."

"To be inspired
is just to breathe properly."

"Yes, yes, the world is an illusion.
But in it, there is truth to be found."

Do you "Have a Life"?
Or are you life itself?

"I swear to do the possible
and only the possible."

"Knowing without application
is not knowing."
"Be detached but not indifferent."

"When people see someone who is sad, they say "Oh feel better, oh you are
okay, cheer up,"
and that makes it worse.
If you see someone who is sad,
go be sad with them.
You will find in no time,
you both burst into laughter."

"If you want
things in your life to change,
you have to change things in your life."

"We are the stamp
of that which created us."

"See and hear
not only with your eyes and ears."

"Everything in motion is still,
and everything still is in motion."

"When in motion, rest in stillness."

"The center of silence
is where motion and stillness are one."

"You can't forget the technique, until the technique is there in the first place."

"You are both the rider, and the horse."

"If you're not totally in transit while in transit,
you create accidents."

"Experts are the ultimate ignorants."

"Transition – a state that is being taken for
granted everywhere."

"Between balance and imbalance
is a void."

"It is better to have
the opposition of a wise man,
than the support of a fool."

"You can't recognize the light,
unless you are the light."

"Take" time to stop and consider
in order to Respond, rather than React
to all life events."

"Obvious Movements
are the secret of longevity
OMSOL."

No Because
If love depends on some cause,
it will not last.
But if one loves
and there is NO BECAUSE,
that is a good sign that it will last.

"The more you pursue happiness,
the more it goes away from you."

People say "I am hungry." That is a lie.
The I AM is never hungry.
The stomach is the one who is hungry.

"Anything that you need to do – Do it now.
Don't postpone your life."

"You must squeeze the grape
in order to get some wine.
Wine and alcohol are also called spirits.
So it is with us, we must be squeezed through
our suffering in life
in order for our spirits to develop,
to get some juice."

"Courage is a cloak you wear
again and again
until every cell in your body
is named Courage."

"Words that come before realization
are unimportant, empty.
Words that come after realization
are gold."

"What you are looking for
is also looking for you."

Saying "I love you" is a lie. Because in that
sentence, I am here and you are there, and
love is between. So there is separation.

When you say "I love you," it's a lie. Why?
Because you are just saying it, it's not you.
You are love itself actually.

"Do you live to eat, or eat to live?"

"People want to find answers,
Instead, we seek to deepen the questions."

"Make New Mistakes.
People are afraid of making mistakes.
Mistakes are useful,
for one can learn from them.
Just be sure you make new mistakes, please."

"If it isn't challenging,
it isn't interesting."

"Do you drive your car,
or do you let your car drive you?
If you let your car drive you,
it will be a disaster.
So you must direct yourself in life."

"If you are completely here,
fulfilling this moment,
then the next one will already be
prepared for."

"Life is now in session.
Are you present?"

"Enlightenment
is taking nothing for granted."

"Movement is the infinite,
directing the finite."

Enjoy your sadness
"If you are sad, enjoy it.
It is a unique experience in life,
and a message too.
It enriches your emotional intelligence."

"Produce more, and consume less."
"Joy is not the lack of sadness.
Health is not the lack of disease.
Silence is not the lack of sound."

"We have been given the power of thought,
but we mostly use it negatively.
The majority of thoughts
are negative or nonsense.
Instead, try thinking only positive
thoughts for a day."

Write Your Own Script
Be the writer, director, and lead actor
in your own life.
Write your own script,
don't let others write it for you.

Three Gates of Words
In my tradition, it is said that before one word
passes our lips, we should ask ourselves three
questions about that which we intend to say:

Is it true?
Is it necessary?
Is it kind?

If we answer "no" to any of these questions,
we should remain silent, for we have nothing
of value to say.

"LIFE IS 99% PREPARATION
AND 1% INSPIRATION."

"DO EVERYTHING AS IF FOR THE FIRST AND
LAST TIME"

Words from Samuel

ABOUT SILENCE

SILENCE IS NOT merely the absence of sound, or noise, it is a state of being at the edge of listening to nothing and something. Silence is not an absence of words; it is a fullness of being. Health is not an absence of dis-ease, it is a state of homeostasis.

Noise and silence have something in a common. Noise is discordant, jarring, unnatural, and produced by us, but is not a part of us. Noise masks the silence but never silences it. Noise also rises and falls, always changes.

Silence is harmonious, soothing, not produced by us, yet pervading our being. Silence is continual, coming forth whenever noise subsides.

When you are in the forest and keep still, it may at first seem hushed. But as the noise in our head diminishes, you hear the forest humming, throbbing with life, and orchestrating a symphony of symbiosis.

Eventually, you may even hear the background silence of your mind, wherein all of your questions arise and are resolved. The inner space is a place where you can listen to that soft voice, a "place" not always quiet, but where silence reigns supreme.

BE YOURSELF

The most difficult and easy thing to do, was, and still is, to BE YOURSELF. This anti-civilization is built and set so that you will never KNOW who you really are. Most educational systems are built in such a way to prevent you from going there, to YOUR BEAUTIFUL SELF. You must really DARE to be who you really want to be and become, right here and now, and not allow any "professors" or "experts," or any external authority, to write your life script for you, or to tell you who you are.

One of the ways to assist you in this essential journey toward yourself is, to stop "explaining" and "talking about it." BE YOUR OWN PERSON and THE BEING YOU WERE MEANT TO BE IN THE BEGINNING. Stop complaining and comparing yourself with any one at all, and use less words in all your communications. You MUST stay focused on your self-development, the way you sense it in your gut.

"This only one of the GATES TO ENTER THAT SPLENDEUR OF YOUR REAL BEING, the other gates you will discover as you advance in this journey toward your true and real being – your sovereign being. Bon courage, my friend."

CONNECTION

Connection is desire. Connection is intimacy.
Connecting is being and becoming.

Connection is getting "into me.
Connection is inhaling and exhaling each other.

Connection is patience.
Connection is having and being each other, with each other, as ONE.

Connection is persistence.
Connection is being important and insignificant with each other.

Connection is a ritual.
Connection is being "here" and "there" at this very moment with each other.

Connection is respect.
Connection is walking the same direction, while being independent of each other.

Connection is reflection.
Connection is to deeply ponder with each other, without shame, guilt or limitations.

Connection is being courageous to be yourself,
in a world that does not allow you to be yourself.

Connection is to be FREE in a masked world of "freedom."

ENOUGHNESS AND THE MORE DISEASE

Many people have a startling sense of emptiness. They always want more. They think when they have more cars, a bigger house, and so on, then they will be happy. But it is never enough. They always want more. I call it the more disease.

The way I was raised was instead with a great sense of enoughness. This enoughness is a discovery for every individual, and it is the most healthy attitude for longevity. This is a basic human characteristic to consider, and it's not difficult to practice. Enoughness is very healing and prevents the disease of being spoiled rotten.

EXPECTATIONS

Do not expect anything, and expect everything. Be comfortable with whatever comes your way, whatever the results may be, and in whatever form. Maintaining this balance will give you a deep sense of being, and can help you to navigate calmly in the "midst of madness."

From the "Fifty (50) Gates of Practical Wisdom" in the book *From Ecstasy to Lunch*

CREATE

"That which you want, **CREATE IT.** Do not wait for others to do it for you, and as a result,

many will benefit from your creative individual initiative, investing in the goodness of the human effort to make this world a better place to be and become."

TO GIVE

"To give is more valuable than withhold and not the opposite which is the "norm" out there, that is rampant in professing that "to withhold is more valuable than to give." We are here to restore the distortions of reality."

GO BE WITH THEM

"When someone is sad, you see that the other person comes and tries to philosophize, "Don't feel bad, life is good. Why are you sad?" When you do that, actually, you depress them more. Go be sad with them. When it is acted sincerely, the sad one turns and says "Are you sad too?" Then they explode with laughter, because they found the edge of it, it's ridiculous. Human healing is exactly there, but we don't activate it."

THE HIDDEN OBVIOUS

The hidden obvious is that which seems as if it is hidden from our awareness, but actually is very obvious. We do not notice the obvious, the state where "miracles" are occurring every breath of our life. Becoming aware of the obvious can reveal to us the "Miracle of life."

KEEP ME SANE IN THE MIDST OF MADNESS

"Keep me sane in the midst of madness
Keep me silent in the midst of noise
Keep me still in the midst of turmoil
Keep me a soft rose in the midst of thorns

Keep me lucid in the midst of slumber
Keep me whole in the midst of parts
Keep me in the vicinity of love in the midst of hate
Keep me an open door in the midst of walls"

(Note: See the book From Ecstasy to Lunch for the full poem)

MOVE SILENTLY

Move silently between the thought and the movement. Pierce the space and stillness with the gentle movements of your body. Think horizontal. Think vertical. Think circular. Integrate both with one conscious movement.

The breath, movement and consciousness, are the power and miracle of being and moving.

MOVING OUT AND RETURNING IN

"The male energy **moves out**, explores the outer dimensions. The Female energy is always in the process of **return**. She shows the way to return to the source of being.

The Male uses the **word, speaks, talks, and explains**. The Female is **the embodiment of silence**. She is just **listening.**

The Male **KNOWS**, the Female **IS**. So, our silence and speech must come from the same root and only source. **All our movement and speech must be permeated by silence and stillness. <u>MAN AND WOMAN IS ONE BEING</u>**

ON MIME

The techniques of mime can help integrate one's mind and body. Harmony of the mind develops through using one's imagination and becoming aware of the movements, actions, and reactions one has used in presenting oneself. When you move truly, you live from your heart. For the line from the mind to the heart to be united, to have a wire of communication from heart to mind, that's fantastic.

The mime condenses space and time to its essence. Mime turns one to the essence of the self, or being, to discover an art that gives total integration in life, as well as genuine artistic self-expression.

SPIRITUALITY

Remember, SPIRITUALITY in Hebrew is a certain way of thinking, and is an attitude of being awake and fully aware of the HERE and NOW, with every breath and with fullness of spirit. The NOW that is available to us now, this very moment, from which arises the sense and the power to ACT.

SPIRIT in Hebrew is, RUAH (רוח) meaning Breath, wind, an inner attitude and the immediate and awakened state of being fully here. Therefore, we do not trust the NOW, we feel threatened by the NOW, that is so powerful to face, escaping to the past, that was already, or the future that is not here yet, escaping to complaining, superstitions, and everything else that we are comfortable, convenient and familiar to escape to.

SUFFERING

You must squeeze the grape in order to get some wine. So it is with the suffering we experience in life. When you "suffer," it is like your grape is being squeezed to produce a change in you, to develop your character. (So your character could be vinegar or wine.) And wine and alcohol are also called spirits. Spirituality is the process of squeezing the grape to make good wine, which means restoring good behavior, sane ethics, and applied wisdom. Applied wisdom comes with practical knowledge. When you practice that knowledge (see "The Three Pillars of Becoming an Artist" in the book, *The BodySpeak Manual*) you have to begin to follow what some great prosperous families have done, to educate their children with all the steps for running their business, so that wealth isn't lost in the generations to come.

THE ULTIMATE IMPORTANCE OF OUR THOUGHTS

With our thoughts, we write our script of life. No one should write your life script with their thoughts of memes. We are what we think, and what our thoughts make us.

Be careful WHAT you think, ABOUT what you think, and HOW you think.

Our words are only the tool, the vessel of our thoughts, with which the manifestation of our thought happens. The speed of thoughts is much faster than the speed of light. Thoughts are very alive, hence the utmost importance of our thoughts.

"Our life depends on what we actually speak.
Speak only words that are true and resonate
with what you desire your life to be.
Speak only when necessary.
Speak few words and act more,
to manifest your words as you think them."
Samuel Avital, Boulder, CO, July 1978.

"Courage is a cloak you wear again and again
until every cell in your body is named, *Courage*."
Samuel Avital, July 1973

"To exist is to change…To change is to mature…
To mature is to go on creating oneself…Endlessly…"
Samuel Avital

"The thought transforms the cell, Thought moves matter;
Thought guides the breath; Breath guides the body."
Samuel Avital, March 2000 in a class session

"Every movement is a preparation for the next movement.
The present moment determines the future moment, which is already here."
Samuel Avital, March 2000 in class session

"Destiny is not a matter of chance. It is a matter of choice.
It is not a thing to wait for; it is a thing to be achieved."
Samuel Avital, in Class session Summer 1999

Here is a French proverb to always remember before uttering a word:
"Si ce que tu vas dire n'est pas plus beau que le silence ne le dis pas"
"If what you are going to say is not more beautiful than silence, do not say it."

One More Thing

Who You Are, and Who They Think You Are	**255**
Excuses and Becauses	**263**
Excuses	**264**
Becauses	**267**
The Hall of Mirrors	**271**
Opposites	**273**

Who You Are, and Who They Think You Are

MOST PEOPLE DON'T know themselves. This is because this self that most people think they are, is actually just who others told them they are. But you are not what others told you. How so? Because actually, it is just a collection of negative memes, programs of thinking, in which they told you that you are this, and you are this, and you are this. And this process started before you were even born.

The parents tell you, "She's such a genius," or "He is good at sports," etc. But actually, all of this is just a dangerous meme, a thought-virus, that brings only the sense of separation. It creates an attitude of "I am better than the other person, I exist, and to hell with them." So, the whole relationship with others is flawed from the beginning. And they keep you busy with that, so you will not know the essential self, which is actually within each and every being on the planet.

There are many examples of this. For instance, maybe they told you that you are talented, and you can be a mathematician – but your inclination is not to be a mathematician. But they continue to guide you toward that. They do this in Academia all the time. If you are a student, you have to do your work the way the professor wants, so they will give you a degree in that field of study. But where are you in that?

The way I understand it is, if I have the inclination to be an artist, or a magician, or an actor, or a dancer, or whatever... then I go for it. Now what happens is, when you go in that path of what you they told you to be, you do succeed. You become that, and you get that degree – but in the process, you lose yourself. What is it to lose yourself? You find that there is no space for that self, because your entire life is packed and filled with those memes, those clogged ways of thinking, that have accumulated over all the years and generations, all over the planet, since before we can remember. So, how do we go to this essential self?

We see this all the time. The parent is an actor and they want their son or daughter to be like them. But they don't know how to let that fresh young being build his or her own wings, according to his or her own essence. All the kids have that tendency to find their own way. That young person wants to invest in studying what they love, but the parents ask what are they going to do with that degree. They always want you to *do* something with it – otherwise you will not be what they want you to be.

I call this the curse of the upgrade. They always want you to "upgrade" in some way. They want to improve upon you in some way. But the upgrade is for the machine, and I say the body is not a machine. The organic, the human being does not upgrade. You cannot upgrade it. It is already created upgraded. But we don't read it properly, because we are not allowed to go to that no space, no time. They keep people busy worrying about this, worrying about that, worrying about that account, worrying about the grade, worrying about that promotion, worrying about that, and that has nothing to do with it. Certainly, these practicalities are a part of things, but that's all. So, I made a map for my students, that you handle this and this, you give 5% to the practicality of me and my little concerns, and then 95% is for living. Everything is taken care of.

Now, we can see that they use a certain intelligence to tell us the story of who we are – which actually we are not. And generally, what they say we are is just what we do. We say that I am an artist and you are an author. But actually, if you are an artist or an author, you create from that essential source we are talking about. Generally, the artists and mystics have access to that inner essential being.

This is why, when the artist paints, and people come and turn the painting this way and that, and ask him what it means, he says "I already created it. Look at it. It is already there for you." But we don't perceive what is right in front of us, because of the great maze of over-conceptualized thinking. And that creates many obstacles.

So, how do we go to this essential self? It is actually so simple. But – nobody will do it. And you will find that there are even many spiritual memes and a lot of spiritual programming out there, and they will not let you go there either. This is why I said to my students throughout the years that they could stop chasing enlightenment. I said, "You are already enlightened. Now, let's do something with it."

And so, **Are you yourself? And what is this self?** Now, the cultures of the world are swamped with these negative memes that we talked about, until the memes have become normal, and now most people consider the distortions good. But this happens because of the reversal of the healthy way of thinking. So, how do we get to that essential self, when everything around us is against that?

First of all, realize that every human being was born to be totally healthy, totally intelligent, to have all the talents of the world. As I have said before, you came here and it is as if you are a secret agent, but a spiritual one. You were given a mission to do. And so, you must use all your resources, you must be prepared. You know that the field is dangerous, but if you develop the sense of observation, you can fulfill your mission.

It is the same thing. We came here, we have all the intelligence we were given, but we don't use it. Instead, the negative memes come and take over, and hijack that, and cloud the gate to that true being.

So, if you want to observe this for yourself, just sit quietly, and look at your life, and see. Recall the ways in which people told you who you are. And you are fulfilling on that. But is that you?... Of course, it is not. But observe this.

In the 70's, I taught many men and women who wanted to be actors, indicating to them how to unearth their innate talent, by connecting with the real self, not the fake self. I told them that the inner essential self does not need an upgrade. The upgrade is for the machines, and the instinct is for the animals. But for us humans, we have intuition and intelligence.

In reality, we have all that we need, but we don't use that intelligence, because of the over-obsession of talking about life, of talking about self, of **talking about it**. Now the human being is a unique creation on the planet, because only the human being has been given the gift of speech. And this actually leads us to something the Zohar mentions multiple times, the relationship between the brain and the heart. Our brains give us the ability to talk, but we mostly talk nonsense. That talent of talking is abused to the edge, right? But the heart doesn't talk. The language of the heart does not talk. It has its own language. As I said in BodySpeak™, when you go to that center of silence, it has a different language. And we have to learn that language. But we don't "have the time" to do it, because we are preoccupied with those governing memes, those programmed thoughts that are so strong, they are almost like an assault.

So, what to do? What do we do? If you observe a tree, a rock, a flower, even an animal, you will see that there is something, a common denominator in the nature of all things. Everywhere you will find that aspect – which is stillness and silence. That is why I called my school **Le Centre du Silence**, the center of silence. But how do we learn this language?

In the school, I created the BodySpeak™ method, in order to teach the language of the body, so students could express beyond conceptual thinking. The authentic artist explores this, no matter who they are. But there are also fake artists and fake actors too. Why? Because they don't use their essence. This is true in any field. Rare are those that have tipped the balance to that essential being, that function from there, moving outward from that essence, and returning back to it. This is a type of back and forth, going out and returning. In Kabbalah they call it Orr Yashar and Orr Hozer, direct light and returning light. They also refer to Orr Makif, surrounding light.

The truth is that we are surrounded by everything we need, but we are totally hypnotized. It is a state of mass hypnosis. The memes and false thoughts are fantastic at hypnotizing, and so everybody goes along with it, and this results in what I call sheep consciousness. You simply direct the sheep where to go, and they go. And so, when I taught BodySpeak™, we included the principles of leaders/followers and motion/stillness.

Let's take this principle of motion/stillness. Begin from complete stillness, then do a minimal essential motion, and return back to stillness. If we breathe with the movement and we do this, we will have begun to open those clogged, clouded gates, to return to that place that has no time, no space, no words, nothing... It is beautiful actually, but we are afraid to go there.

And so, there was a poem by Apollinaire that I used to read in the workshops:

> ""Come to the edge," he said.
> "We can't, we're afraid!" they responded.
> "Come to the edge," he said.
> "We can't, We will fall!" they responded.
> "Come to the edge," he said.
> And so they came.
> And he pushed them.
> And they flew."

This is an invitation to get out of the limitations of being obsessed with duality. They were afraid, but he kept asking, and at one time, they came, and they flew. At a certain time, you have to face it, to fly. This is a strong metaphor.

We can do that through stillness, by not moving. And in that not moving, we breathe. Now, you will find that kabbalistic thought is the grand paradox. It accepts duality and unity in such a way that can drive people crazy. This is one of the ways of exploring that. In the workshops, we explored it directly, and discovered that in that motion, there is stillness; and in stillness, there is motion.

Naturally, we all want to experience this for ourselves. So, if you are by yourself, just sit. Close the gates of this world, the eyes, and just be silent. Is that difficult? No. But the monsters of the world are going to interfere, all the thoughts and distractions. But the more you do it, gradually, little by little, the more you are going to enter into that silence. Because in Hebrew, silence and stillness are the same word, Shetika (**שתיקה**).

Now what this means, simply, is to be in touch with your heart. Simple. The heart doesn't talk. So, let's be with it. But how to be with your heart? Here we are indicating how to find this path to that no space, no time, no silence, no stillness, nothingness...

Little by little, you have to set this for yourself, but you have to make a time for it, even if you are busy. Because actually there is no such thing as time. Even scientifically, they have now proven that time doesn't exist. Time and space don't exist. We are just vibrational, emotional intelligences trying to relate to one another. And in that process, if people don't follow that law of oneness, then they clash with each other, and they kill each other, and who will make peace between them?

So just sit and enter that no space. You can sit however you want to sit, as long as you are relaxed. Here the physical body is totally relaxed and still. To do this, you have to overcome the mountain of memes that have been planted there. You do this, little by little. Just use that intelligence to watch those thoughts passing, like birds or clouds in the sky, just let them pass. The amazing thing is that it does not take long to do this. There is such a simplicity to this, but the human tendency toward overdoing everything will not allow you to go there. But go there anyway. Because it's here, actually.

Essentially, this means to get in touch with the heart. How do I know my heart? Let's begin first with the physical heart, before we go to the spiritual heart. Actually, this is the path to go to the spiritual heart, through the physical heart. The physical heart is the center of the whole body, it is the King of the whole system, not the brain. The brain has its role too, but if the brain doesn't use the heart, what it does is futile. And the heart that doesn't use the brain, that's futile too.

This is one of the ways to go to what we spoke about. And there is one simple thing here that is difficult. If you get to that degree of silence, you will begin to hear the pulse of your heartbeat. You can feel that. That's a beginning, because very few hear and feel their heartbeat, very few. Try it now. Just try it. Be totally still and just breathe naturally, and try to hear your heartbeat. You will find that you have to make some effort, because that communication is clogged.

Right now, we are just talking about the physical heart. That physical heart beats in spite of you, doesn't it? Here we are speaking about duality and unity. The duality is breath. If you inhale and you don't exhale, you die. If you exhale and you don't inhale, you die. So right here is an example of the great paradox. In spite of ourselves, we breathe. That is why in Pirke Avot, it says "for in spite of yourself you were born, and in spite of yourself you live, and in spite of yourself you die."

That's the first step, be with your physical heart. Just make a little effort to be with it totally and please, try to feel the heart-beat. People do not listen to their heart, and so it is no wonder that the great illness in the world today is heart disease. And this is one of the spiritual ways to prevent that, to be with your heart. Later on, we will learn how to speak from the heart, but not with words. I'm emphasizing this, we have to learn this step by step. First step, hear how the heart beats. And over time, you can begin to coordinate your breathing with that. It's very simple, nothing new. This is just a translation of certain things on how to return to yourself, to go back to your essence, which in Hebrew we call Teshuvah (תשובה). Or as they say in the classic Torah portion about Abraham, Lekh Lekha (לך לך), go to yourself.

The more you practice this simple thing, the more it will have an effect. However, most of us don't like simplicity. As I mentioned in my classes throughout the years, simplicity is the most difficult thing to do. Granted, there is difficulty to doing this – And, we can go over that seeming difficulty. And then, you get to yourself, and you just stay there, in total silence.

In the beginning, you make this effort until you master it. It doesn't take long, just a few weeks. And when you go to a place of no time, no space, you don't time it, you don't put an alarm on it. And you don't think of what you are going to do next. You are totally in the now, totally. I don't think it is too much to dedicate 15 or 20 minutes to this steadily. It is not difficult.

Listening to the heart. You begin with the heartbeat, just listen to the heartbeat. Until, when you close your eyes, even in the noisiest cafes and noisy places you can hear it. The more you listen to it, the more you resonate with that rhythm.

This is one of the ways to answer the call, to go back to yourself, to go back home, as they say. But that home is not anywhere, it's here inside of you, your heart. But are you aware of it? Are you aware of it? For example, we make many movements automatically, without being aware of them. We take for granted that we breathe, we take for granted that we walk, we take for granted that we talk. And now, fake creativity is rampant all over the world, spreading false memes, false thoughts in all fields of knowledge.

When you begin to feel the benefits of this exercise, you will be careful of what you talk about. You will use the silence in between your sentences. You will be more considerate of others, because they are just like you – and most people are struggling to go to this place, but they don't "have time" to explore this.

So, the challenge, according to the Zohar, is to unite the duality and the oneness, and go beyond it. I've said many times to accept that paradox. Both of these aspects have to be there. But we are for this, and against that. So we have to accept it. Many have studied this.

But when we use words to say "I don't have time for this practice," that's a lie. In the same way, when you say "I'm hungry," it's a lie, or when you say "I love you," it's a lie. Why? Because you are just saying it, it's not you. You are love itself actually. And if you tune with your heart this way, it will affect everything. You will reexamine your life, no matter how old you are. In one second, or two minutes to realize this, it's a new life. But as I always suggest, don't believe it until you experience it. And remember please, that you are not the story other people told you of who you are.

Know thyself is not to know the story of what other people said you are. That is something else completely. Actually, it is the things you know, without knowing that you know. This needs some reflection. And when you do these exercises, then you know that you know that you don't know. So who knows you? Because those who think they know you, what they think you are is actually not that at all.

We explored this principle in the first session of the BodySpeak™ workshops, in which students first had to introduce themselves with words, and then without words, through movement and expression. With words, you describe yourself, you use 500,000 words to say how many PhDs you have, and all that you do. But all the students agreed that without words revealed much more of the person, beyond just their titles. These are the things that you know, without knowing you know.

And out there, they love to describe everything. They tell you that you are too short, or you are too tall, or you are too smart, or not smart enough, or all the limitations. They are trying to shape you. And so, you go with it, but that's sheep consciousness. Then you don't have your integrity. And actually, we are talking about the path to true freedom here.

The heart has a language, the body has a language, and it has nothing to do with words. I said many times over the years that words are one of the most primitive ways to communicate. But no one pays attention to this heartbeat within us, it is not known. And that's where the secret is. But no one has time to go there, because we are clogged by, and snatched by the thousands and millions of memes that formed us, and we believe what they tell us we are. No, I am not that. You are not that. As I wrote in one my articles, "Who am I to say I am Nothing?"

That is beyond time and space. But by trying to physicalize the beat of the heart, you can at least begin to feel it. And believe me, if you function from that, you will not just succeed, but you will overcome all the difficulties, all the challenges of the duality. But as I tell my students, I am the biggest liar of them all, don't believe me. Try it and find out for yourself. Taste it and see if you discover something.

So, this practice is for the ones among you who are really sincere, and ready to delete the millions of those negative thought viruses that people used to tell us who we are. Because you are not what other people think you are. I repeat: You are not what other people told you stories that you are.

And so, if you dear reader, are sincere to know who on earth you are, it's in your hands now. And it's in your heart. If you are more than just curious, then explore, and bon courage.

• • •

כֵּן אִם אֲנִי כָּאן הַכֹּל כָּאן

תַּנְיָא אָמְרוּ עָלָיו עַל הִלֵּל הַזָּקֵן כְּשֶׁהָיָה שָׂמֵחַ בְּשִׂמְחַת בֵּית הַשּׁוֹאֵבָה –

אָמַר כֵּן אִם אֲנִי כָּאן הַכֹּל כָּאן וְאִם אֵינִי כָּאן מִי כָּאן

הוּא הָיָה אוֹמֵר   כֵּן מָקוֹם שֶׁאֲנִי אוֹהֵב שָׁם רַגְלַי מוֹלִיכוֹת אוֹתִי אִם תָּבֹא אֶל בֵּיתִי

אֲנִי אָבֹא אֶל בֵּיתֶךָ אִם אַתָּה לֹא תָבֹא אֶל בֵּיתִי   אֲנִי לֹא אָבֹא אֶל בֵּיתֶךָ

שֶׁנֶּאֱמַר בְּכָל הַמָּקוֹם אֲשֶׁר אַזְכִּיר אֶת שְׁמִי אָבֹא אֵלֶיךָ וּבֵרַכְתִּיךָ: סוכה נ"ג א :ג'

If I Am Here All Is Here…

They said of Hillel the Elder, when he was happy during The Celebration of Rejoicing of Drawing the Water, "*Simchat Beit HaShoeva*" – שִׂמְחַת בֵּית הַשּׁוֹאֵבָה

He said this: If I am here, everything is here; And if I am not here, who is here?
To the place that I love, there my feet take me.
And he said: If you come to my house, I will come to your house;
If you do not come to my house, I will not come to your house.
As it is stated "In every place that I cause my name to be mentioned,
I will come to you and bless you." (*Exodus 20:21*)
– *Talmud, Sukkah 53:3*

Note: "In every place that I cause my name to be mentioned, I will come to you and bless you." This quote was later interpreted as that the presence of the Shekhinah (the divine feminine presence) is activated and present when two or three are dwelling with the Torah.

To the western ear, this quote "If I am here, everything is here" may sound pretentious, simplistic, or nonsense. But for the careful, sane, and balanced thinker, it may make sense, especially if you are versed in the Zen arts. S.A.

The celebration of the drawing of the water for the Temple altar is called in the Talmud(*Sukkah* 50b) both "*Simchat Beit HaShoeva*"- ("the rejoicing of the house of the important one"), since it is an important *mitzvah*, and ""*Simchat Beit HaShoeva*"- ("the rejoicing of the house of water-drawing.")

"And you shall draw water in happiness out of the wells of salvation"
Isaiah 12:3

Excuses and Becauses

IDENTIFY THE <u>EXCUSES</u> and **<u>Becauses</u>** in your life. Know the memes (the programmed ways of thinking) that stop you and limit you from creating, acting and being. This will help you in all areas of life. It will help you to be full of initiative, and not wait for someone to tell you what to do, which is what most have been trained to do.

When you identify the excuses and becauses, then you are free from them. But you have to become aware, for instance when that little sentence comes to say 'I can't do that,' and instead to say "No, I can. I'm able to. If it's a problem, I can solve it." And amazingly speaking, if you begin to generate this inside you, it has a big effect. You may not feel it in the beginning, so even if what you want doesn't happen, just continue it. At one moment, it will happen, and you will be amazed that the eyes can see.

If you nourish this inner dialogue of yourself, you will succeed in everything you do, in your relationships, in your work, in everything. And you will begin to notice who these thoughts are that sway you from your direction – the becauses and the justifications of things. Those are the enemies. But remember, no one is at fault for it, because those thoughts were planted there unconsciously, and so many negative memes have become instilled that it becomes the usual thing. These are the tools of the obstacle. But with a little awareness, when they come you can laugh and overcome them.

Excuses

The "Poem of Excuses"
The Obstacles creating total confusion and self-denial
The poetry of self-disaster and creating problems where they don't exist

PLEASE SIT DOWN and go to the list of excuses. If you find that some of these are in your everyday vocabulary, you are ready to explore and correct your vocabulary now, before the trouble starts.

Suggestion: Create your own list of these excuses to know yourself a little better. This will help you to achieve the situation of correcting your mistakes immediately, as soon as you make them. Thus, this will make you super aware, to do your own restoration, Tikkun.

I can't
I don't have time
I don't know how to
It's not possible
It's too hard
I'm busy
I forgot
I'm not strong enough
I will do it later
I don't have the energy
It's pointless
I'm too stressed out to do it
I have other things to do
It's fine as it is
It will take too long
Someone else will do it
It is too complicated
I'm not good at it
What if it fails?
What if I look bad?

What if people judge me?
The government should do it
Someone else should do it
I'm not to blame. It's someone else's fault.
I won't like doing it
It will be stressful
I'm too tired
It didn't work when I tried before
Someone told me I'm not capable to do it
I don't have enough money
It's my parents' fault
It's too expensive
What if I get hurt?
Something bad could happen
I'm depressed
I don't feel like it today
My parents or relatives or friends or girlfriend or boyfriend or people I know don't think it's a good idea

My parents or relatives or friends or girlfriend or boyfriend or people don't think I will succeed
I don't feel good
My schedule is already booked
It will be boring
What's next?
I've got to go. I've got an appointment
I'm not tall enough
I'm not smart enough
I'm not successful enough
I'm not famous enough
I'm not attractive enough
I'm not old enough to do that
I'm too old to do that
They don't like me
The traffic is bad
It won't work anyway
I hate doing things like that
Maybe next year
I need more money to do that
I'm too good to do that
I'm not good enough to do that
Only rich people get to do that kind of thing
I don't have an advanced enough degree
People will laugh at me
I won't make enough money at it
People of the opposite sex won't find me attractive if I do that
I will look dumb
I've got another appointment then
I've already done everything I can
It's someone else's fault
My alarm clock didn't go off
Traffic was bad
My dog ate my homework
The "computer system" is down
I need to get an approval to do that
I don't have the authority to decide that
I don't make the rules
My cat was sick
My car isn't working
Nobody else is doing it, so why should I have to?
I've already got enough on my plate
I've already done enough
I'm not allowed to
It's impossible
It's too cold
It's too hot
It's too soon
It's too late
I don't want to face it
I'm just going with the flow
I'm just taking it day by day
It's not fair
I'll do it when I have more time or money
I can't handle it
I don't want to deal with it

We don't have space to add all these excuses, we would circle the earth just itemizing them. So we just added a few here.

Learn to observe the excuses. Are you used to using some of these? If so, roll up your sleeves, and fasten your seatbelt – welcome to the madness of this world.

Just observing these justifications will help you not to do them. Because they are a waste of time. These excuses and justifications are just memes (false thoughts) to program you into having a distracted personality.

If you are using any of these, be careful, you are in a mine field. Now, you have to increase your awareness to never use them. Because when you use them, you cause them to happen. If you say you don't "have time," you will find that indeed, you don't have time to do what you really wanted to or to realize your dreams. You postpone your happiness. But by changing your vocabulary, you can avoid many unnecessary obstacles. And remember, what you decide today is your tomorrow.

List of Becauses

I like you, because you have a nice figure
I marry you, because you have money
I tell you I love you, because I want you to sleep with me
I am your friend, so you will support me when I have problems
I take you out to dinner, because I want you to give me that contract
I compliment you, because then you will be attracted to me
I am your friend, because you validate me
I hold parties, because I want to be popular and well-liked

I do a favor for you, because then you will do a favor for me
I befriend many people, so I can become powerful
I work, because I want to make a lot of money
I dress a certain way, because I want others to approve of me
I do a good deed, because I want to be good
I compliment you, so you will like me
I am friends with you, because I want attention

I am nice to you, because you are famous
I am nice to you, because you are rich
I am nice to you, because you are powerful
I am your friend, because you are famous
I am your friend, because you are rich
I am your friend, because you are powerful
I do what you want, because you are famous
I do what you want, because you are rich
I do what you want, because you are powerful

I love you, because you give me pleasure
I get into a relationship with you, because I want you to "make me happy"
I get into a relationship with you, because I am lonely
I get into a relationship with you, because I am scared of being alone
I invite you to dinner, so you will invite me to dinner next week
I give you a present on your birthday, so you will give me a present on my birthday

I am attracted to you, because you have a yacht
I am attracted to you, because you are powerful
I am attracted to you, because you have a nice chest
I exercise, so I can have nice abs
I like being with you, because you're good in bed
I say I care about you, so you will do what I want

I do what my boss says, because I want a promotion
I will be your boyfriend or girlfriend, for the free rent
I am in this relationship, because I want the other person to take care of me
I am in this relationship, because I don't want to have to be responsible

I put a promotion on the table, so you will work insane hours without complaining
I offer up something you want, so you will do what I want

I want my child to be an actor, because I wanted to be an actor but failed
I want my child to be good at sports, because I wanted to be good at sports
I want my child to succeed, so they can take care of me
I want a big house, because it will impress the neighbors
I act good, because it will impress the people at church

I avoid committing crimes, because I don't want to be arrested
I treat you with respect, because you have money
I am not lazy, because I don't want to be fired
I like you, because you are "on my side"
I go to church, because I want to be good

I make myself beautiful, so others will be impressed
I am getting rich, because I want others to be impressed
I have a fancy car, because women will be more attracted to me
I honor my grandparents, so they will put me in their will
I have 12 PhD's, because it will prove I'm good
I donate to charity, so everyone will know how generous and good I am

I am a doctor, because my parents will finally approve of me now
I became a lawyer, because everyone will be impressed
I wear Versace, so everyone will think I'm cool
I love you, because you give me expensive jewelry
I love you, because you give me pleasure
I am friends with you, because you agree with my political beliefs
I am friends with you, because you agree with my religious beliefs
I am friends with you, because you agree with me
I will make you part of my friend group, so you will feed my ego
I will make you feel "less than," because I want to control you
I get a partner, so they will take care of me when I'm old
I remind my kids what I did for them, so they will take care of me
I work hard to succeed, because I want to "be someone"
I write a book, because I want to be famous
I hire those people, because their work will make me rich
I write those politicians a big check, so they will pass laws that benefit me

I will honor you, because you have higher status
I will be mean to you, because you have lower status
I invite you on a lavish vacation, so you can make me rich
I am a musician, because girls will be attracted to me
I am an artist, because I will make a million dollars
I am a religious figure, so everyone will know how holy I am
I am successful, so everyone will know how great I am

I say I am there for you, so you will trust me
I offer you things, to make you dependent on me
I tell you a sad story, so you will be sympathetic with me
I love you, because you give me what I want
I do that work, because it pays, even if it is harmful

I validate all your fears, because I want you to vote for me
I offer to protect you, so you will let me control you
I repeat false messages, because I want to control you
I paint others as villainous, evil, and stupid, so you will believe the messages of "our group" and be easily controlled

I encourage you to fear others, because it will make me more powerful
I tell you what you want to hear, so you will support me
I lie to you, because then I can get what I want
I tell you that you misunderstood, because then you won't catch on that I'm lying
I make others "wrong, because then I can be "right"
I convince you it's good, so you will not see how bad it is
I tell you that it's your duty, because then you will kill others for my agenda
I convince you that you have no power, because then you will be in my power, instead of being free

The Amusement Park and The Hall of Mirrors

IN THIS WORLD, there is such a thing as an amusement park, and in the amusement park, there is a section that they call the hall of mirrors. Now imagine yourself in the amusement park, and you go to the house of mirrors. In a hall of mirrors, you see your image different ways – short, tall, fat, skinny, multiplied over and over in different reflections. You see your image all kinds of different ways. But my question is: Are you that?

This is the comparison – in the world we live in, we experience the total distortion of words, and that's how we see the world. They classify everyone: He is tall, you are short, he is fat, and she is thin. We describe this matter that is constantly changing. And as soon as you describe that, it produces different kinds of images in our minds. But is that you? That is the question here.

We see the existence of these changing images, and we think we are that. But what we learn from the hall of mirrors is that you are not that. The world is seducing us to see ourselves in a distorted way, and we accept that distortion. Yet, we are not that. It's just a hall of mirrors. This world is a hall of mirrors.

You classify that person as tall, black, white, skinny, short, big, brown-haired, blond-haired, smart, ignorant, poor, rich, happy, sad, etc, all these ways they categorize people. And as soon as you meet somebody, you are applying all those categories. But the question is: Is that the person? No.

So, we live in an amusement park, in which we see a distorted picture of ourselves from all those different images. As a result, we get lost in compulsive consuming, and compulsive senseless images, and we think we are that. They try to tell you many things about what and who you are. Sure, there are many descriptions of you. But are you all those things – are you multiple personalities? No, of course not. You are not a hall of mirrors.

Yet the whole world seems to us like a hall of mirrors, with all the names and categories and justifications, and all that. But that is not you, just like you wouldn't call your shirt or your pants you. But unfortunately, most people think that is what they are.

Mirrors. With my students, we spoke about this many times, that even physically, you cannot see yourself. The most you can see is your arms and legs, but you cannot see your whole body. Yes, you can look in a mirror, but you don't see yourself there, just the reflection of your image. So, actually, you will find that there is no way to see yourself, only by seeing the other. And everyone's body is different. Yes, we both have two hands, but I use my hands differently than you use yours. We have the same eyes, but you see differently.

In BodySpeak™, we had an exercise, and the aim is to begin with this treasure called the body. When you observe the other person's form, you can immediately detect the attitude of the person, outside, inside, everything. But you don't do this to say "You're stupid," "You're tall," etc. The purpose is to learn to communicate. How? By knowing that there is a good thing behind that house of mirrors. Because that person is more than a house of mirrors, more than what you see.

In other words, we are living in a house of mirrors, but we don't know it. Because we get caught in the illusion of it. When you come to this world, you are programmed to the hall of mirrors. The mirror that shows you that you are tall and you are short and you are fat, etc. This is the world we live in, sorry. You see through that hall of mirrors. And then you lose touch with the moment, because you are busy escaping, because you miss this elusive obvious.

So, you decide. Do you want to live in a hall of mirrors? Do you want to live in "this world" of the house of mirrors? It is a distortion, period.

Opposites Duality

Meditation Instructions

1	Happiness	Sadness
2	Having	Being
3	Wanting	Needing
4	Disease	Health
5	Giving	Receiving
6	Being	Becoming
7	Initiative	Passive
8	Leader	Follower
9	Pleasure	Pain, Suffering
10	Good	Bad
11	Warrior	Coward
12	Awakening	Sleeping
13	Awareness	Slumber
14	Living	Sleepwalking
15	Being	Talking about being

AS WE BEGIN to work systematically with this list of apparent paradoxes, we can shift from the puzzle of the great paradox, to no paradox at all. That is a state of being, in total balance with yourself and others. It is a state of being in total balance, actually, with everyone and everything around you. It is the secret of accepting. It will perhaps assist you, the reader, to find your purpose in this life.

Note: This list is a drop in the sea of the categories of opposites and we can't write them all. But you will find them everywhere and you can include your own.

Begin by taking a sheet of paper and drawing a line down the middle. Starting with the first set of opposites, write "Happiness" down on one side, and "Sadness" on the other. These are two obvious things that most people take totally for granted, and that nobody gives attention to. Happiness and sadness.

Explore happiness and sadness in your own life. Focus on each of these during the week, and write down your observations. These are things that are taken for granted by most humans, but instead, explore them a little. Let it occupy you. Observe them in your own life. See what you think happiness and sadness are, from your own way of thinking, looking at it both physically and spiritually.

Take the line of happiness. What is happiness? Describe it and write down observations from your own experience. When I'm healthy, I am happy, etc. Do the same process looking at sadness. When you are sad, what is happening? Explore it.* Maybe it is bad news, or injustice. Or maybe that person told me something, and then I felt sad.

And after you explore your happiness your way, begin to practice it, and don't talk about it anymore. Because if you talk about it, you lose it, somehow.

As you explore these opposites, starting with happiness and sadness, the exploration will start with because, feeling that way for a reason, but it will take you to no because. First you feel happiness because of something, or sadness because of something. But later it will be with no because. This is why I always told my students, when you are sad, enjoy it. Why? Because that's the only unique moment when you feel that feeling.

It can happen to you that you feel sad, but not because you lack something. Or you feel happy for no reason. First I'm happy because I have food, I have shelter. But when you go to the edge of that experience, you bounce to the opposite, and then you can choose. (Also see the article Balance, the Middle Way of the Tree of Life, in the Kabbalah section for more exploration of opposites, extreme positive and extreme negative).

And when you feel happy, don't talk about it. Sad to say, if you talk about it, you don't live it. So you end up talking about life and not living. Once you've decided that this is your happiness, your own way, I suggest don't talk about it, experience it. This way you will discover untold ways of being happy in this world.

Create the sheets of your opposites. Observe these from your essential being, seeing them from your physical and spiritual aspects. This is a way to look into yourself.

---

* See the article "Practical Happiness" in the Mime section for more about the state of happiness.

Exploring these opposites will take you to the obvious, and then beyond the obvious. Go to the edge of that thing you are exploring. And you will actually discover new things.

Take an example of any of these, and take it to the edge. For example, "When I see a beautiful green field, I feel good." Repeat it 1 million times, stretch it to the edge of reasoning, until finally there is no because. When I have money, I'm happy. Take that reasoning and explore it, and after some work, you can come to the edge of it. When I see that green field, I feel happy. Repeat it 1,000 times, until you get sick of green.

Maybe I feel sad because I see a homeless person. It is sad, because they don't have a home, they don't have food to eat, they don't have shelter. Keep exploring it. The more you explore it, the more you find the opposite. You do have shelter, you do have food to eat, you find the other side of it. When you come to the edge of it, you want to give charity. So it reveals to you how to deal with the duality. But you don't give charity because you pity that person, or because you want your name written on a hall in a university.

If you do this work, you will find out how the obvious is being revealed, and how to work out these dualities without being confused or stressed. Because they are all just inventions, they don't exist. Stress doesn't exist, but they invented that idea, so they can sell you pills and stress-release devices.*

Take one thing that really brings you happiness or really bothers you. At the edge, you will come to an impasse. When we do that, we actually find out how comical we are, and how stupid we are. I will be happy when I have a romantic partner to love me. When you take it to the edge, you realize it is futile, you don't need it. I'm unhappy because I don't have a Mercedes. Take it to the edge. And at the edge of it, you will laugh. What is the focus? Having or being?

We explored this in the mime workshops. If a person is sad, don't come up to them and philosophize and say, "Don't feel bad, life is good. Why are you feeling sad?" When you do that, actually you depress them more. Instead, just go be with them in their sadness. And when it is acted sincerely, the sad person turns and says "Are you sad too?" and they both explode with laughter. Because they found that at the edge of it, it is ridiculous. Human healing is exactly there, but we don't activate it. What to do? Increase it.

Over my years of teaching, we talked about the pursuit of happiness. That is the greatest recipe for sadness, stress and misery. As it says in the Talmud, if you pursue happiness, happiness will run away from you. If you pursue honor, honor will flee from you.

---

* See the article, "Fear Does Not Exist" under Articles

From this you can understand what I always said – If you are sad, enjoy it. That breaks all the logic. But it is true, actually. It is an invitation to shift, to experience the opposite, and to be happy. It is the ability to shift from this to that.

This is how we can experience this simple kabbalistic knowledge from the Torah now. Being with it. Be with your sadness sometimes. Really, you will find it is interesting. Look at it, be with it, take it to the edge, and it disappears. But don't believe that until you experience it yourself.

Take happiness and sadness to the edge. If you are sad, go to the edge of it, you will find yourself experiencing a happiness that you can't even describe that doesn't depend on anything.

Maybe there is a time that you want to do something. But when you go to do it, it's impossible. So what do you do? Well, if you are that original happiness, you will do it, and it will succeed. But if you are operating from your situation of sadness, or obsession with having, the focus is on that, not on what you are doing. You are busy feeling sad, rather than shifting.

So here are a few of these dualities and how you can work with each of them. You can begin with Happiness/Sadness, and then move on to explore the other opposites on the list. This will work no matter how old you are, as it has nothing to do with age or personal history or even cultural conditionings. This is a true private work with your being. These suggestions will assist you to make that shift, at least for yourself. And if you practice them, you can feel that change in no time. But don't believe my words, instead consider and contemplate this, and don't believe it until you yourself have practiced and experienced the results for yourself. If you implement these suggestions, you may be amazed at what you discover.

And I suggest that whatever you are exploring, don't talk about it, live it. Because if you live it, you'll enjoy it. But if you talk about it, you will doubt it.

Do you see how many words I used in this article about happiness? Have mercy. Count them and be happy. Or as you say in America, count your blessings and be happy. That is an obvious "secret" to entice you to practice. Because it has to come from within you. It is not, as they say in the culture "one-size-fits-all."*

---

* See the article "What is BodySpeak?" in the book the BodySpeak™ Manual. It explores how we each have to integrate the learning in our own unique way and understanding, through the phases of the intellectual, physical, and the integration and application of the learning. This can help you understand how we circulate the actual work to experience these principles and many others.

Defintuitions

Defintuitions

Consider these terms, words, expressions and suggestions, from various sections of the book, defined via intuition and experience working with students

Very Important Note:

These new definitions are one of the tools of Samuel's teachings, and are directly connected to specific exercises. The intention here is that there are words that are taken for granted and have become clichés, and so we suggest creating new definitions. Defintuitions point out corrections of certain terms, so we can become aware if the definitions or ideas we have of things are of benefit, or actually not of benefit.

Some of these new definitions may appear obvious, and that is actually the point. From this, you can come to the conclusion that the obvious is actually the key to balance; physical, mental, and spiritual.

Here we redefine obvious words. Why? Because most of the languages of the world are filled with memes (programmed ways of thinking), both positive and negative, which are accepted as natural and built into the ideas we want to express. So, I think that languages are a big trap of constantly introducing those memes and they are glued into the everyday language that everyone speaks. So if you are ready to find a new definition of things, in an intuitive way, welcome to Defintuitions.

In this way, Defintuitions are a technique to maintain presence in what you do. They are a tool for a healthy change of your being. They are an introduction to build your island of sanity, in the midst of a confused and perplexed world.

"ALEPH" HIGHWAY	The highway a person travels on to reach a specific destination. Sometimes one gets hungry and takes a side exit to a restaurant to eat and rest, assuming that, obviously, they will then return to the Aleph highway. But unfortunately, often we are on our way and stop to consider something temporarily, and we tend to stay on the sideway, forgetting to go back to the highway and our true destination.

APPLICATION	The situation or an occasion where one manifests the learning, thus making the abstract concrete. Understanding by doing and being the learning.
ARTISTIC ZERO	Natural posture. Physically, standing as a perfect vertical line. Being focused and totally present mentally and spiritually in all living situations. A state of being 100% totally in the present moment, as a preparation to be in the inner Artistic Zero.
BALANCE	Balance is a state of mind. This state includes modest movements, respecting objects in space, etc, and hints to us to correct certain negative characteristics in oneself. This can be practiced especially on an awkward day, when one drops things, or is awkward handling objects in one's environment.
BENESTROPHE	Expect benestrophes rather than catastrophes. Bene is Latin for "good." Strophe means "to turn." <u>Thus, to turn everything for the good</u>. We can say that as we focus our imagination constantly on generating benestrophic events in the future, so it will be – by our positive attitude in action. By overcoming the negative with the positive, by filling the darkness with light, by finding balance and peace within, one can indeed remain sane, happy, and calm while sailing one's ship amidst madness and turbulent waters.
BETWEEN	Working in the space between thought and action, between the yes and no. <u>The music happens between the piano keys</u>. To be always in the state of between, the state of transit, as all is passing and nothing is permanent.
BEWILDERNESS	A place or state of unrefined energy where one lives in confusion, or fusion.
BILL OF DUTIES	We have the **BILL OF HUMAN RIGHTS**, which are now more important than the "Human". And this connotes the rights to have, to receive, and NOT to give. It is about time now that the **BILL OF HUMAN DUTIES** must be written to balance the giving and receiving in our consciousness. It is not just to receive, but to give. This is a very important principle for balanced and just living for all.

I am daring to hope that some intelligent and consciously awakened humans on this planet are busy writing this very important DOCUMENT OF DUTIES. It will likely appear when most humans evolve and awake from the unconscious slumber of "these days."

CAT CONSCIOUSNESS Alert, like a cat; using the knowledge you have on time, when you need it

CAMEL CONSCIOUSNESS Being able to see your own hump as well as the humps of others.

LE CENTRE DU SILENCE A neutral space/time in absolute silence and stillness, from which clarity of sight can be manifested on all planes with an amazing simplicity. The **Centre of Silence** is an invisible dot in an infinite circle. It is a good place/time to function from, in total calm and poise, in any situation you are in. Teach yourself to always respond to life from a **center of silence**.

CIRCULAR THINKING Circular thinking is one of the tools to use in order to possess a high I.Q. Most of the western world is based in linear thinking. The nonlinear was left only to artists and mystics. So therefore, the two hemispheres of the brain are not equally practiced in every way of thinking.

So, it is like "playing the violin with one hand". In so many areas of life, people don't embrace the whole, because they don't have the circularity of thinking.

COLLAPSATION Collapsation is built of two words: corruption and collapse. Collapsation is a process that has been present in many ancient and new cultures on this planet. It is a word that suggests corruption and the collapse that happens as a result of it. It is what happened in Rome and in many ancient cultures which ultimately disappeared. Knowing the symptoms of it throughout history could warn us not to repeat those tragic outcomes.

COMPULSIVE THINKING AND DOING We know that most of our tendencies lead us to be compulsive consumers, and to engage in compulsive thinking and compulsive doing. From that state, we tend to react rather than respond, thus creating problems where they do not exist.

CONDORIANS AND TURTELIANS

Condorian – One who perceives reality with its wholeness, as from the Condor's view, and so can make healthy decisions both artistically and in life.

Turtelian – The opposite of the Condorian. One who is lazy and perceives reality from the "boat" view, seeing things in a limited way and lacking vision and courage to act.

CONSCIOUS INNOCENCE

A living state and a natural quality of being, where one is totally at one with their child innocence, and is consciously aware of it. A paradox, yes. But, when one knows with "certainty" that paradox does not exist, then this state of conscious innocence can be totally understood, experienced, and lived with every breath, thought and action.

Clowns, genuine artists, musicians, painters, writers, actors, and yes, mimes, also have this beautiful quality of being, which is a great source of true and potent creativity. It is a kind of innocence, but aware. Einstein and some other scientists had it. It is known that the gaze of a consciously innocent being is the most powerful in the world. It can be, what people call a "**miraculous**" event.

If you did not lose your innocence after childhood, you will begin to know it and understand it from the depth of your being.

COSMIC ACCORDION

The journey between the infinitely small and the infinitely great, back and forth, and back again. Expansion and contraction. The ebb and flow of the breath, the dance of balanced being

COW CONSCIOUSNESS

Knowing how to chew, vomit, swallow and digest information properly.

THE DOORS ARE ALWAYS OPEN

When a door bangs shut, most people are attracted to the noise and get distracted by where all the attention is. However, the time when the door is shut is the **exact moment** when you should be looking for the next door that is now opened before you.

There is no need for "keys." But if you feel you need a "key," remember, YOU are the key. Use it and enter the door.

ELASTICIZING THE PRESENT	Stretching the moment, elongating the moment. Being 100% present, breathing the Great Breath.
ELEPHANT-IN-THE-DARK MENTALITY	Seeing only the part, not the whole.
ENDARKENMENT	The exact opposite of enlightenment, meaning the unconscious state of sleep and slumber most humans are always in, away from the essential self and especially from this present moment.
ENOUGHNESS AND THE "MORE" DISEASE	Many people have a startling sense of emptiness. They always want more. They think when they have more cars, a bigger house, and so on, then they will be happy. But it is never enough. They always want more. I call it **The "More" Disease**. **Enoughness** is a discovery for every individual, especially in American culture. To live with enoughness is the most healthy attitude for longevity. This is a basic human characteristic to consider, and it's not difficult to practice. Enoughness is very healing and prevents the disease of being spoiled rotten.
EVERY LITTLE SMALL MOVEMENT COUNTS	Be aware that every movement you do is very important and counts. Do it slowly. That way, you can preserve your energy and act without effort. The effort of sudden movement is not needed unless it is an urgent and necessary movement.
EXPERTS ARE THE ULTIMATE IGNORANTS	"Intelligent" people who specialize only in one topic, that pretend to know, and speak nonsense based on supposition and guessing.
FARFELU	One who is asleep; doing things halfway.
FEAR	Fear is the tool to enslave humanity. Please see the article Fear Does Not Exist.
FIRST THOUGHT, LAST THOUGHT (FTLT)	Become aware of your first thought when you awake in the morning and your last thought before you sleep. Before you sleep, do a **daily review** of your thoughts and experiences of the day, and resolve to sleep well with a clean conscience of having lived that day with awareness and honesty. Practice this while still in bed, before awakening and as you are going to sleep.

FROM ECSTASY TO LUNCH — The ability to always return to the Artistic Zero from any state, at any moment. The ability to remain totally here, while transiting from here to there, from sadness to joy, from inhaling to exhaling, etc. The state of "between".

GIVE IT FIRST — If you want something in this life, give it first.

THE GREAT SECRET OF THE UNIVERSE! — We often forget and take for granted the everyday movement, because we forget to breathe.

<u>**Remember**</u>! I asked you once in every session—

What is the great and the most obvious secret in the universe? Always remember to breathe!

THE GREAT SHIFT — The Great Shift is the acceptance of changes and paradigm-shifts in all fields. Our resistance of change is the root cause of all human problems, both individually and globally. So, the more we resist, the more we create problems where they don't exist. (See the article The Great Shift)

In other words, there are moments in life that we make a decision without knowing that the effect is destroying us. Therefore, study well your decisions, and also what words you use to communicate with yourself and with other people.

Actually, most of the decisions one makes are based on different memes (programmed ways of thinking), so they create false decisions that are not effective for the outcome you envision.

HIDDEN OBVIOUS — That which seems as if it is hidden from our awareness, but actually is very obvious. We do not notice the obvious, the state where "miracles" are occurring every breath of our life. Becoming aware of the obvious can reveal to us the "Miracle of life".

So if you want to understand yourself, study your definitions for what is obvious and maybe there you will find yourself, if you notice it. For the treasures of wisdom in life are in the hidden obvious. As the saying goes – hidden in plain sight.

I CAN'T	Use of the words "I can't" was forbidden in my workshops – because it blocks the creativity of human talent, and blocks the total view of that moment. Sure, we can't fly. But that's another topic, which was "solved" by inventing the airplane. In my workshops, I had my students raise their right hand and say "I swear to do the possible and only the possible."
THE IMPERMEABLE	The Impermeable is a practical exercise that I suggest to maintain a mental state in which one does not allow events to affect one's balance and harmony. The exercise cultivates the ability to be involved, yet remain detached and objective. Visualize yourself wearing an invisible raincoat. Any rain-drops slide off, leaving the inside dry. The water of the rain does not affect the coat. This applies to whatever comes to you from the outside world, be it negative thoughts, chaotic emotions, hecticness; they all just slide off, leaving the inside unaffected. Learn to become calmly detached, but not indifferent, to interacting with the world. Remember well: **Detached, but NOT indifferent**.
INHALE IMPORTANCE, EXHALE INSIGNIFICANCE	This is a suggested practice, to balance between importance and insignificance. With it, you delete the pretense of being.
THE JOURNEY FROM THOUGHT TO ACTION **Making the Invisible, Visible**	Jump into yourself. Un-block. Translate thoughts into words, and bright ideas into action. Transform the ordinary into the extraordinary. Make the abstract concrete. Improvise. Be spontaneous. Condense the time/space between thinking and doing. Tap your creative resources in a magical, entertaining, Body*Speak*™ learning event.
JUMP INTO THE FIRE	Do that which you are afraid of. Face your fears. Dare to experience the edge. **Envision yourself totally fearless**.
JUMP INTO YOURSELF	Dare to be yourself, awake and ready, being the real being you were meant to be – Living your purpose to be here at this time.

JUMPING FROM STREAM TO STREAM	When one does not follow the path one has chosen to walk, instead going from one path to another, jumping from stream to stream, and thus getting nowhere.
"KEEP ME SANE IN THE MIDST OF MADNESS"	This practice of "Keep me sane in the midst of madness" is based on a specific experience that I encountered in New York when I came to this country. It is a practice to stay balanced and free in an unbalanced world. (Please read the article Madness and Sanity on Broadway for details).
	Later, in the study of some Hebrew prophets, I found the same message with different words. These are my own words, based on that ancient attitude that the Hebrew prophets spoke about.
"KNOW YOUR PLACE"	

אַל־תְּבַהֵל עַל־פִּיךָ וְלִבְּךָ אַל־יְמַהֵר לְהוֹצִיא דָבָר לִפְנֵי הָאֱלֹהִים
כִּי הָאֱלֹהִים בַּשָּׁמַיִם וְאַתָּה עַל־הָאָרֶץ עַל־כֵּן יִהְיוּ דְבָרֶיךָ מְעַטִּים
קהלת ה״א

**Keep your mouth from being rash,
and let not your throat be quick to bring forth speech before God.
For God is in heaven and you are on earth;
Therefore, let your words be few.**
Kohelet (Ecclesiastes) 5:1

This is an essential question — do you really know your place? This is not just a rhetorical question — it is an essential question to know who you really are; your physical, spiritual, and mental place. This is to be explored and practiced through this quote we found in the book of Kohelet/Ecclesiastes.

These words are addressed to sincere and honest people who really care about themselves and who know how to think independently themselves. Why? Because most human communication at this time is automatic thinking and parroting, built on the obvious negative memes that were instilled in us while we were unaware, even from birth.

To explore this topic even more deeply, go to Pirkei Avot/The Wisdom of the Fathers 6:5 and 6:6 to read the 48 ways to study the Torah. And the book of Me'Am Loez commentary on Pirke Avot is recommended to explore this in even greater depth.

MAKE NEW MISTAKES

Mistakes are useful, because we can learn from them. After you are **perfect**, then you make mistakes again, so why wait? Enjoy your mistakes, and master the ability to correct them.

Do not be afraid of making mistakes. Please, I am just asking you to always be sure to **make NEW mistakes**, now that you know how to correct them creatively.

MEDITATION ANESTHESIA

"Meditation" is hazardous for your health. In the 70's, I witnessed an exaggerated obsession about the terms "enlightenment" and "meditation", and I personally observed that is not enlightenment, that is endarkenment. Because when the meditation was transported from eastern cultures to the American culture, the good meaning of many words and terms was distorted, creating negative and distorted ways of thinking. So instead of helping you to wake up, they convince you to just relax and go to sleep. (See the article Meditation Anesthesia). Meditation anesthesia is also a tried tool for creating cults.

MEME

The original definition of meme is a "thought virus." Memes are words or suggestions of behavior, that influence a person to accept ideas as truth, without investigation or examination. Human languages are full with many, many thousands of memes, both positive and negative.

Memes often contain half-truths, which have been accepted as "common sense". They are implanted especially when we are unaware, from the time we are young. And they are very subtle and easy to accept, because not everyone examines the words that one speaks.

A meme can be a poisonous suggestion to change and distort the human condition. It also could distort human intelligence, confusing good and evil as opposites – that good is bad, and bad is good – that white is black, and black is white, etc. They can confuse your perceptions. It seems that this is being accepted by humans today. Memes can be both positive and negative, but unfortunately, the negative is the most common.

MENTAL CONTROL

Observing reality **AS IT IS**. Become aware of your thoughts as an observer, and the one who is being observed. Develop your mentality in a healthy, balanced way. Use your faculties of thinking creatively, with no limitation. **SEEING THINGS AS THEY ARE** will become natural.

MINIMUM MOVEMENT, MAXIMUM EXPRESSION

Small gestures can be the most meaningful. Dramatics serve their purpose, but can be left at the stage door. Economical movements are more effective than big movements, very expressive and powerful.

MOVING BOX MEDITATION

A unique, artistic approach to meditation that enhances personal space awareness. This meditation demonstrates that you don't have to sit still to calm the mind, reduce stress, and improve your ability to focus and concentrate. Slow motion is the key here.

Hold an imaginary box between your hands, and simply move around, carrying the box, and placing it in different locations, maintaining the same distance between the hands. You can move it up, down, right, left, forward, and backwards, and can switch hands to hold it from below and above, the sides, etc.

Move slower that you think. Establish a very calm presence with easy and natural breathing.

NO BECAUSE

כָּל אַהֲבָה שֶׁהִיא תְלוּיָה בְדָבָר, בָּטֵל דָּבָר בְּטֵלָה אַהֲבָה, וְשֶׁאֵינָהּ תְּלוּיָה בְדָבָר, אֵינָהּ בְּטֵלָה לְעוֹלָם.

"Whenever love depends upon something and it passes, then the love passes away too. But if love does not depend upon some ulterior interest, then the love will never pass away."
Saying of the Ancestors 5. 19.

I call this "BECAUSE." If love depends on some cause it will not last. But if one loves and there is **NO BECAUSE**, that is a good sign that it will last.

NOTHING	See the article "Who am I to Say I am Nothing?"
NOWHERE	"Nowhere" is a term newly used in Le Centre Du Silence, for that which is beyond space and time, beyond silence, and beyond spiritual transmission teachings. It is also a state of mind to aspire to, to protect oneself from this perplexed and confused world.
O M S O L	**O**bvious **M**ovements are the **S**ecret of **L**ongevity.
ONE DAY OF SILENCE	Fast from words and fast from food to strengthen the immune system.

A suggestion: In a world full of noise, choose one day a week not to use words to communicate. Simply practice silence. Go about your everyday activities, and observe your essential presence at work. You can choose half a day instead, but do it regularly, the same day each week.

In addition, one of the great hidden secrets of longevity, as practiced by conscious kabbalists, is fasting from food. Done on a regular basis, one day every week, or every two weeks, this will prevent many diseases. It regenerates your digestive system, allowing it to rest. If possible, combine the day of silence and the day of fasting.

"PARADOX"	"Paradox" is a deeply imposed conflict of intelligence that is directed only to one small aspect of being. In reality this is a tool in the hands of people who manipulate others for their own benefit. Go ponder on this and you will find whatever you will find.
PERFORMER, PEFORMING, PERFORMANCE ARE ONE	The one who is doing it, that which is being done, the state of being in it, and watching it at the same time, all becomes one whole reality.
PRESENCE	Charisma is the force of the personality. Presence is the life force of manifesting itself in the now. There is ONLY this moment where all and everything is happening right in this very moment.
THE PRESENCE ZONE: <u>The Posture of Enchantment, The Turnkey Posture</u>	This Presence Zone practice is closely connected with the practice of the Artistic Zero. The idea is to integrate the two in order to sense the power within yourself. For this practice you are free to choose any comfortable movement. You can sit, walk or stand, lean against a tree, etc. Notice your calm breathing. Just watch your thoughts passing through, like birds flying past. Observe them from this state. Let them go, and just be.
RELAXATION	A state of being conscious and ready to respond not react. A state of being totally here, ready to be active and creative. Consciously respond, rather that reacting from an emotional state.
RESPONSIBILITY	The ability to respond—immediately. The ability to respond, creatively and appropriately to the immediate activity at that moment.
75/25	75/25 is an exercise in which 75% of your attention is completely engaged in what you are doing, while you use the other 25% to observe yourself. Practice this in order to function from objectivity and to consciously direct your actions. 75% Doer, 25% Observer.
SENTIMENTAL	Send the mental somewhere else when it is not needed.
SHEEP CONSCIOUSNESS	"Sheep consciousness" is when, in the face of the insanity and imbalance we increasingly meet everywhere, we tend to follow like sheep, rather than being the shepherd, the self-leader. I call that "sheep consciousness." Sheep consciousness is following someone or something, or some ideology or mindset that is not yours. It is something that you didn't decide. It was imposed on you. And that is what is happening for 99.9% of humanity now.

We have been given the power to be self-leaders and to use our self-governing ability. We came to this world to LIVE in it, and to overcome that which is not balanced for us.

SILENCE	State of total peace where one can hear all sounds. A zero of invisibility.
SLOW MOTION	To experience and do things slowly, slower than you think. This state of "Moving Meditation" can be done with the Moving Box meditation.
	Move slowly, like a cloud – it moves so slowly if you are not watching, you do not even notice its motion.
SPIRITUAL RATATOUILLE	Ratatouille is a French salad that has many different ingredients mixed together. When this ratatouille is done with spiritual understanding, it is a clever and negative escape meme to flee from the essence of now. (See the Article "Spiritual Ratatouille" in the book *From Ecstasy to Lunch*)
SQUEEZING THE GRAPE	For me, the word spirit is the result, the juice from squeezing grapes. When you squeeze a grape, it produces juice that later becomes what we call wine. Looking at the true spiritual meaning, the squeezed grape can refer to the suffering of humans. Metaphorically, the juice that is produced is the essence of the grape. In the human being, after extreme suffering, caused by ourselves, there arrives a time after suffering, which is the learning from the experience, after being squeezed.
STOP AND CONSIDER	The way to shift from reaction to responding. This practice will lead to a great way to move only when necessary, and not to do unnecessary movement. Economy of energy is attained through less movement.
THIS TOO SHALL PASS גַּם זֶה יַעֲבוֹר	This well-known Hebrew proverb is a nugget of applicable wisdom. It suggests that nothing is permanent. When we are always present, we realize everything will pass. If you are sad or joyous it will pass, so enjoy the present moment of now.
THIS TOO IS FOR THE GOOD גַּם זוֹ לְטוֹבָה	This saying and the above saying, "This too shall pass," are two ancient Hebrew practices to balance one's life. We suggest to practice these two and benefit from this ancient wisdom.

THREE GATES BEFORE YOU SPEAK	<u>There is a proverb from the Kabbalistic tradition, which says, that every word should pass through three gates before being uttered.</u> At the first gate, the gatekeeper asks, "**Is it true**?" At the second gate he asks. "**Is it necessary?**" At the third gate he asks. "**Is it kind?**" If you answer in the positive, go ahead and utter it.
UNKNOWN VERSUS <u>NOT YET KNOWN</u>	Remember the "unknown" is some event that "is not yet known." It has the potential to be known, if only you look for it, because it is there and always looking for you.
"THE VIEW FROM THE HELICOPTER AND THE BOAT"	The ability to see things as they are from two levels: The objective (the helicopter-whole) and the subjective (the boat-details) to integrate and see the whole.
	From the boat, your view is personal, limited, with blinders. From the helicopter, you can see the whole from different angles. It is beneficial to make decisions after exploring both of these ways of seeing.
	Relax your body in any position you choose, while seeing yourself AS IF you are in the helicopter or the boat. Consciously do this 3 times a day, 5 minutes each time until it is established as a consistent state of being.
WHO IS WRITING YOUR SCRIPT?	Be the Author and Play the Lead Actor in your life, Now. This is a **Body*Speak*™** exercise to unleash the Fearless Creative Power Within You.
WORD HONESTY, BODY HONESTY	You can twist the meaning of words and take them out of context, being dishonest. But you cannot do this with the body.
	You can't turn your head 360 degrees, without **discovering** your spine. You do that by going to the edge of your limit in turning your head right or left. To go beyond that limit of turning, you discover the **pivot** of the whole body, and the rotation of the **spine.**
WORDER/WORKER	One who <u>talks</u> (<u>words</u>) about doing versus one who <u>does</u> (<u>works</u>). Develop the habit to speak less, preserve energy, and do more. Remember, the abuse of words can lead to verbal and physical terrorism.

WHAT IF?	"What if" is a subtle meme that can go in both directions, positive and negative. But we mostly use it on the negative side. "What if it doesn't work?" "What if I fail?" etc. In other word, you are creating a false imagination – using the gift of imagination in a negative way.

However, what if could be a source of positive creativity for the world – "What if I am able to create something new?" "What if I explored a new field?" "What if it works?" |
WHAT'S NEXT?	A subconscious clever escape from the now.
WHATEVER	"Whatever" is a way of postponing your happiness and distorting your communications instead of deciding exactly what you want. You use it when you don't want to face something. "What do you want to do today?" "Whatever." That is a clever escape of deciding what you want in life. See the article "Maybe" and "Whatever."
YOU DO NOT HAVE THE RIGHT TO BE SICK	This is a sane suggestion for my students that I emphasized over the years: The body is born to be totally healthy, and disease comes only according to the degree of our awareness, or lack of awareness, in how to nurture the body with healthy foods, healthy thoughts, healthy actions, and healthy behavior. When we interfere with our exaggerated imaginary thoughts that have nothing to do with authentic reality, one gets a dis-ease either mentally or physically. When you know this, you do not have to be afraid of the current health-scare system of western society.

Last Word

Last Word

Has Intelligence Left the Planet? 299

Madness and Sanity on Broadway 304

Has Intelligence Left the Planet, Or Is It Still Here?

Or is this world the greatest insane asylum?

"IN THESE TIMES" when the abuse of language has increased to the point that it conditions ones basic and balanced way of thinking and understanding reality – the urgency and importance of how we use language now seems obvious. Because language structures our reality. Otherwise, there would be no philosophy or shared understanding, just physical living, back to basic survival only.

The continual abuse of language has created a state of confusion. This gives us the impression that intelligence is non-existent in communications between humans. And as many human values are now being erased from dictionaries all over this planet, one must be careful of how to use words. I say this as a performing artist in America since the early 60's, who has been able to observe people's language and behavior over time.

I also say this because English is not my first language. Being more oriented with the Hebrew language, I know that language structures our reality. It can structure our thinking in a way that is balanced or in a way that is imbalanced – and that way becomes the norm.

Growing up with respect for this original language of Hebrew, I approached the new language I learned when I came to this country with the same kind of respect. But over the years, I did not absorb the idiosyncrasies of the way English is used in these United States. And as I made the shift from the Hebrew culture I grew up in, I observed the language my students spoke.

Therefore, from one of the aspects of my traditional Jewish upbringing, I can sum up the human conflicts of relationships, that I observed in my years of teaching here, since 1965. This view taught me to respect every human, because they are the sacred image of the Creator – because the human was created in the image of the Creator.

Therefore, in my travels, my consideration was to develop human friendships, and always consider the other as sacred as the Creator, as a friend. So, this attitude helped me to develop beautiful relationships with people of this country and helped me to adjust to this culture. I considered each of my students as a book that I could learn to read. Which chapter and which sentence, and which word were they expressing in this particular time in their life?

I observed from experience the source of conflict in human relationships. That source is lack of respect to the other. The other is considered as an enemy, and therefore the relationships are conditioned by that fact.

Observing this, I recorded my story, "Madness and Sanity on Broadway," which follows this article, about my experience in New York in the 60's. I used my performances then to reflect the disordered behavior I observed. But the image of that disordered reality of behavior shook my being. It was then, I began to think, should I be considering it as if I am living in a great insane asylum?

Now, in our very times, I try to insert and teach in my classes, the respect of the other. In the classes, we learn this through movement. The time and space of the other is to be respected. And therefore, I could balance my life to that sane reality.

But life slaps you in the face. That is what happened to me there in New York then, as I share in the story.

There in New York, I encountered such a dense linear architecture, with no curve or dome anywhere, and barely any trees or green growing things. It was a violent architecture, as I called it then. It made me feel physically insignificant, like nothing. And the only poor trees that grew there were surrounded in metal enclosures, so I thought they were in prison. Now, trees and green growing plants are an example of healing structures that surround us. So, when you grow up in a spacious mountainside, you see things very differently.

In New York, that linear and square architecture was pervasive. Meanwhile, I found circularity to be a key to healing of basic relationships between humans. And so, all my artistic work was focused by the idea of curvature – circular language, circular movements – for that is the true nature of every human being, and of our physical universe and physical bodies. There is curvature to everything in the human body: the shoulder, the knees, the head, the eyes, the joints, etc. And learning circular movements is a way this physical structure can be reeducated.

Below, you can see a sample of a circular text I created in BodySpeak™. You will find that most of the words there are physical exercises of balance. In the workshops, we attempted to find a balance, both physical, mental and spiritual. (See the article Balance: The Middle Way of the Tree of Life, under Kabbalah Articles.)

Those who are familiar with my artistic works and the teachings of BodySpeak™ over the years, can recall specific exercises that introduced that shift from linear thinking to circular thinking. And that influences the balance of the body, as I envisioned it with the artists, mimes, actors, and many different people who came to the workshops. You can refer to my early books for specific exercises on balance and circular thinking, which help us in dealing with the disbalance we encounter every day in the world.

For in every human field nowadays, it is hard to find a suggestion of balance. This is because we form our reality by how we think, and that means language: How do we speak? How do we name things? How do we foul our mouths? Etc. All of this is important. But now it is à la mode, even in higher education, people are regressing to speaking street language, instead of good English. Because they want to be like everyone else. And so, women begin to speak like teenagers, and men begin to behave like little boys in those fraternities and sororities. It is as if they never grew up.

So, my work was discovering and setting and suggesting a new attitude of working with the human body. One main exploration was, balance, balance, and balance. I developed many exercises of balance. And when we develop that attitude of balance at an early age, you respect how to tie your shoes properly, and how to put a stamp on an envelope in its right place so it will get to its destination. These are components of balance actually. And that balance can be learned at any time, no matter what age you are.

In the workshops, when you learn the balance of the body, it influences your thinking in a very interesting and subtle way. Sometimes the people in the class don't even realize at first the effect it has had, until later they begin to see things in a new way. (See the detailed exercises for developing balance in my early books.)

Culturally, I suggest beginning to treat each other with respect, friendliness and cooperation. You have to respect what the other says, it is natural. And the intention for the other to be a friend, not as an enemy. So the root of human conflicts is the other as enemy, not as a friend. And I say this knowing there are bad people on this planet.

In my classes, I tried to develop that experience. Almost all of my students immediately had that impression, that in this space, in this small group, which I called a microcosm of humanity, I made sure to introduce an atmosphere of safety and no criticism.

The BodySpeak™ method that I developed, I call it also physical philosophy. We physicalize the philosophy with the body, instead of just using words. And for that, you have to condense the thought you have and go to the essence of it.

I call it the physics of philosophy. In other words, it is exploring the great questions of life, by exploring and physicalizing it with your body. Because in the body, you have to be exact. Every movement should be essentialized, and in the meanwhile, you are killing 500 birds with one breath, understanding 500 things that you couldn't understand before.

For more details, you can look at the BodySpeak™ Manual: Moving Body and Mind – A Collection of Writings and Exercises for Developing Kinesthetic Intelligence. Available on Amazon. There are many exercises there to explore what I am speaking about here.

And so, after coming to America, knowing the imbalance of our human behaviors, over the years, I began to wonder, are there some intelligent people left on this planet? And that is a very sad thing for me to say. Thus, after encountering these confused ways of thinking and being, and my encounter with "Madness and Sanity on Broadway," I developed my motto:

שְׁמוֹר נָא לִי אֶת שְׁפִיּוּת דַּעְתִּי בְּעוֹלָם מְטוֹרָף זֶה

KEEP ME SANE IN THE MIDST OF MADNESS

This is one of the mottos that keep me functioning healthy and balanced so that I can function in "this unbalanced society." And hence, I developed the sense of questioning everything – becoming a walking question mark.

אַל־תְּבַהֵל עַל־פִּיךָ וְלִבְּךָ אַל־יְמַהֵר לְהוֹצִיא דָבָר לִפְנֵי הָאֱלֹהִים
כִּי הָאֱלֹהִים בַּשָּׁמַיִם וְאַתָּה עַל־הָאָרֶץ עַל־כֵּן יִהְיוּ דְבָרֶיךָ מְעַטִּים:

**Keep your mouth from being rash,
and let not your throat be quick to bring forth speech before God.
For God is in heaven and you are on earth;
that is why your words should be few.**
Kohelet (Ecclesiastes) 5:1

holy workspace
• **the centre of silence** • jump
into yourself • symphony of being •
mind-body harmony • essence of yourself • dot in
space • drop in the sea • think movement • still as a
mountain • a l'italienne • the body cannot lie • slower than
that • timing the space • spacing the time • blah blah blah • the
tragedy of focus • you are the text • joke number 36½ • **burn, but
not to ashes** • suicide, but don't die • swim but don't drown • listen to
your body • **thank you for being here** • center yourself • **from ecstacy to
lunch** • **the one who** • relax in it • unarchy • freak in • everyday movement
• 2 stones get stoned • find your axe • line of work • **alert like a cat** • **claying
around** • out of it • **be your own mirror** • sharpen your sword • **send a telegram** • **perfection in action** • brick by brick • build a mold • measure your energy • **verbal fast** • **day of silence** • fingers of the feet • jump into the fire • go
mad with it • be sincere with it • such mastery! • **be a whole in the detail and
the detail in the whole** • always come back to zero • it was not projected • no
leader, no follower • don't panic • **the genesis of the self** • one breath class •
thought to action • no philosophy • do the unexpected • no mediocre
movement • do not manipulate • moving mandala • digest the food • take
a picture • be sincere with it • instrument • it must project • be with
yourself here • the body as a brush • a pinpoint of light • **to be and
not to be** • tubes of vision • tubes of communication • dancing
diaphragm • a circle inside itself • **echo of a whisper** • crystallized thought • **serve the idea** • it can be seen • be
true to yourself • penetrate space • explore the
space • cut through space • don't rape the
space • it is known • **you are
unique** • names

Circle of BodySpeak™ Terms 1975

Madness and Sanity on Broadway

Encountering America's state of mind of the mid 60's

THE EVENT OF 60 years ago that gave me the first clue or sign of what America was all about remains vivid in my mind today. It was a first encounter that prepared me for America's state of mind then as well as now. I came to understand through great effort the meaning of this event only after much struggle.

I Remembered few years earlier in Paris, watching the assassination of JFK on French television. With the astonishment of that momentary emotion I wondered, why would a great and rich country kill its president? I developed a keen sense of observation while living in America during the turbulent 60s.

I arrived in New York City via Montréal from Paris in June of 1964, as a visitor of my friends Moni & Mina Yakim, with whom I resided until I found my own apartment.

As an innocent immigrant, not yet knowing English, American history or culture, I just dived in. New York was a jungle of confusion for me. I focused on learning the language fast so I could catch up with my self-education and face the realities of my new adventure, the discovery of my America.

In 1965 I have my first American performance at the theatre of La Mama. etc. downtown in the neighborhood of Second Ave. I offered classes in different schools, spoke enough English to get by, and read a lot.

Some of my performances depicted in silence and movement those personal observations, made through the artist's eyes. These were my own efforts to "understand" the western culture in which I chose to learn and develop my artistic career.

Then one day a street encounter gave me a real clue of the diseased symptoms and the way of thinking of America in its un-united "state."

I was walking on Broadway between 82nd and 84th streets, happy but contemplative about the strangeness of being here. I considered myself to be a physically, mentally, fit and healthy individual, and I was simply glad to be in this country.

I met a friend, actually an acquaintance whom I had known some time ago, and as we greeted each other, I asked him where he was going. He said, "I am going to see my psychiatrist." I thought to myself that to see a psychiatrist one must be mentally unbalanced or unable to cope with reality. So, I said with honesty, "Is something wrong?" He then reacted very defensively, "No" he shouted, "If you don't have a psychiatrist then something is wrong with **you**," he said and disappeared into the crowd.

I was transfixed, planted firm on the ground, as dumbfounded as if I had just been struck by lightning on that beautiful and sunny day. My mind went blank. Shocked to the core, I thought about the irrationality of this person's behavior, his twisted logic, and his distorted perception of reality.

I couldn't understand then, that such a mentally disturbed individual, could jump to a false conclusion about me and dare to judge me as abnormal because I did not have a psychiatrist. I found it to be utterly outrageous and insulting to my intelligence.

My thoughts raced for a conclusion or resolution as I woke up out of my stupor. Smiling to myself, I processed and absorbed this event. I identified and analyzed what had just occurred with my natural sense of objectivity, in order to make sense of it without being mentally injured by the distortion I had just witnessed. I found myself greatly amused with a deeper smile.

I realized and told myself, "My dear Samuel, you have just witnessed a glimpse of insanity and twisted reality. Now, you know that you have come to an immense insane asylum. This asylum is caught in a trap of false identities, distorted realities that have become a norm that relies on psychiatrists and external authorities, using them as an escape from facing the truth as it is."

This innocent nouveau immigrant suddenly understood the scope of his survival: That one has to be mentally strong and healthy to face the irrationalities of the majority – irrationalities which are considered a norm in this society.

I developed a safety valve called,

"KEEP ME SANE IN THE MIDST OF MADNESS"

This valve of thinking objectively with common sense kept the flame of sanity alive in me, in spite of the imbalances that I had to deal with. I sharpened my intellect more to carry my artistic work creatively.

I developed a keen sense of observation, an ability to identify irrationalities and reject them in order to keep my sanity alive. I used my objectivity to stay logical and practice honesty in spite of the popular belief that it does not pay.

I identified reality as it was in regard to my emotions, the cheating and lying that were commonplace, and the "mystical" ideas that create problems where none exist. My experiences and involvement in my newly adopted and discovered country, made it possible for me to practice freedom of thought and action.

So my motto was and is to actively say to myself:

"KEEP ME SANE IN THE MIDST OF MADNESS"

Stay alert and consciously awake to any winds of change, and be armed with a healthy sense of life and determination to be creatively happy, and above all, increasing kindness to all.

That event – an immigrant's encounter with madness and sanity on Broadway, New York City of 1965, gave me a shining glimpse of what was going to be my American Experience and a great lesson in my life.

Front Cover of the Mime Workbook

Biography

Biography of Samuel Ben-Or Avital 311

**Heritage of my Families Abitbol, Ezekri, and Elbaz
Partial Lineage Legacy** 315

Biography of Samuel Ben-Or Avital

"He teaches a Kabbalistic Tai-Chi in which God and Man are fused in MIME."
Reb Zalman Schachter-Shalomi. Boulder, Colorado.

Samuel Ben-Or Avital was born in the small village of **Sefrou**, near **Fez**, in the Atlas Mountains of Morocco. He was educated in the home of a simple and remarkable family, which traces its lineage to **15th Century Spain** and before. This line carried with them, from father to son, in the **Sephardic tradition,** the ancient, beautiful and practical wisdom of the Hebrew Science of the **Kabbalah**.

At a young age, Samuel embarked on the first of many adventurous journeys, which led him to Israel and later to Paris, France, Europe and Scandinavia, and then to the United States. During his travels from East to West, Samuel encountered and explored different schools of knowledge, including Alchemical and Sufi traditions, which he absorbed, and later synthesized into his own organic and Cosmic Kabbalistic learning.

Over the years, he accumulated the knowledge of a few languages, which assisted him in living in the Western world. At the age of 16, Samuel traveled to Israel where he lived in a kibbutz and in Jerusalem, studying physics, agronomy, theology, arts and theatre.

His innate interest in the arts eventually drew him to Paris, where he studied dance and theatre at the Sorbonne. There, he discovered the world of mime in the teachings of the masters, Etienne Decroux and Marcel Marceau. Having met his art form, Avital threw himself into what he found to be the very essence of human expression. Decroux, Marcel Marceau, and others were all to have a profound influence on the formation of his own artistic expression. He soon began touring with the Mime Company of Maximilien Decroux and performing his own solo performances in Paris, France.

In 1964, Samuel joined his friend Moni Yakim in New York, performing with him in his Pantomime Theatre of New York and also in the off off-Broadway theatres, as well as teaching mime in the New York City schools. He performed in many countries and shared his knowledge with all who have orbited in his vicinity. He has toured in North and South America, and Canada, and in 1969, he was invited to teach Mime and Movement Theatre as an Artist-in-Residence at SMU, Dallas, Texas.

In 1971, he established **Le Centre du Silence Mime School** in Boulder, Colorado. The following year, he created the **Boulder Mime Theatre** with his most dedicated students. The **BMT** performed during the next thirteen years in local, state and national engagements.

In 1974, Avital initiated the International Summer Mime Workspace, an annual intensive course attracting students worldwide. The same year, he published his *MIME WORKBOOK* followed by a second edition in 1977, a third printing in 1982, and *MIMENSPIEL* a German edition out of Frankfurt. Hohm Press in Prescott, Arizona, published his second book, *MIME & BEYOND: The Silent Outcry,* in **1985**. Inner Traditions, Rochester, VT, published *The Conception Mandala* by Samuel Avital and Mark Olsen. His video, *The Silent Outcry: The Life and Times of Samuel Avital,* was produced in **1992**. In 1985 Samuel was nominated for the Colorado Governor's Award for Excellence in the Arts.

His **Book**, *The BodySpeak Manual™,* was published in August 2001 by Author House. The recently revised and republished version is available now on Amazon.

Samuel's book "*THE INVISIBLE STAIRWAY: Kabbalistic Meditations on the Hebrew Letters* was privately published in 1982 in Hebrew and English, for possible limited distribution for close students and friends, and is now available in an English-only version on Amazon.

Samuel Avital, at a Workshop Introduction

Over the years, Samuel developed his unique method of teaching, called ***BodySpeak™ Moving Body and Mind.*** He has also contributed numerous articles, interviews and essays in several languages to diverse publications throughout the U.S. and abroad. Currently, Avital lives in Boulder, Colorado, where he continues his artistic activities, and offers seminars, workshops and public talks on the sacred knowledge of Kabbalah.

תולדות משפחות אביטבול, אזכרי ואלבאז ממרוקו.

שמי שמואל בן-אור אביטל לבית אביטבול. נולדתי בשנת תרצ"ב - 2391 בצפרו - Sefrou בדרום במרוקו הידועה בשם "ירושלים הקטנה" כבן משפחת אביטבול, אזכרי ואלבאז. אני מקדיש מלים אלה לזכר אבותי ואבות אבותי שלשלת החכמים הדיינים, הסופרים, והמקובלים לתולדותיהם.

גזע המשפחה הוא בעל שלושה ענפים של קדושה וטהרה בשם טוב ותהילה בעץ חכמת החיים של מורשתנו המפוארת בהיסטורית עמנו. משפחות אביטבול אלבאז ואזכרי נֵרָם יָאִיר, היו מפורסמות לא רק בעיר התורה ויראת שמים, צפרו ("ירושלים הקטנה") הידועה ברבניה, משוריה, פייטניה ובתושביה התמימים והישרים, ולא רק בארץ מרוקו בלבד אלא בכל קצוי העולם היהודי.

ממשפחת אביטבול העֲנֵפָה יצאו ממנה חכמים, דיינים, מפרשים, מנהיגים רוחניים ומקובלים, אנשים מכובדים בתורה ובקהילה, ששמה הטוב יוצא לפניה בתבל. משפחת אלבאז ידועה לפי המסורת שיצאה מסוריה, וגם משפחת אביחצירה בשמה האמיתי הוא "אלבאז". (אבוחצירה הוא רק כינוי בגלל הנס שקרה לאב המשפחה רבי שמואל אלבאז זצ"ל). (עיין באנציקלופדיה יודאיקה*)

מצד אימא חנה אורובידה הרחומה והאהובה, בת שמחה בת הרב אבא אלבאז זצ"ל, רב גדול ומורה צדק עשרות בשנים כדיין ופוסק בעירנו צפרו המהוללה. משפחת אזכרי הברוכה ברבנים, סופרים, משוררים ומקובלים בעלי הלכה ושרה ואהובים על הציבור. ממנה יצאו תלמידי חכמים גדולים ומקובלים בעלי חזון, כמו בעל ספר החרדים רבי אליעזר אזכרי זצ"ל שהיה ממקורביו של האר"י, מהרח"ו רבי חיים ויטאל והרמ"ק רבי משה קורדובירו זצ"ל בצפת עיר המקובלים בזמנו.

ומצד אבא מארי משה עמרם וסבא יקירא אליהו יעקב זצ"ל יקירא למשפחת אביטבול, והרב הגאון רבי עמור אביטבול זצ"ל, מצאצאי גולי קסטיליא בספרד, פרשן דרשן איש ענק בקדושתו ובהדרת כבודו, בעל החיבורים המפורסמים, עומר מן ושירת העומר שיצא לאחרונה במהדורה מיוחדת. וכן מצד הסבא רבי אבא – הרמ"א – רבי רפאל משה אלבאז זצק"ל הפוסק והמקובל והפייטן הגדול, בעל הספרים עדן מקדם, מיני מתיקה, ארבעה שומרים, עטרת פז, דרש משה, שיר חדש, כסא המלכים, באר שבע על שבע חכמות, וספרים אחרים עוד בכתב יד. הוא היה משורר ומקובל רב עוצמה המצויין בשירתו המרנינה ובעלת תוכן עמוק ונפלא.

ליקוב"ה – ויהיו לרצון אמרי פי והגיון לבי ואהבת בוראי מקובלים לפני כסא כבודו. ויהיו דברי זכרון אלה מוקדשים לעילוי נשמתם הצרורה בצרור החיים, ויהיו מחשבותי, דברי ולימודי לתיקון נשמותיהם, לתיקון עצמי ולתיקון עולם ומלואו. ויהיו כוונותי הטהורות מכוונות להשפיע מטובו של הבורא באור העליון, לכל בני משפחתי באשר הם, לשלומם ולשלום כל עם ישראל בנצח ההויה בכל העולמות אמן כן יהי רצון. יהי זכרם ברוך.

הערה: ליקטתי וערכתי אני ע"ה שמואל בן-אור אביטל הי"ו אכי"ר בן חנה אורובידה אזכרי, ור' משה עמרם אביטבול זצ"ל בן ר' אליהו יעקב אביטבול זצ"ל.

<u>הערה</u>: שניתי את שמי ל-אביטל בהיותי בקיבוץ אילת השחר, ובבית הספר החקלאי במקוה ישראל בשנת ה.תש"ט 1949 שנת עליתי לארץ ישראל. הָאוֹתִיּוֹת הַזּוֹהֲרוֹת

Heritage of my Families Abitbol, Ezekri, and Elbaz Partial Lineage Legacy

For the name ABITBOL, See Encyclopedia Judaica, Volume 2, A-ANG
For the name ELBAZ, See Encyclopedia Judaica, Volume 6, DI-FO

MY NAME IS (Samuel) Shemuel ben-Or Avital*, of the house of Abitbol. I was born on the 23rd of the month of Tevet 1932 in Sefrou, (near Fez) Morocco, which was known then as "Little Jerusalem." As a son of the families Abitbol, Ezekri, and Elbaz, I write these words as a testament to my ancestors and for the lineage of the wise rabbis, kabbalists, and their spiritual heirs.

My family has three sacred branches of honor from the tree of wisdom, adding to the splendid heritage of our people. These are the families Abitbol, Ezekri, and Elbaz, may their light illumine us. These saints were revered by the honest and pure people of the city of the Torah, Sefrou, but were also known throughout Morocco and in many other parts of the world.

From the Abitbol family branch, there were many rabbis, judges, interpreters, spiritual leaders, and renown Mekoubalim, who were honored by the community, as those whose good name always walked before them in the world.

The Abitbols were descendants of the Megorashim – exiled in 1492 from Castille, Spain. In the line of my father, Moshe Amram, and my beloved grandfather, Eliyahu Yaakov, blessed be his memory, is the HaRav HaGaon, Rabbi Amor Abitbol. He was an interpreter of the Torah, a Dayan, and giant of holiness, in whom dwelt a true splendor of being. He is the author of Omer Man and Shirat HaOmer, a new edition of which was just republished in Israel.

Through my mother, Hannah Robidah and the family of Ezekri, there were also many learned and wise Kabbalists of great vision, such as the author of the Sefer Haredim, Rabbi Eliezer Ezekri, blessed

---

* I changed my name to AVITAL when I was in kibbutz Ayelet Hashahar (high Galilee) in 1949, the year I immigrated to Israel (March 20, 1949). I now use the name of Samuel Avital.

be his memory. He was a disciple of the Great ARI, Rabbi Hayim Vital, and Rabbi Moshe Cordovero in Tsafet, the city of Kabbalists, at the time.

The family of Elbaz is well known, and according to a tradition that comes from Syria, the family of Abu-Hatsirah is in truth Elbaz (Abu-Hatsirah being a name given to Rabbi Shemuel Elbaz ZL, after the miraculous event he was known to have caused). Rabbi Shemuel Elbaz was famous as a powerful healer throughout the world. Many people still visit his place of burial to ask for healing.

Now, my mother, Hannah Robidah, was the daughter of Simha, who was the daughter of the great rabbi, Abba Elbaz, blessed be his memory. He was a great rabbi and teacher of justice, for many years a judge and posek, one who decides on how to interpret the Halachah of Jewish law. He said once, that my mother Hannah Robidah, the beloved and merciful of the family Ezekri, would be blessed with a good family and children.

The cousin of Rabbi Abba Elbaz was the great Rabbi Raphael Moshe Elbaz, called RAMA (his acronym). He was a great visionary, miracle-maker, and famed Kabbalist, who authored many classic books like, The Ancient from Eden, Things of Sweetness, The Four Guardians, The Crown of Gold, The Words of Moshe, New Songs, Throne of Kings, The Seven Wisdoms, and many other works that are still in manuscript.

He was a poet of great renown, and a kabbalist of great powers, a revered miracle-maker. His beautiful songs, in the style of the classic Andalusian music, are marked by a marvelous depth and content, and have become prayers, used many Jewish Sephardic communities around the world. Some of them are included in the repertoire of the Israeli Andalusian Orchestra.

Samuel Avital, Founder and Director Le Centre du Silence Mime School,

Websites:
www.bodyspeak.com
www.gokabbalahnow.com

What are "They" Saying About Samuel Avital?

Rabbi Zalman Schachter-Shalomi	**319**
Zohara Hieronimus	**319**
Marcel Marceau	**320**
Kenneth Cohen	**322**
Maximilien Decroux	**323**
Masheikh Wali Ali Meyer	**323**
Dr. David Passig	**323**
Mark Olson	**323**
Melissa Michaels	**324**
Moni Yakim	**324**
E.J. Gold	**324**
Shalom Kalfon	**325**

What are "They" Saying About Samuel Avital?

Rabbi Zalman Meshullam Schachter-Shalomi
Founder of Aleph: Alliance for Jewish Renewal,
Emeritus Temple University.
Boulder, Colorado, USA.
April 10, 2001 and June 11, 1975

"How do the Sephiroth dance? What is the face of Gevurah? How does one walk on Netzah and Hod? Shemouel Avital teaches a Kabbalistic Tai-Chi in which God and Man are fused in Mime. If only my teachers could have Mimed the world of Yetzirah, how much more I would know of the light today. Shemouel is a Kabbalist's Kabbalist."

"Rabbeynu Shemouel Ben-Or Avital, descendant and disciple of Moroccan Kabbalists, has opened access to the content of the sacred kabbalah and the very studies of the sacred letters... He not only addresses the mind, but also the soul.

Being the master of Le Centre du Silence Mime School, he views the body as the "Merkaba," "chariot" of the spirit, and as a generous soul, readies you for the ride. May the letters connect you, the reader, to the Great Word."

J. Zohara Meyerhoff Hieronimus DHL
Author of Kabbalistic Teachings of the Female Prophets (2008) and
Sanctuary of the Divine Presence (2012)

Samuel Avital is a truly wise man. Combining his lifetime of practice as Mime performer and teacher and as a true and devoted lover of Torah, his offerings are like the holy dew of creation. Whether parable, wisdom teaching, or personal story, Avital's insights spark each person's mind and soul in finding truth in their own lives and in the world around us.

Few are the truly enlightened who can combine wisdom, understanding and knowledge to reveal truth and beauty. Avital does just this, using words especially chosen for their task of showering gems of meaning for the reader.

As each person who has the privilege of coming into rapport with Samuel or his writings discovers, his love of life, good humor and impeccable talent of observation, whispers like the spirit into the heart and soul of every sincere seeker.

Marcel Marceau
World-Famous Mime Artist, BIP
Paris, France, November 20, 1971 and Denver, Colorado, 1980

"I think that Samuel's work is important. He brings awareness to the soul of people and gives the young dedicated artists who work under his direction the need, dedication, and love for the world of silence and the beautiful art of movement."

"Mon cher Samuel, Les mots seront toujours pauvres a coté de notre silence, mais ils ouvrent les portes a notre esprit silencieux. De tous Coeur."

"To my dear Samuel, words will be always poor besides our silence, but they will open doors…to our silent spirit."

—Marcel Marceau
World-Famous Mime Artist, BIP

> À mon cher SAMUEL AVITAL
> Les mots seront toujours pauvres à côté de notre silence, mais ils ouvriront des portes... À notre esprit silencieux.
>
> De tout cœur
>
> Bye 🌸
>
> Marcel Marceau
>
> Denver, Co. March 22. 80.

Kenneth Cohen
Author of The Way of Qigong
Boulder, CO, 2009

"Samuel Avital's classes are inspiring and transforming. Instead of offering ultimate truths, he awakens his students with words that cut away falsehood and hideouts. He would rather have his students ask great questions than settle for dogmatic answers. With flair and style, he demonstrates the importance of a flexible approach to life. He reminds us that we can play many roles in life, but whether in mime, theatre, or everyday life, let's not allow the masks to get stuck to our faces! In a world that increasingly looks at surfaces and that judges a book by its cover, how refreshing to find a course with real depth and content."

Maximilien Decroux
Internationally Known Mime Artist,
École Internationale de Mimodrame de Paris
Paris, France, 1961

"Samuel Avital – whom I have known since his first years with my company in Paris – I suspected would become one of the great mimes. He has fulfilled that promise. He was among the first to reveal to me what creative interpretation could be, surpassing the creativity of the art of mime in order to become a human being who dares to be different. This great artist has discovered an extraordinary relationship between being an artist and becoming a true teacher of his own method. Our acquaintance has brought the greatest joy and surprise to my life and art."

Masheikh Wali Ali Meyer
Sufi, February, 1975

Samuel Avital is a lover of God-in-man. Many mystical schools teach that the real transmission takes place in and through the silence – through breath, heart, glance, and atmosphere. The danger lies when we make this a mere philosophy; the fulfillment comes when we make it a reality in our art, in our lives. I believe Samuel Avital's teachings are a real step in this direction.

Dr. David Passig
Futurist, Bar Ilan University, Israel, 2003
Author of "The FutureCode: Israel's Future Test" and "2048"

"Shemuel has found an original way to deeply touch the eternity of our physical and spiritual existence…..an authentic way to express Kabbalistic and Cosmic ideas with the medium of the human body. With the soul's means, he has pierced many ways to The Great Wisdom."

Mark Olson
Professor, Juilliard Drama Division NYC, NY
March 17, 1999

"Samuel Avital is an artist of conscious life, conscious theatre and cosmic laughter. When the madness of the world starts to get me down, I am lifted by the knowledge that men like Samuel exist. He remains unique, elusive, profound, demanding, dedicated, theatrical, passionate, and one of the most vibrant teachers I have encountered."

"Samuel's teaching goes directly to the heart of each person, challenging them to formulate their vision with unflinching honesty, chart their action with verve, take responsibility for their choices with relish, and then to free their imaginative powers from conditioned self-imposed restrictions."

Melissa Michaels
Movement Educator and Author

"I think "Samuel has created simple tools that absolutely awaken the spirit and ground the body. Each learner is initiated into the reality that coded in the physical body are key principles for living a creative and purposeful life. He is a grandfather in this field of using conscious movement for one's inner practice."

Moni Yakim
Movement Theatre Director,
Juillliard Drama Division NYC, NY

"Mr. Avital is a remarkable man of astonishing depth and an artist of great magnitude and achievement. His profound knowledge of physical expression, teaching and performing is vast, rich and highly creative; his artistic fervor is contagious and his mastery is impeccable and practical.."

"If you seek some truth or direction in life or art, stay close to Samuel for he might just then crawl out of his shell and give you of his soul."

E.J. Gold
E. J. Gold presents Samuel Avital, June, 1977

"A thin, tiny sparrowlike man perches at the door, peering into the gloomy reddish glow of the room. He hesitates only a moment and then strides in.

Within the room he finds elements of new space. Everything he once held secure he has dropped at the door, for he no longer needs them.

The Man who dares – the wild explorer of equally wild spaces, is Samuel Avital – distinguished by no title, no diploma, no degree, no special honors, no awards of recognition – but only the fact that he is genuinely, truly alive.

The great contribution is that others who have been touched by him, even though they were asleep and walking in shadow, also become alive by virtue of his gift.

Is he a mime? Only if Solomon, Merlin and Gandalf were mimes. He does not move through space, he creates it as if solid and real.

He finds new uses for old things, and make new things with new uses. The universe does not exist for him beyond the moment, and for those who walk with him, the universe becomes new, freshly made, and ancient beyond memory.

He forms mass, makes it appear in space, moves within and around it, stirs up realities that never were, until he thought of them; reflects absurdities that no one looked at until they appeared in his mirror of life; conjures people that no one has seen because they are the self...in short, he is master of the universe, yet can be claimed by no object within it. He knows, remembers, understands, feels, senses with all his heart. What more is there to say about a man?"

SAMUEL REMAINED FAITHFUL TO HIS ROOTS
by Shalom Kalfon

About Shmuel we can say that he lives the verse 2:4 from the prophet Habakuk: "**The righteous shall live by his faith.**" – "**וצדיק באמונתו יחיה**".

His faith in Hebrew is (**אמונתו**) **EIMUNATO** and his art is (**אומנותו**) **UMANUTO**. It's a play on words that fits his personality so well. Shmuel lives his faith as he lives his art, originality and faithfulness. His faith includes all the gamut of the Jewish Civilization in its colors and richness. His art includes all facets of art with emphasis on mime.

I have known him since childhood in Sefrou, Morocco, where we grew up together, and afterwards in Jerusalem where he started his interest in theatre and appeared with different groups. Shmuel was always gifted with great talent, seriousness and originality. I met him again in Paris where he followed his vocation steadfastly by studying with the great masters of his field, the art of mime.

I met him again in New York where he was struggling to forge his personal style in his art. What distinguished him from other artists I know is his faithfulness to our heritage, to his roots. While advancing and progressing in his art, he also followed and deepened his studies in Judaism. He published essays in kabbalah in a very distinguished and refined literary Hebrew. His essays were published in the Hebrew weekly (**הדואר**) "Hadoar," edited and published in New York.

I had the privilege to be present in the opening class in Boulder, Colorado (USA), of one of his international seminars that he conducts yearly. On this occasion, I was surprised to listen to him reciting in Hebrew with such serenity (אלוהי נשמה) "Elohai Neshama" from our daily prayer book. This prayer, we recite every morning, to thank The Creator of The Universe for his gift to us, the gift of our pure soul. In this prayer, we express our nothingness and our humility in the face of our short life in this vast universe. It expresses our faith and optimism in the worth of life itself...

Shmuel recited this prayer with such spiritual intensity that all his students, myself among them, were mesmerized, even though they did not understand Hebrew. They were captivated by the spiritual radiance emanated from each and every word that he articulated slowly, with his eyes closed.

Shmuel lives his art and his Jewishness with grace and pride. He kept his spiritual and cultural heritage and remained faithful to his roots. This is reflected in his many books, which are a spiritual inspiration to all his many readers, disciples and admirers.

In his books one will find his wisdom and his outlook on life. His theories enclose the richness and the wisdom from both civilizations in which he is so well rooted. His views are expressed with literary talent and with a deep knowledge of the philosophy of consciousness. He touches upon the problems of our confused and perplexed generation.

To know Shmuel and talk to him, one will learn about the richness of his life experiences and his achievements through consistency and suffering without compromising his integrity as a Jew and as an artist. Throughout his life he remained a faithful friend and a genial and uniquely original human being.

Vancouver, B.C. Canada
Monday, Dec 16, 2002
יום שני י"א טבת, תשס"ג

Shalom Kalfon is a native of Sefrou, Morocco. He immigrated to Israel illegally at the time of British rule. He was a soldier in Israel's war of independence, lived in a Kibbutz, studied philosophy, literature & political science. An author & educator, he has served as a Rabbi and taught Hebrew at the University of Victoria.

He was VP of the Zionist Organization of Canada and VP of its charitable fund. He has served as a member of the Board of Governors of the Conservatory of Music and as a member of the Executive of the Canadian Zionist Federation and the United Jewish Appeal of Canada. He has published various books and essays in Hebrew, French and English. He is married to Rebecca and father to Edna, Itay and Vardit, and currently lives in Israel. Shalom is a well-known Israeli author, documenting the unique culture of his birth-place in Sefrou Morocco.

Memorial To Suzanne Fountain

A memorial to Suzanne Fountain, my former student, who was among the 10 deaths in the Boulder Massacre in the King Soopers Grocery Store on March 22, 2021.

Dear friends and colleagues,

What happened in our Boulder community's King Soopers mass killing on Tuesday, March 22, 2021 was a massacre of innocent people.

Among those 10 souls that departed was a dear student of mine. I noticed this when they published the names of the people killed in that criminal attack. When I saw her name in that list, I recognized immediately that she was one of my dear students who participated in our 44th Mime workshop of Le Centre du Silence Mime School. I held these evening workshops in the early Spring, from March 13 to April 12, 1984, in the evenings, for four weeks, in Boulder, Colorado.

Her name is Suzanne Fountain. She was a remarkable woman, and with her creative attitude was eager to learn and improvise actively in our class then. I used to speak her last name in the French way, she was 59, may her soul rest in peace. I verified her name in my past students list of that year, 1984.

I offer her family condolence and hopefully justice will be done soon of this evil criminal event. I am sorry to let you know this piece of this news. May it be that peace and justice will return to earth very soon.

With my love and compassionate heart to you all,
Samuel Avital

Wednesday, March 24, 2021

Suzanne Fountain

"Fountain, 59, was a financial counselor who loved theater," The Denver Post reported.

"She was a very well-known actress in town," Brian Miller, who worked with Fountain in a show several years ago, told the publication. "She was absolutely lovely, a natural, someone you simply didn't forget."

Hilarie Kavanaugh, owner of Medicare Licensed Agents in Boulder where Fountain had been an agent since 2018, described Fountain as a "very genuine person with tons of integrity."

"She was just always bright and incredibly warm," Kavanaugh told the Post. "You could just see it in her eyes."

From the local press.

Books by Samuel Avital

Mime Workbook. 1975
Mimenspiel. German edition of Mime Workbook, 1985
Mime and Beyond: The Silent Outcry. 1985
The Conception Mandala: Creative Techniques for Inviting a Child into Your Life. 1992, co-authored with Mark Olsen.
The Silent Outcry: The Life and Times of Samuel Avital (DVD) 1992
The BodySpeak™ Manual. 2001
The Invisible Stairway: Kabbalistic Meditations on the Hebrew Letters. 2003
Passover Haggadah – Haggadah Shel Pessah, 1982, revised 2010
From Ecstasy to Lunch, 2020
Messages from "Nowhere", 2024

www.ingramcontent.com/pod-product-compliance
Lightning Source LLC
Chambersburg PA
CBHW080422230426
43662CB00015B/2182